Simplifying Response to Intervention

to

FOUR *Essential* GUIDING PRINCIPLES

AUSTIN BUFFUM | MIKE MATTOS | CHRIS WEBER

Solution Tree | Press

a division of

Solution Tree

555 North Morton Street
Bloomington, IN 47404
800.733.6786 (toll free) / 812.336.7700
FAX: 812.336.7790
email: info@solution-tree.com
solution-tree.com
Visit **go.solution-tree.com/rti** to download the reproducibles in this book.

Printed in the United States of America

15 14 13 12 11   1 2 3 4 5

Library of Congress Cataloging-in-Publication Data

Buffum, Austin.

  Simplifying response to intervention : four essential guiding principles / Austin Buffum, Mike Mattos, Chris Weber.

     p. cm.

  Includes bibliographical references and index.

  ISBN 978-1-935543-65-7 (perfect bound) -- ISBN 978-1-935543-66-4 (library edition) 1. Remedial teaching--United States. 2. Response to intervention (Learning disabled children) 3. Slow learning children--Education--United States. 4. Learning disabled children--Education--United States. I. Mattos, Mike (Mike William) II. Weber, Chris, 1948- III. Title.

  LB1029.R4.B786 2012

  371.9'043--dc23

                          2011034298

Solution Tree
Jeffrey C. Jones, CEO & President

Solution Tree Press
President: Douglas M. Rife
Publisher: Robert D. Clouse
Vice President of Production: Gretchen Knapp
Managing Production Editor: Caroline Wise
Cover and Text Designer: Jenn Taylor

Acknowledgments

RTI is about using the collective knowledge and skills of an organization to benefit students. The creation of this book followed the same premise; it was truly a collaborative effort to help children. To that end, there are many people whose contributions were invaluable to our efforts. We must first acknowledge the outstanding professionals at Solution Tree. Under the leadership of our friend and colleague, Jeff Jones, Solution Tree has become the preeminent provider of educational resources and staff development in North America. It is an honor to collaborate with a company that is truly committed to the mission of getting proven research and resources into the hands of educators. We owe a debt of gratitude to Gretchen Knapp for her exceptional editing of both of our books. She has the rare ability to simultaneously grasp our vision, challenge our assumptions, unite our ideas, and evaluate the effectiveness of every sentence, phrase, and word. Our two books are infinitely better due to her advice and expertise. As much of our recent learning has been gained through our work with schools and districts throughout North America, we thank Terri Martin, Shannon Ritz, and the entire Professional Development and Institutes departments for their support of our model, pyramid response to intervention. Without the efforts of the entire Solution Tree family, this book would not have been possible.

Additionally, we have had the privilege of working with some of the finest educators in America. These dear colleagues, many of whom serve as fellow Associates for Solution Tree, have graciously shared their knowledge, their materials, and their friendship. We would specifically like to thank Janet Malone for her assistance with the assessment portions of this book—this work is much richer because of her contributions. We also thank Anthony Muhammad for his influence on the school culture elements of this book. We were blessed with the opportunity to work closely with Anthony a few years back, and his research had a significant impact on our work.

Taking this book from a rough draft to the final copy was like polishing a precious gem. We thank Anita Mattos for her editing of our initial manuscript. She is a distinguished educator in her own right, and her efforts helped refine and clarify our prose. We also thank Connie Galliher for her technical editing of our first draft.

Finally, both of our books would not have been possible without the support we have received from Rick DuFour, Becky DuFour, and Bob Eaker. Our view of RTI has been framed through the lens of their Professional Learning Communities at Work™ model. Their contributions to our profession are profound, and their impact on our work is indelible. We are honored to consider them mentors, colleagues, and dear friends.

Solution Tree Press would like to thank the following reviewers:

Alane E. Adams
Principal
Tanglewood Elementary
Fort Myers, Florida

Matthew K. Burns
Professor of Educational Psychology
  and Co-Director of the Minnesota
  Center for Reading Research
University of Minnesota
Minneapolis, Minnesota

Megan Dooley
Intervention Specialist
Upper Arlington City Schools
Upper Arlington, Ohio

Kris Quinn
Principal
Horace Mann Elementary
Iowa City, Iowa

Sherry L. Reed
Curriculum Coordinator
USD 437 Auburn Washburn
Topeka, Kansas

Philip Ruetz
Special Education Teacher
Casa Grande Elementary School District 4
Casa Grande, Arizona

Jackie Webb
Executive Director of Learning
  Services
Sheridan School District
Denver, Colorado

Tammy S. Wolicki
Director of Curriculum, Instruction,
  and Assessment
Greensburg Salem School District
Greensburg, Pennsylvania

Visit **go.solution-tree.com/rti** to download
the reproducibles in this book.

Table of Contents

Reproducible pages are in italics.

About the Authors

Austin Buffum, EdD, is former senior deputy superintendent of the Capistrano Unified School District, which enrolls more than fifty thousand students in South Orange County, California. Dr. Buffum attended the Principals' Center at the Harvard Graduate School of Education, where he was greatly inspired by the work of its founder, Roland Barth. He later led Capistrano's K–12 instructional program on an increasingly collaborative path toward operating as a professional learning community (PLC). During this process, thirty-seven of the district's schools were designated California Distinguished Schools, and eleven received National Blue Ribbon recognition. Dr. Buffum is coauthor of *Pyramid Response to Intervention: RTI, Professional Learning Communities, and How to Respond When Kids Don't Learn* and *Generations at School*. He also contributed to the anthology *The Collaborative Administrator*.

Dr. Buffum has served as a music teacher and coordinator, elementary school principal, curriculum director, and assistant superintendent. He was selected 2006 Curriculum and Instruction Administrator of the Year by the Association of California School Administrators. A graduate of the University of Southern California, Dr. Buffum earned a bachelor of music and received his master of education with honors. He also holds a doctor of education from Nova Southeastern University in Fort Lauderdale, Florida.

Mike Mattos is recognized throughout North America for his work in the areas of response to intervention and professional learning communities. He is coauthor of *Pyramid Response to Intervention*, which was a 2009 finalist for the Distinguished Achievement Award from the Association of Educational Publishers. He also contributed to the anthology *The Collaborative Administrator*.

Mike is former principal of both Marjorie Veeh Elementary School and Pioneer Middle School in Tustin, California. In 2004, Marjorie Veeh Elementary, a school with a large population of at-risk youth, won the California Distinguished School and National Title I Achieving School awards.

A National Blue Ribbon School, Pioneer is one of only thirteen schools in the nation selected by the GE Foundation as a Best-Practice Partner and is one of eight schools chosen by Richard DuFour to be featured in the video *The Power of Professional Learning Communities at Work™: Bringing the Big Ideas to Life*. Based on standardized test scores, Pioneer ranks among the top 1 percent of California middle schools and in 2009 and 2011 was named Orange County's top middle school. For his leadership, Mike was named the Orange County Middle School Administrator of the Year by the Association of California School Administrators.

Chris Weber, EdD, is a consultant and administrative coach for Chicago Public Schools and the Oakland (California) Unified School District. As principal of R. H. Dana Elementary School in the Capistrano Unified School District (CUSD) in California, together with his staff, Dr. Weber lifted the school to remarkable levels of success. Designated school-wide Title I, with more than 60 percent of all students English learners and Latino and more than 75 percent socioeconomically disadvantaged, R. H. Dana consistently exceeded adequate yearly progress (AYP) goals. The school's gains over four years were among the top 1 percent in the state, and it was the first school in the decades-long history of the CUSD to win the State of California's Title I Academic Achievement Award. Under Dr. Weber's leadership, R. H. Dana earned the first California Distinguished School Award in the school's history. After the percentage of students meeting AYP in English and math tripled in four years, the school was named a National Blue Ribbon School.

Dr. Weber has taught grades K–12 and served as a site administrator for elementary and secondary schools. He was director of instruction for the Garden Grove Unified School District in California, which was the 2004 winner of the prestigious Broad Prize for Urban Education. During this time, all groups of students in the district's forty-seven K–6 schools achieved double-digit AYP gains in mathematics and English language arts.

Dr. Weber is a coauthor of *Pyramid Response to Intervention* and *Pyramid of Behavior Interventions: Seven Keys to a Positive Learning Environment.* He earned a master's degree from California State University, San Marcos, and a doctorate of education from the University of California (Irvine and Los Angeles). He is a graduate of the United States Air Force Academy and a former U.S. Air Force pilot.

A Sense of Urgency

In our first book, *Pyramid Response to Intervention: RTI, Professional Learning Communities, and How to Respond When Kids Don't Learn* (Buffum, Mattos, & Weber, 2009, p. 1), we proclaimed in the first sentence: "This book is written for practitioners by practitioners."

Once again, we repeat this assertion. We remain resolute in our belief that response to intervention (RTI) is our best hope to provide every child with the additional time and support needed to learn at high levels. RTI's underlying premise is that schools should not delay providing help for struggling students until they fall far enough behind to qualify for special education, but instead should provide timely, targeted, systematic interventions to all students who demonstrate the need. To achieve this goal, we remain equally convinced that the only way for an organization to successfully implement RTI practices is within the professional learning community (PLC) model. Our conviction has only grown stronger as we have witnessed unprecedented levels of learning at schools that are effectively combining these two complementary, research-based models into a singular process focused on student learning—a process we refer to as *pyramid response to intervention* (PRTI). Educators across North America continue to validate that the practical examples and proven tools provided in our first book are helping them meet the needs of all students.

While we firmly support the ideas and recommendations described in our first book, we have learned a great deal since its publication. A number of factors led to our new understanding and insights. First and foremost, we have remained practitioners, continuing to work directly on the educational front lines. Through this work, we have gained greater clarity of thought and have developed additional tools to help schools improve student achievement. We have had the privilege of collaborating with educators throughout North America as they work to transform their schools and districts. Our travels have taken us from one-room schoolhouses on the frozen tundra of Alaska to large urban secondary schools in the economic decay of America's inner cities. We have learned how schools with markedly different student demographics, resources, and local requirements are successfully applying pyramid response to intervention practices to meet the diverse needs of their students.

Equally important to our learning is the work we have done with schools that are struggling to implement the changes needed to successfully respond when students don't learn. The reasons for these struggles are as varied as the places we have visited.

Through all of these challenging experiences, we have gained a better understanding of the obstacles many schools face in implementing RTI. We have learned that to successfully implement RTI, a school must not only provide its educators with a new set of tools to help students learn, but must also help them develop a new way of thinking about their roles and responsibilities.

Complementing our firsthand experience is a wealth of new research, literature, and instructional materials in the area of RTI. This new information challenges us to re-examine our ideas, refine our thinking, and revise our recommended resources. In some cases, we find ourselves in strong disagreement with the products and suggestions being "sold" as RTI best practices. We will outline our objections to these claims, as we are concerned that the powerful promise of RTI is being undermined by misguided recommendations and rigid protocols that fail to support and empower educators in their efforts to help all students succeed.

Regarding the foundational role of professional learning communities in the RTI process, we have been most fortunate to continue to learn from the three architects of PLC at Work practices, Richard and Rebecca DuFour and Robert Eaker. They continue to generously share their unmatched expertise, respond to our questions, and help us to better understand exactly how connected and powerful are the concepts of professional learning communities and response to intervention.

Most importantly, our efforts to write a second book have been driven by the same motivation that inspired the first: a sense of urgency. Never have the demands on our educational system been greater or the consequences of failure so severe. Consider for a moment what the future will look like for students who fail at school:

- In 2008, more than 1.2 million students dropped out of school (Swanson, 2008).
- Dropouts on average earn about $12,000 per year, nearly 50 percent less than those who have a high school diploma (Muennig & Woolf, 2007).
- Dropouts are 50 percent less likely to have a job that offers a pension plan or health insurance (Muennig & Woolf, 2007).
- The National Institute for Literacy estimates that approximately 70 percent of adult welfare recipients have lower level literacy skills, and about 47 percent of adult welfare recipients have not graduated from high school (USDOE, 2003).
- Eighty-five percent of juvenile delinquents are functionally illiterate (USDOE, 2003).

With stakes this high, a quality education is no longer a privilege, but a moral responsibility we owe to every child. It is our sincere hope that this book will provide our fellow educators with additional tools, practices, and most importantly, the right *thinking* needed to meet this noble task.

CHAPTER 1

A New Way of Thinking

What worked yesterday is the gilded cage of tomorrow.

—PETER BLOCK

Gone are the days when hard work and elbow grease were enough for the average person to make a living. To prepare for successful adult life in a competitive global marketplace, today's students must learn more than the three Rs; they must also master the higher-level thinking skills required to continue to learn beyond high school. Those who do will find numerous paths to success. In stark contrast, many students who fail in school will go on to adult lives characterized by poverty, welfare, and incarceration, as we saw in the preface. With such high stakes, today's educators are like tightrope walkers without a safety net—responsible for meeting the needs of every child, with very little room for error.

We know one thing for certain: we are never going to get there doing what we have always done. Our traditional school system was created in a time when the typical educator worked in a one-room schoolhouse and served as the only teacher for an entire town. Today it is virtually impossible for a single teacher to possess all the skills and knowledge necessary to meet the unique needs of every child in the classroom. But even the one-room schoolteacher was not expected to achieve that outcome, as throughout most of the 20th century fewer than 20 percent of all jobs required even a high school diploma (Hagenbaugh, 2002).

Our current reality dictates that *every* student succeeds in school, and so we must face the facts: our current system has never produced these results—not in the past, not now—nor will it in the future.

Fortunately, we know what to do differently. Our profession has never had greater clarity and consensus on what schools must do to ensure that all students learn. As Mike Schmoker (2004, p. 424) states, "There are simple, proven, affordable structures that exist right now and could have a dramatic, widespread impact on schools and achievement—in virtually any school. An astonishing level of agreement has emerged on this point."

Compelling evidence shows that response to intervention can successfully engage a school's staff in a collective process to provide every child with the additional time and support needed to learn at high levels (Burns, Appleton, & Stehouwer, 2005). In the RTI process, schools do not delay in providing help for struggling students until they fall far enough behind to qualify for special education, but instead provide targeted and systematic interventions to all students as soon as they demonstrate need. Hundreds of schools are effectively implementing RTI practices to achieve record levels of learning for their students.

Yet in spite of this knowledge, most schools continue to struggle to meet the needs of all their students, especially the ones most at risk. Most schools continue to function like one-room schoolhouses, with individual teachers responsible only for "their" kids. Some schools mistakenly view RTI as merely a new way to qualify at-risk students for special education and focus on trying a few token general education interventions before referring struggling students for traditional special education testing and placement. Others implement RTI from a compliance perspective, doing just enough to meet mandates and stay legal. For still others, RTI efforts are driven by a desire to raise test scores, which often leads to practices that are counterproductive to the guiding principles of RTI. Finally, some schools defiantly refuse to take responsibility for student learning, instead opting to blame the kids, parents, lack of funding, or society in general for their students' failures. Far too many schools find the cultural beliefs and essential practices of RTI such a radical departure from how they have traditionally functioned that they are uncomfortable or unwilling to commit to the level of change necessary to succeed. While the specific obstacles vary, the underlying cause of the problem is the same: too many schools have failed to develop the correct *thinking* about response to intervention.

To fully realize the benefits of RTI for our students, we must develop a new way of thinking about how schools should work and redefine our responsibilities as educators. This new way of thinking is critical for two reasons. First, we observe too many schools that take proven research-based practices and misapply them due to misguided principles and priorities—they implement some of the right practices, but for all the wrong reasons. For example, a well-known characteristic of RTI is its emphasis on fidelity when implementing research-based instructional practices. To this end, districts often purchase a research-based core language arts program and then, in the name of "program fidelity," dictate that this program constitutes the only instructional materials that district teachers can use. The quest for fidelity then becomes so rigid that each teacher is required to be on the same lesson, on the same day, following the same script. While we agree that scientifically research-based resources should be implemented within the proven protocols of the program, we also know that not all kids learn the same way.

Second, no matter how many practical examples and proven interventions we provide in this book, there is no way we could possibly list examples of every intervention a school will need to meet the unique needs of every at-risk student. New ways of thinking about RTI will empower schools to adapt research and proven practices to meet the individual needs of their students using the distinct talents and resources of their sites. We want you to become like a master jazz musician: able to play the correct RTI melody, but also able to improvise and, ultimately, create your own music.

Throwing Out the Old Questions

How do we develop a new way of thinking? We must start by asking the right questions. The right questions shape organizational thinking and lead to answers and actions that improve learning for all students. Unfortunately, we find that far too many schools are asking the wrong questions.

How Do We Raise Our Test Scores?

This is the most pervasive misguided (and misguiding) question. While high-stakes testing is an undeniable reality in public education, this fatally flawed initial question leads to the wrong answers for achieving deep levels of student learning. We are constantly confronted with situations in which district leadership gives lip service to RTI while reinforcing the need for schools to "get the scores up now, or else." As a result, schools often seek out the quick fix that will result in a sudden bump in test scores rather than investing in the long-term work.

Many districts that focus first on raising test scores have concluded that strictly enforced pacing guides for each course of study are needed to ensure that all required state standards are taught prior to the high-stakes state tests. Usually, these guides determine exactly how many days each teacher has to teach a specific standard. Such thinking makes sense if the goal is to *teach* all the material prior to the state assessments, but not if the goal is to have all students *learn* essential standards. As educators, we know that students don't learn at the same speed, so when arbitrary, predetermined amounts of time are allocated to achieve specific learning outcomes, students who need additional time to learn the concept will be left in the wake as the teacher races to cover all the material.

This faulty thinking also leads to misguided intervention decisions, such as focusing school resources primarily on the "bubble kids"—those who are slightly below proficient. This policy is based on the conclusion that if the bubble students can improve a little, the school's aggregated proficiency levels will likely make a substantial short-term jump. Consequently, the students far below proficiency often receive less help. If the primary goal of the school is to raise test scores, the bubble-kid approach, although morally bankrupt, makes some sense because the lowest-achieving learners are so far behind that providing them intensive resources will likely not show immediate gains in the school's state assessment scores. But if the goal is to help all students learn at high levels, this approach will do nothing for the students most in need.

These examples demonstrate thinking and practices that are contradictory to the underlying principles of RTI and the values of a learning-focused school. This is not to suggest that RTI will not raise test scores—on the contrary. When schools focus on *all* students learning at higher levels, improvement in standardized assessments *will* occur.

How Do We Implement RTI?

We often work with schools that view RTI as a mandated program that must be "implemented." District leadership creates implementation checklists, protocols, and timelines and tells school staff what they must do to "implement RTI." Typically, these protocols suggest how many weeks a student should remain in a tier and when the referral for special education assessment might begin. Like obedient soldiers, site educators take their RTI marching orders and begin to complete the items on their RTI to-do list, such as administering a universal screening assessment, regrouping kids in tiered groups, or creating an intervention period.

This approach is fraught with potential pitfalls. It reduces RTI to a list of disconnected tasks to cross off, rather than a set of ongoing *processes* to improve teaching and learning. The specific things we ask educators to do in response to intervention are not ends in themselves, however, but means to an end. For example, a school's goal should not be to administer a universal screening assessment in reading, but rather to ensure that all students are able to read proficiently. To achieve that goal, it is essential to start by measuring each student's current reading level, thus collecting vital information needed to identify at-risk students and differentiate initial instruction. Universal screening is a *means* to help achieve the *end* of student learning.

To secure the benefits of RTI, we must do more than provide teachers with new protocols, assessments, and intervention programs. For real change to occur, we must sufficiently address attitudes, beliefs, and behaviors, as Seymour Sarason (1996) argues. Michael Fullan writes:

> Most strategies for reform focus on structures, formal requirements, and event-based activities. . . . They do not struggle directly with existing cultures and which new values and practices may be required. . . . *Restructuring* (which can be done by fiat) occurs time and time again, whereas *reculturing* (how teachers come to question and change their beliefs and habits) is what is needed. (Fullan, 2007, p. 25, emphasis in the original)

It is not necessary for district leadership to make a choice between structural and cultural change; both are absolutely necessary. But in many districts, efforts to uniformly implement RTI place a greater emphasis on compliance with paperwork and protocols than on high levels of engagement and ownership among its teachers. RTI is as much a way of thinking as it is a way of doing; it is not a list of tasks to complete, but a dynamic value system of goals that must be embedded in all of the school's ongoing procedures. This way of thinking places a higher priority on making a shared commitment to every student's success than on merely implementing programs.

How Do We Stay Legal?

Because RTI was part of the reauthorization of the Individuals with Disabilities Education Improvement Act (IDEIA) in 2004, many schools view RTI implementation from the perspective of *legal* compliance. This concern is certainly understandable, as special education is one of the most litigious segments of public education, and the potential costs of being out of compliance or losing a fair hearing can be crippling to district resources.

However, if this question is the first consideration when creating an RTI system, it leads to a number of unfortunate outcomes. For example, we find many districts creating unnecessarily complicated, time-intensive documentation processes for every level of student intervention out of fear that the data may be needed someday if a specific child is referred for special education identification. Teachers required to follow this

Byzantine paper trail tell us that they often decide against recommending students for interventions because "it isn't worth the paperwork." Other teachers complain that they hate RTI because they spend more time filling out forms than actually working with at-risk students. Additionally, we have worked with districts that refuse to begin implementing RTI until there is a greater depth of legal interpretation and case precedent—meanwhile, their traditional special education services continue to achieve woefully insufficient results in student learning.

If there is one thing that traditional special education has taught us, it is that staying compliant does not necessarily lead to improved student learning; in fact, the opposite is more often the case. Since the creation of special education in 1975, we have spent billions of dollars and millions of hours on making sure that we meet timelines, fill out the correct forms, check the correct boxes, and secure the proper signatures for special education. The vast majority of schools are compliant, but are kids learning? Consider these facts:

- Nationally, the special education redesignation rate (the percentage of students who are officially deemed no longer in need of special education services) is 4 percent (USDOE, 1996a).
- According to the U.S. Department of Education, the graduation rate of kids with special needs is 57 percent (USDOE, 2001).
- Up to an estimated 50 percent of the U.S. prison population was identified as having special needs in school (NCSET, 2006).

By almost any measure, there is no evidence to suggest that greater levels of legal compliance lead to greater levels of learning. So while staying legal is a necessary consideration, the first question we should pose is not how do we stay legal, but rather, how do we help this child be successful? When their children succeed in school, parents rarely file for fair hearing.

What Is Wrong With This Student?

This has been the first question of our special education system for nearly a half-century. At most schools, when a student consistently struggles in the general education program, the school's systematic response is to refer that student for special education testing. As special education expert David Prasse (2009) states, traditionally schools have believed that "failure to succeed in a general education program meant the student must, therefore, have a disability." Does special education testing assess the effectiveness and quality of the teaching that the child has received? Rarely, if ever; instead, the entire focus is on discovering potential avenues by which a student might become qualified to receive special education services.

Response to intervention is built on a polar-opposite philosophy from traditional special education. When a student struggles, rather than assume there is something wrong with the student, we first assume that we are not teaching the child correctly. We turn our attention inward to ask how we can find better ways to meet this child's specific learning needs. Unless a school is able to move beyond asking, "What is wrong with this student?" it is unlikely that school will ever see RTI as anything more than a new way to identify students for special education.

Asking the Right Questions

If a school begins with the mindset that RTI is a means of raising test scores, implementing mandates, staying legal, and/or identifying kids for special education, then those outcomes will guide staff thinking throughout the process. In turn, these misguided principles will often lead to misguided actions. The purpose of RTI is to ensure high levels of learning for every child, and our actions must be guided by that purpose.

If the previous questions are the wrong questions to guide our thinking and actions, then what are the right questions to lead our work?

Why Are We Here?

As Judith Bardwick recommends, "the most important question in any organization has to be 'what is the business of our business?' Answering this question is the first step in setting priorities" (Bardwick, 1996, p. 134). If this is the case, educators must begin by asking, why are we here? Our schools were built neither to give educators a place to teach nor to give government officials locations to administer high-stakes standardized tests each spring. If we peel away the various layers of local, state, and federal mandates piled on schools, the core mission of any school system is to provide students with the skills and knowledge they will need to be self-sufficient, successful adults.

As educators, we should provide every student the type of education we would want for our own child. Ask parents what they want school to provide, and it is doubtful they'd answer, "I just want my child to score proficient on state assessments," or "I want my child to master standard 2.2.3 this year." As parents, we see the bigger picture. Learning specific academic standards and passing state tests are meaningless if the child does not ultimately become an intelligent, responsible adult who possesses the knowledge and quality of character to live a rewarding adult life.

What Knowledge and Skills Will Our Children Need to Be Successful Adults?

If the fundamental purpose of school is to prepare our children to be successful adults and citizens, this is logically the next question we should ask. To be sure, the world for which we are preparing our students today is not the world most educators entered when we transitioned from childhood to adulthood. During the 20th century, the United States became the most powerful economic force on earth based on an economy driven by industry and agriculture. One hundred years ago, almost half of America's adult population farmed for a living, while another third worked in factories (Hagenbaugh, 2002; U.S. Department of Agriculture, Utah State University Extension, & LetterPress Software, n.d.). These honorable, labor-intensive professions did not require a high school diploma or college degree, yet provided sufficient wages and benefits for most Americans to maintain a middle-class standard of living.

Today, less than 1 percent of our population directly farms for a living, and less than 10 percent works in factories (Hagenbaugh, 2002; U.S. Department of Agriculture et al., n.d.).

Our new economy is driven by technology, innovation, and service. Because technology and human knowledge are changing at faster and faster rates, educator Karl Fisch (n.d.) states: "We are currently preparing students for jobs that don't yet exist, using technologies that haven't been invented, in order to solve problems we don't even know are problems yet." Due to this acceleration of human knowledge, Alvin Toffler (Toffler & Toffler, 1999) says the definition of literacy in the 21st century will not center on whether a person can read and write, but rather on whether a person can learn, unlearn, and relearn.

How do we prepare students for jobs that don't exist? How do we teach our students knowledge that has not been discovered? Teaching comprehension and computation skills will not be enough; we need our students to be able to analyze, synthesize, evaluate, compare and contrast, manipulate, and apply information. Our state tests measure these skills inadequately at best. Think how low we are setting the bar for our students if our only goal is to get every child to be proficient on state assessments. If we truly focus our efforts on the higher-level thinking skills that our children need for their future, state tests will be downright easy for them.

How Effectively Are We Preparing Students for These Future Challenges?

Because our traditional educational system was designed to prepare students for an economy driven by farms and factories, it was assumed that only a small percentage of students would learn beyond high school. Consequently, schools did not expect all students to learn at high levels, but instead ranked and sorted kids along a bell-shaped curve, identifying those few expected to reach higher education. In such a system, it is reasonable to expect that "a few people will excel, most will be satisfactory or average, and a few will fail" (Fendler & Muzaffar, 2008, p. 63). This approach assumes that student learning is more a function of each student's innate ability and socioeconomic status, and a teacher's job is not necessarily to develop each student's academic ability, but rather to reveal it. Yet as Benjamin Bloom (1971, p. 49) states:

> The normal curve is not sacred. It describes the outcome of a random process. Since education is a purposeful activity in which we seek to have the students learn what we teach, the achievement distribution should be very different from the normal curve if our instruction is effective. In fact, our educational efforts may be said to be unsuccessful to the extent that student achievement is normally distributed.

It is unrealistic to expect our traditional school system to ensure high levels of learning for every child with practices designed to have only a small percentage of students achieve at these levels. In fact, "the bell curve serves as both a model and a fitting symbol of an archaic public education system. It describes a broad swath of mediocrity flanked by a sliver of excellence and a ribbon of failure" (Wallace & Graves, 1995, p. 24).

What Must We Do to Make Success the Reality for Every Child?

Once we have embraced the belief that the fundamental purpose of our schools is to ensure that every student learns what he or she needs to know to become a successful adult, and we clearly understand the skills and knowledge that our students will need to be competitive in the world they will inherit, then our final question would be, what must we do to make this a reality for every child?

While this question sounds daunting, the answer is within our grasp. There is tremendous evidence and consensus on what schools need to do to ensure that all kids succeed. As Ron Edmonds said more than thirty years ago: "We can, whenever and wherever we choose, successfully teach all children whose schooling is of interest to us. We already know more than we need to do that. Whether or not we do it must finally depend on how we feel about the fact that we haven't so far" (Edmonds, 1979a, p. 23).

Implementing the Formula for Learning

So what do schools need to do to unlock the potential of every child? If we took the research on effective teaching and condensed it into a simple formula to ensure student learning, the formula for learning would look like this (Bloom, 1968; Guskey & Pigott, 1988):

Targeted Instruction + Time = Learning

It is a universally acknowledged truth in education that all children do not learn the same way. Because learning styles and instructional needs vary from student to student, we must provide each student *targeted instruction*—that is, teaching practices designed to meet the *individual* learning needs of each student. We also know that all children do not learn at the same speed. Toddlers do not learn to walk or talk at the same rate, nor do students learn to read, write, or solve equations at the same time. We know that some kids will need more time to learn.

While few educational researchers, policymakers, administrators, or teachers would disagree with this formula for learning, very few schools have designed the instructional day to provide every student differentiated instruction and flexible time to learn. In reality, most schools operate in ways that are counterproductive to these outcomes. Consider for a moment how our traditional school system currently works:

- Each student is randomly assigned to a teacher for each grade (elementary level) and/or subject (secondary level).
- Each teacher is responsible for meeting all the learning needs of every student assigned to him or her.
- The teacher provides daily instruction, usually in a whole-group setting.
- Instruction is provided within a predetermined, finite amount of time, most often determined by the school's master schedule.
- If the teacher's instructional style and methods match a student's learning style, and if the class period provides the student with enough time to learn, then the student will be successful.

- If either the teacher's instructional style and methods or the time allotted do not meet an individual student's learning needs, then the student will likely fail.

Traditional school practices are in direct conflict with the formula for learning. The failure to differentiate instruction to meet the needs of individual students makes *instruction* a constant; likewise, finite amounts of time for all students to learn new material make *time* a constant. In the traditional formula for learning, if instruction and time are constants, only one remaining element can be variable—*learning*!

As educators, we can't be surprised that our schools are leaving kids behind. The traditional model ensures this outcome. It worked perfectly for preparing students to be adults in 1950, but we are no longer preparing kids for life in Mayberry; we are preparing them for life in the age of BlackBerry. If our new mission is to ensure high levels of learning for all students, learning must be the constant, while instruction and time must be varied to meet the needs of every student. That is the purpose of RTI: to systematically provide every child with the additional time and support needed to learn at high levels.

While the underlying premise of the formula for learning is easy to understand, most schools find that putting this principle into daily practice is not nearly so simple, due to their overemphasis on raising test scores, compliance-driven decision making, one-size-fits-all directives, and implementation practices that are too burdensome for the site educators who actually do the work. We have carefully and purposefully designed this book to address these obstacles by focusing on two critical outcomes.

First, we strongly believe that changing our schools must start by building a culture of commitment, empowerment, and site ownership. We create this culture when we find balance between (1) expecting schools to abandon outdated traditional school practices and implement the proven practices necessary to ensure that all students learn and (2) allowing schools the autonomy to tailor the implementation of these practices to meet the individual needs of their students, using the distinct talents and resources of their local sites. We must be "tight" about *what* schools must do to help all students learn and "loose" on *how* they carry out these concepts and practices (DuFour, DuFour, Eaker, & Many, 2006). This balance of responsibility and site ownership empowers schools. Second, we must adopt guiding principles and practices that are simple, practical, and doable. Our focus on these two vital outcomes has profoundly affected our rethinking and refining of our recommendations in this book. Nowhere is this more evident than in our efforts to simplify our thinking about RTI into four essential guiding principles.

Understanding the Four Cs of RTI

If our goal is to create the right way of thinking about our work as educators, then what are the essential principles that must guide our actions? What practices must we follow if we want all students to succeed? We believe there are four; we call them the four Cs of RTI. They are:

1. **Collective responsibility.** A shared belief that the primary responsibility of each member of the organization is to ensure high levels of learning for every child. Thinking is guided by the question, Why are we here?

2. **Concentrated instruction.** A systematic process of identifying essential knowledge and skills that all students must master to learn at high levels, and determining the specific learning needs for each child to get there. Thinking is guided by the question, Where do we need to go?

3. **Convergent assessment.** An ongoing process of collectively analyzing targeted evidence to determine the specific learning needs of each child and the effectiveness of the instruction the child receives in meeting these needs. Thinking is guided by the question, Where are we now?

4. **Certain access.** A systematic process that guarantees every student will receive the time and support needed to learn at high levels. Thinking is guided by the question, How do we get every child there?

We contend that these four Cs are the essential guiding principles of RTI.

Consider for a moment the meaning of the word *essential*. When something is essential, it is absolutely indispensable, so important to the whole that the whole cannot survive without it. Without each of the four Cs, it is impossible for a school to achieve high levels of learning for every child. The four Cs work interdependently to create the systems, structures, and processes needed to provide every child with additional time and support. All other practices and specific recommendations flow from these four essential guiding principles, as we'll explore in the rest of the book.

Rethinking the Pyramid

In thinking of RTI, the most common image that comes to mind is the RTI pyramid (see fig. 1.1).

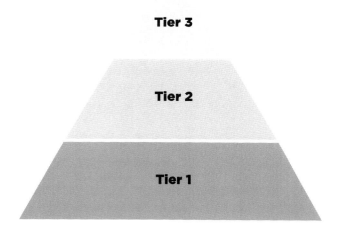

Figure 1.1: The traditional RTI pyramid.

Working with schools throughout North America, we have found that this graphic has been both a blessing and a curse. When used properly, it is both a powerful visual representation of the RTI process and a useful structure to assist in organizing a school's core instruction and support resources. The pyramid shape is wide at the bottom to represent the basic instruction that all students receive. As students demonstrate the need for additional support, they move up the pyramid, receiving increasingly more targeted and intensive help. Fewer students should need the services offered at the upper levels, thus creating the tapered shape of a pyramid. The pyramid is also traditionally separated into tiers, with Tier 1 representing grade-level core instruction, Tier 2 supplemental interventions, and Tier 3 intensive student support.

When used as a visual model to capture these guiding ideas, the pyramid has proven to be a helpful tool for schools implementing RTI. Unfortunately, far too often we have seen schools and districts misinterpret and misapply the pyramid structure. Rather than create an intervention system that is fluid, flexible, and sensitive to the needs of each child, schools and districts implement the pyramid as a rigid, protocol-driven program. Student identification, placement, and duration in each tier are predetermined based upon screening assessments, cut scores, and program decision protocols. Often, the upper tiers are disjointed and misaligned to the school's core instruction. School resources and responsibilities are frequently divided, with Tiers 1 and 2 designated for general education and Tier 3 for special education.

Considering these concerns, we have carefully re-examined the RTI pyramid. We still believe there is tremendous power in using a pyramid as a visual representation of the way in which we should think about RTI, but we believe a more accurate way to capture the right thinking is by inverting the pyramid, as in figure 1.2.

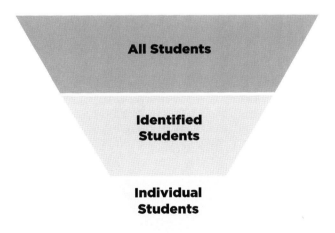

Figure 1.2: The inverted RTI pyramid.

If we consider the formula for learning, we know we must focus our efforts on the unique needs of each child. The inverted pyramid continually focuses a school's collective attention and resources to a single point: the individual child. We still believe that the pyramid should be wide at the top to represent access to the core grade-level curriculum that all students deserve and need. We also strongly support the RTI belief that a school's initial core instruction must be designed to meet the needs of most students and should include differentiation. Beyond this initial instruction, when some students demonstrate the need for more targeted instruction and additional time, the school responds by focusing on the needs of each of these students.

In addition to making the pyramid too rigid and focused on special education identification, schools consistently make another damaging misinterpretation and application of the traditional RTI pyramid. Too often, the process of creating a schoolwide system of interventions has reinforced a belief in general education teachers that they are responsible for only the initial teaching in Tier 1. If students require help after initial teaching, the classroom teacher's response is, who do I send them to? Especially at schools with a large number of at-risk students, this practice overwhelms the intervention team, site intervention resources, and the RTI process.

In response to this problem, many districts have responded by dictating that classroom teachers cannot refer a student for schoolwide interventions until they can document a set of predetermined interventions that must first be tried in their classroom. This approach places the initial response of Tier 2 interventions with the classroom teacher.

The problem with this approach is that every student does not struggle for the same reason. The reasons can vary from just needing a little extra practice on a new concept, to lacking necessary prerequisite skills, to requiring assistance with English language, to severe attendance and behavioral issues. It is unlikely that each teacher has all the skills and time needed to effectively meet every need—making initial Tier 2 response an impossible responsibility for classroom teachers. This approach fails students *and* educators.

The answer to the dilemma of how to best meet the child's needs, given limited resources, lies not in determining who is responsible for intervening when students don't learn—classroom teachers *or* the school's intervention resources—but in determining the responsibilities of these specific groups to ensure that *all* students succeed. To visually capture this thinking, we have divided the RTI pyramid into two distinct areas of responsibility: interventions led by collaborative teacher teams and interventions led by schoolwide teams (fig. 1.3).

Collaborative teacher teams are teams of educators whose classes share essential student learning outcomes; these teachers work collaboratively to ensure that their students master these critical standards. The structure for teacher teams could include grade-level, subject/course-specific, vertical, and/or interdisciplinary teams.

While teacher teams focus on specific grade/subject learning outcomes, we recommend that two *schoolwide collaborative teams*—a site leadership team and an intervention team—be responsible for coordinating core instruction and interventions across

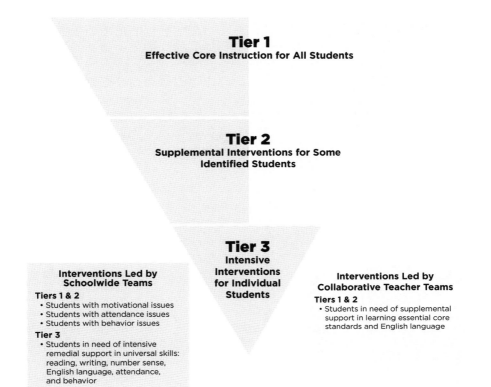

Figure 1.3: Team responsibilities in the inverted RTI pyramid.

the school. Specifically, we will make the case that a *school leadership team* should be responsible for building consensus on the school's mission of collective responsibility for student learning, coordinating individual and team efforts across the school to meet this goal, and allocating the school's limited resources to best support high levels of learning for all students. While this leadership team is responsible for the larger schoolwide structures that support student learning, the *school intervention team*'s primary responsibility is to coordinate the school's efforts to meet the needs of individual students requiring intensive support.

The structures, roles, and responsibilities of both teacher and schoolwide teams will be thoroughly explored throughout this book. Providing greater clarity on exactly how to share responsibility for student learning will make RTI simpler, more focused, and more doable for educators—and more effective for children.

The RTI pyramid is more than a visual representation of a system of interventions; it is a practical tool that will help transform thinking into action. It has the flexibility to help both district leadership plan for systemwide interventions and grade-level teams plan to teach specific standards. Throughout the book, we will use this collaborative vision to frame content, connect ideas, and lead schools to achievable outcomes.

What's Next

The rest of this book explores the four Cs, the RTI pyramid, and their implications. Each chapter concludes with activities and tools to further your learning; these are also available online (visit **go.solution-tree.com/rti** to download them). By the end of this book, you will understand how to:

- Use the four essential guiding principles to guide thinking and implementation
- Create a school leadership team to lead the shift to a culture of collective responsibility and allocate resources for the work of collaborative teacher teams and the schoolwide intervention team
- Build team structures for collaboration
- Utilize collaborative teacher teams to define essential learnings and deliver concentrated instruction and Tier 2 interventions in core standards and English language
- Develop a system of convergent assessment to *identify* students for intervention, *determine* their unique needs, *monitor* progress (the effectiveness of the instruction and intervention each child is receiving), and *revise* interventions or *extend* learning based on progress
- Create a toolbox of effective interventions
- Utilize a schoolwide intervention team to address complex issues such as severe motivation, attendance, and behavior issues as well as English language proficiency and intense academic struggles
- Ensure certain access and monitor the success of your RTI program
- Re-envision the role of special education

In his book *Good to Great*, Jim Collins says that great organizations "maintain unwavering faith that you can and will prevail in the end, regardless of the difficulties, and, at the same time have the discipline to confront the most brutal facts about your current reality, whatever they may be" (Collins, 2005, p. 13). We have shared the brutal facts of our traditional educational system's ability to prepare our students for the new realities they will face as adults. Now that we understand our current reality, know our destination, and have defined our path to get there, let us begin the journey.

CHAPTER 2

Collective Responsibility: Why Are We Here?

> **Collective responsibility:** *A shared belief that the primary responsibility of each member of the organization is to ensure high levels of learning for every child. Thinking is guided by the question, Why are we here?*

A successful journey does not begin with taking a first step, but with facing the right direction. Likewise, transforming a school or district does not start with implementing a sequence of tasks, but with creating clarity on the organization's direction: its fundamental purpose. In his book *Transforming School Culture*, Anthony Muhammad describes this difference in terms of "technical changes" and "cultural changes." Technical changes are made to tools such as a school's master schedule, instructional materials, and policies. Cultural changes are shifts in the norms, values, assumptions, and collective beliefs of an organization. Substantial cultural change must precede technical change, he argues, "for while technical changes are necessary to improve our schools, they produce few positive results when the people using them do not believe in the intended outcome of the change" (Muhammad, 2009, p. 15).

The fundamental purpose of response to intervention is to provide every child with the additional time and support needed to learn at high levels. This is an ongoing commitment, and for the technical steps of RTI to work, we believe they must be executed within a culture of collective responsibility. A culture of collective responsibility is guided by a shared belief that the primary responsibility of every member of the organization is to ensure high levels of learning for every child. Professional learning communities call this a *focus on learning*: the "educators within the organization embrace high levels of learning for all students as both the reason the organization exists and the fundamental responsibility of those who work within it" (DuFour, DuFour, Eaker, & Many, 2010, p. 11). This collective purpose sets the direction for the organization and serves as a compass to guide its actions. It is the answer to the question, why are we here?

Answering that question may seem an exercise in stating the obvious, as virtually every school has a similar mission statement that references making students "lifelong learners," "responsible citizens," and "prepared for the 21st century." In reality, this kind of generic mission statement is little more than a tired slogan on a school's let-terhead and has little meaningful impact on the values, beliefs, and daily actions of the educators in the building. In many schools, the stated mission of the school and the actual beliefs voiced in the staff lounge are two different things. This conflict between existing school culture and the fundamental assumptions of collective responsibility is a significant obstacle to most schools and districts struggling to successfully imple-ment RTI.

Thomas Sergiovanni (1996) says, "The heart and soul of school culture is what peo-ple believe, the assumptions they make about how school works" (pp. 2–3). Embedded within a culture of collective responsibility are two assumptions. The first assumption is that we, as educators, must accept responsibility to ensure high levels of learning for every child. While parental, societal, and economic forces impact student learning, the actions of the educators will ultimately determine each child's success in school.

The second assumption is that all students can learn at high levels. We define "high" levels of learning as "high school plus," meaning every child will graduate from high school with the skills and knowledge required to continue to learn. To compete in the global marketplace of the 21st century, students must continue to learn beyond high school, and there are many paths for that learning, including trade schools, intern-ships, community colleges, and universities. But a high school diploma *alone* is a ticket to nowhere (Waller, 2001).

For the technical changes of RTI to be successful, a school's culture must be aligned to these two fundamental assumptions. Unfortunately, many schools have devel-oped a school culture that is misaligned to these beliefs. Let's consider the dichotomy between the fundamental assumptions of collective responsibility and the traditional culture of our current school system.

Taking Responsibility for Student Learning

Ask a school faculty if they believe all kids can learn, and the answer will likely be a unified and confident *yes!*

But then some educators will start to qualify their responses with *ifs*: "Yes, all kids can learn . . . *if* the students want to learn . . . *if* the parents are supportive . . . *if* our school had more resources . . . *if* the district, state, and national policymakers would stop hampering our efforts." Too often, the "ifs" are all conditions beyond the school's control, conditions that ultimately release the educators from responsibility for their students' learning.

There is no question that factors outside a school's control impact student learning, and it is understandable why educators can feel like victims due to these parental, soci-etal, economic, and political realities. In light of these factors, is it fair for educators to hold themselves responsible for student learning? Frankly, yes! If a student attends school from kindergarten through high school and still cannot read, who should be held most responsible? Was it the child's responsibility—are children expected to teach themselves how to read? Was it the parents' responsibility—are parents expected to be credentialed reading teachers?

Some blame the school's lack of resources. However, there are schools with extremely limited resources operating under similar state, provincial, and national regulations that have successfully taught their students to read. As a profession, we have almost four decades of Effective Schools research by Ron Edmonds, Larry Lezotte, Wilber Brookover, Michael Rutter, and others that proves conclusively that all children can learn when provided effective teaching. In *What Works in Schools*, Robert Marzano (2003) stated that an analysis of research conducted over a thirty-five-year period demonstrates that highly effective schools produce results that almost entirely overcome the effects of student background. In spite of this overwhelming evidence, some schools continue to act on ineffective school beliefs—beliefs that are in direct conflict with our formula for learning.

Compounding these cultural obstacles are counterproductive leadership practices. Many administrators and lawmakers believe that technical change alone can transform our schools. This has led to a litany of educational reform initiatives over the past four decades. These technical changes come and go, creating little impact on student learning and feeding a "this-too-shall-pass" mentality among many veteran teachers. From their perspective, RTI looks no different than the myriad of other previously failed district, state, provincial, and federal mandates.

Site educators have understandably developed a resistance to new change initiatives, and this has led to our current accountability movement, in which change is mandated under the threat of Draconian consequences. There is no better example of this approach than *No Child Left Behind* (NCLB). At best, this top-down change process has created a culture of compliance and failed to develop the deep levels of commitment and ownership needed to truly transform our schools.

Cultural change cannot be gained through force or coercion (Muhammad, 2009), and it is difficult and sometimes painful process. Throughout our travels, we have found that confronting our profession's current reality with fellow educators has evoked feelings ranging from anger and despair ("How dare someone blame educators for the failing of our current system?"), to acknowledgment and hope ("Now I understand why my tireless efforts are not working—it's not me, it's the limitations of our traditional system of schooling"). Education attracts people with the noblest intentions. Educators achieve a level of education for which they can make much more money doing something else, yet they choose to serve children. They work tirelessly, care deeply, and sacrifice their own personal time and resources for the benefit of their students. Teachers do not begin each day thinking, how can I disregard the professional evidence and hurt my students? Site and district administrators do not make decisions by thinking, how can I create policies that will make it more difficult for teachers to do their job?

Our purpose is neither to place blame nor to challenge the motives or integrity of educators. Yet until we are willing to examine and acknowledge that our traditional assumptions and beliefs about our work are outdated and detrimental to the challenges we face today, we will never get better results for our students.

This honest conversation about educational culture begins when an organization asks itself, are we here to *teach*, or are we here to ensure that our students *learn*?

Many schools believe it is their job to provide their students the *opportunity* to learn. This teaching-focused philosophy is best captured by the common school mantra "It is the teacher's job to teach, and the student's job to learn." It is virtually impossible for RTI to succeed in this school culture, as the very purpose of RTI is to provide students additional time and support when they don't succeed after initial teaching. A teaching-focused school believes that its responsibility for student learning ends once the child has been given the opportunity to learn the first time. But a learning-focused school understands that the school was not built so that teachers have a place to teach; it was built so that the children of the community have a place to learn. Learning-focused schools embrace RTI, as it is a proven process to help them achieve their mission.

Believing All Kids Can Learn at High Levels

Again, ask a school faculty if they believe all kids can learn, and the answer will likely be a unified and confident *yes*!

But ask the same faculty if they believe all kids can learn *at high levels* (high school plus), and you will launch a heated debate. Virtually all educators believe that kids can learn, but many feel that how much a student can learn varies depending on his or her innate abilities and demographic background. This belief creates a sliding scale of student expectations—that is, children who come from parents who are economically stable, English speaking, actively involved, and highly educated are perceived to be more capable of learning at high levels, while children who come from families that are economically disadvantaged, non–English speaking, uninvolved, and uneducated are seen as less capable of meeting rigorous learning expectations. These beliefs are not expressed formally in the school's mission statement or policies, but they are carried out in school practice every day. Across North America, minority students, English learners, and economically disadvantaged students are disproportionately represented in special education (Brantlinger, 2006; Ferri & Connor, 2006; Skiba, Poloni-Staudinger, Gallini, Simmons, & Feggins-Azziz, 2006; Skiba et al., 2008) and underrepresented in gifted and honors programs (Donovan & Cross, 2003).

Are minority students born with a diminished capacity to learn at high levels? Does learning any language besides English at birth genetically alter a student's ability to learn at high levels? Does poverty irreversibly alter a student's potential to learn? Of course not! A student's ethnicity, native language, and economic status do not reduce the child's innate capacity to learn. These misconceptions are part of the cultural beliefs and assumptions of far too many schools, however, and they become a self-fulfilling prophecy for the students these schools serve. The students perceived as being capable of learning at high levels are placed in more rigorous coursework, taught at advanced levels, and expected to achieve, and thus are much more likely to learn at this level. Conversely, the students perceived as being incapable of learning at high levels are placed in below-grade-level curriculum, taught at remedial levels, and expected to achieve at lower levels and, to no one's surprise, will most likely learn at low levels. These outcomes falsely confirm the school's initial assumptions and reinforce their misguided practices.

Does "All" Really Mean "All"?

Committing to take responsibility for every student's academic success is a daunting proposition. But if a school settles for anything less than all, then which students deserve no realistic chance at a successful adult life? How many failing students are "acceptable"? As educators, we should provide every student with what we would want and expect for our own child. No parent would view her child's failure as acceptable simply because the majority of other students succeeded. Our response as educators should be no different.

Many schools struggle with the dilemma of applying this expectation to students with diagnosed disabilities. At almost every school, a small percentage of students have such severe disabilities that it may be virtually impossible for them to reach the standard of high school plus. In these instances, it is unfair to ask teachers to take responsibility for these students to learn at high levels. But again, once a school makes an exception to all kids learning, where does the school draw the line on permitting students to achieve anything less than high school plus? Do we draw that line at students with profound disabilities? Students with a specific learning disability? Students with attention deficit disorder (ADD)?

We offer this reply: *all* includes any student who will be expected to live as a financially independent adult someday. For these students, achieving anything less than high school plus will make it virtually impossible to thrive as adults.

If a school has determined beyond a shadow of a doubt that a student is incapable of living independently, it would be appropriate to modify that student's learning outcomes to better prepare the student for the needs of his or her unique adult life. In no way are we suggesting that these students will not have meaningful adult lives, or that the school is void of responsibility to meet their needs. It is the school's job to help them maximize the potential for their adult lives, and so the school may need to modify its learning goals accordingly. In all likelihood, these students are severely disabled—a very small percentage of the student population. The majority of students qualified for special education do not meet this criterion, for most of these students will not pay "modified" rent or "accommodated" bills someday. With these rare exceptions, *all* really must mean *all*.

Leading School Cultural Change

Clearly, the fundamental assumptions behind collective responsibility are not the current reality in most schools. Through our work across North America at sites struggling to implement RTI, schools often acknowledge that a shared commitment is lacking. But the question we hear most often is again the wrong question: "How do we get 'buy-in' from our staff?"

We don't like the term *buy-in*—it sounds like a Texas Hold 'em tournament. More importantly, it carries the wrong connotation. The purpose of RTI is to help children, and the concern that staff won't "buy into" it suggests they are resisting RTI because they want to know what is in it for *staff*. But there is hardly an educator who does not work with the best interests of students in mind. Educators are attracted to this field by what they have to give, not by what they expect to receive.

We suggest that the correct term is *ownership*: how does a school create a sense of staff ownership of the RTI process, especially in light of the cultural hurdles described in this chapter? Frankly, it is hard—really hard. As Muhammad states, "Cultural change is a much more difficult form of change to accomplish. . . . As human beings, we do not have the ability to control the thoughts and beliefs of others, so cultural change requires something more profound" (2009, p. 16).

Rational adults resist change for many reasons, and many educators often raise legitimate concerns regarding the professional conditions and personal commitments needed to make RTI work, so there is no silver bullet to overcoming resistance and developing staff ownership. Complex problems require multiple solutions. We suggest that school sites take the following actions to cultivate the sense of collective responsibility that is the foundation of RTI; in subsequent chapters we will address the structural changes necessary to allow collective responsibility to flourish.

Build an Effective School Leadership Team

Leadership is not a solo act. As Harvard researcher John Kotter states,

> No one person, no matter how competent, is capable of single handedly developing the right vision, communicating it to vast numbers of people, eliminating all of the key obstacles, generating short term wins, leading and managing dozens of change projects and anchoring new approaches deep in an organization's culture. Putting together the right coalition of people to lead a change initiative is critical to its success. (Kotter, 2010, p. 52)

To this end, we recommend that schools create a school leadership team to guide the change process. The composition of the team is critical. Every school has key individuals who have influence on campus. To give the coalition credibility, these individuals must be included, as well as those who may traditionally resist change. The coalition should also represent all relevant points of view and campus expertise, including the administration, each department and/or grade-level teacher team, and classified staff. For districts that have employee unions, we suggest proactively engaging union representation.

This guiding coalition is not the school "dictatorship committee" but a team that learns deeply about best practices, assesses candidly the school's current reality, determines potential next steps to improve the school, identifies possible obstacles and points of leverage, and plans the best way to create staff consensus and ownership. To accomplish this, the team must meet frequently, especially at the beginning of the process. In the end, if a school cannot get even a small group of people to agree on a common direction, it is unlikely that group will be able to convince the entire school. This team will be discussed at more length in chapter 3; see page 25 or visit **go.solution-tree.com/rti** for *Building a School Leadership Team*, an activity to help a principal or administrative team select members.

Learn Together

People tend to come to the same conclusions when they base their decisions on the same facts. Regrettably, many schools make decisions by averaging opinions. Because every staff member enters the RTI discussion with different prior experiences, priorities, and perspectives, it is often difficult to reach consensus. More often than not, the loudest and most aggressive voices win, and those resistant to change are usually the most vocal in this debate process, as Muhammad's (2009) research found that resisters to change are usually the most aggressive at stating their beliefs.

In a learning community, by contrast, members arrive at consensus on vital questions by building shared knowledge instead of averaging opinions. They engage in collective inquiry into both best practices and their school's current reality (DuFour et al., 2010). The guiding coalition should serve as the "lead learners." They should dig deeply into the areas of focus, identify powerful research and relevant information, and determine the best format to share this information with the staff. See page 27 or visit **go.solution-tree.com/rti** to access *Creating Consensus for a Culture of Collective Responsibility*, a list of guiding questions the school leadership team can use to get started.

Provide the Why Before the What

Too often, change initiatives are introduced by describing what needs to be done, without first providing a compelling reason why the change is necessary. In his study of educational "fundamentalists" who actively fight change, Muhammad (2009) found that many resist because they were never provided a clear rationale for change.

If school leadership cannot provide a compelling *why*, the staff will not care about the *what*. In our experience, raising state test scores and staying out of program improvement do not provide a compelling rationale to teachers. Muhammad recommends using data to create a catalyst for change in an inspirational way, and we have found that many successful schools don't look solely at data such as the percentage of students below proficient on state assessments or the number of kids reading below grade level. Instead, these schools connect these data to individual kids—in other words, instead of telling teachers that 12 percent of the school's students are below proficient in reading, they connect those numbers with a list of the specific kids who make up the 12 percent. These connections resonate with why we joined the profession: to help kids.

Create a Doable Plan

The most compelling reason for change will be irrelevant if the staff view the goal as impossible. A few years ago, a newly selected Teacher of the Year was interviewed on television. She served as a language arts teacher at an inner-city high school and was getting tremendous results with extremely at-risk students. When asked what the key to her success was, she said that many of her students came from transient, often homeless families. So, in her personal time, she started a homeless shelter!

While the cause was compelling, and the teacher's results in student learning were obvious, it is hardly feasible to ask every teacher to start a homeless shelter—or to give up family or personal time, for that matter. It is critical that staff receive a doable plan that defines specific responsibilities and includes the resources needed to meet these expectations. If teachers view RTI as a demand to do the equivalent of starting a homeless shelter, they have the right to resist. Later chapters will explore the details of an RTI process that is achievable.

Expect the Best

It is easy for school leaders to view potential resisters as the enemy. This view often becomes reality, as the leader may pre-emptively take actions to disengage the perceived threats, thus silencing those voices and increasing their distrust and animosity.

Consider for a moment what a school would do for a *student* deemed at risk. Before the student entered a new unit of study, from the first day of instruction, the school would most likely create a scaffold of support. The school would not prepare for failure, but rather provide pre-emptive supports to make it difficult for the student to fail. This is what effective leaders do for "at-risk" staff members: provide the professional development, resources, and ongoing support they need to feel immediate success. Effective leaders see the potential for difficulty and assume that if they create the right supports, there is every expectation the staff member can succeed.

Confront the Worst

Once reluctant staff members have learned the compelling reasons to change and been provided with a doable plan and every opportunity to succeed, then they have no professional, logical, or ethical justification to resist the proposed changes that a majority of the staff has deemed necessary for the welfare of their students. By this point, they have neither the right to stop the plan from proceeding nor the option of refusing to participate. Leaders must be willing to confront these resisters and demand that they meet their responsibilities to the collective school efforts. Failure to do so will empower the resisters to continue their destructive ways and damage trust with the majority of staff members who support the changes.

While the school administration must take the lead in confronting hard-core resistant members, our experience is that the greatest coercive pressure comes from peers who are willing to take a stand. At most schools, a silent majority is willing to change, and an aggressive minority will do whatever it takes to stop change. Many of these extreme resisters mistakenly believe that they speak for the majority of the staff, because they share their combatant opinions in the staff lounge every day, and their peers sit there silently and don't say a word. That silence seemingly condones the comments and emboldens resisters. The individual actions of each staff member shape the collective culture of an entire school. Unless the silent majority begins to have some courageous conversations with the aggressive minority that is holding their school hostage, it will be difficult to truly transform the school's culture. Because influential staff members comprise the school leadership team, these faculty leaders can be especially effective at achieving this goal.

Start!

Most people become committed to a process once they see that it works, not before. This creates an interesting dilemma: you can't start until you build consensus, but you never get true commitment until you start. Consequently, taking months and months planning for change and getting everyone to feel ownership in the process follows the laws of diminishing returns. If you wait for everyone to "get on board" before starting, the train will never leave the station. What it takes to start is consensus—everyone has had a say, the will of the group has emerged, and it is evident, even to those who disagree (DuFour et al., 2010).

Once consensus has been reached, start! Proven results will ultimately create the ownership needed to promote and sustain the RTI process. There will be no moment of epiphany when staff members suddenly "see the light" and are converted into believers. Instead, the faculty will start to do the work and will see a little improvement in student learning. These results will confirm their efforts and make them a little more committed to the process, which in turn will lead to even better results. Eventually the school will reach a tipping point when enough staff members have experienced the positive results of RTI that the new thinking becomes "just the way we do business."

Leading District Cultural Change

The individual school site bears most of the burden for building a sense of collective responsibility among its faculty. But district leadership also plays a role in developing and sustaining schools' ability to help all students achieve success through response to intervention. In their well-intentioned efforts to create a sense of collective responsibility among schools, some districts have instead encouraged compliance with paperwork and protocols rather than high levels of engagement and ownership among its teachers. We believe that Joan Talbert's words, focused on the development of professional learning communities, apply equally well to RTI:

> A "bureaucratic strategy" uses traditional management tools of directives and rules, prescribed routines, and sanctions for compliance as ways to promote change. A "professional strategy" uses tools of decision-making structures, professional expertise and knowledge resources, and leader modeling and feedback to engender change. (Talbert, 2010, p. 6)

These professional strategies directly address the potential problems outlined earlier and present an alternative view of the role of district leadership in supporting RTI.

Build a Shared Vision and Leaders' Capacity to Support Change

The first step toward developing a culture of collective responsibility occurs when district leadership comes together to develop a shared vision of what RTI will mean in the district. This vision is developed through ongoing conversations between general and special education administrators from both school sites and the district office. This forged vision is then shared with individual school staff by a subset of this same group, general and special education leaders. Ideally, this sharing of the district vision for this change is a dialogue rather than a monologue. This dialogue will deepen everyone's understanding of what it means to implement RTI in a way that helps students experience greater success.

A major area of focus for district leadership during this phase of implementation is creating a dialogue about RTI among school site administrators as well. District leadership should provide time for school site administrators to share their struggles and learn from one another about how to develop a sense of collective responsibility for the learning of all children. Beyond the structures created by district leadership, school site administrators need to build their own capacity to sustain the work of their teachers through regular and ongoing access to a support network.

Establish Mutual Professional Accountability

Nothing provides a stronger impetus for collective responsibility than accountability to one's peers. District leadership plays a key role in helping schools and collaborative teams move toward holding each other accountable for the learning of each student. This requires a long-term view of change and certainly represents a huge cultural change for most schools today. District leadership should de-emphasize state accountability reports and instead consistently promote (1) using common formative assessments to measure student performance on key targets and (2) designing and then using interventions when students struggle. In doing so, district leadership sends a powerful message that shifts the accountability for student learning away from the state and toward each school site and its collaborative teacher teams.

Finally, Talbert warns us that this kind of "professional change" is not easy:

> At its crossroads, the international education movement to develop a new paradigm for teaching—one that features . . . greater professional control and accountability—will grow and be sustained to the extent that local systems take up the challenges for change outlined here. Administrators and leaders at all system levels will need to resist tendencies toward bureaucratic habits of mind and strategies and invent new ones, adapted to their particular system context, that are grounded in . . . professional approaches to system change. (Talbert, 2010, p. 14)

To assess your progress as a district in supporting RTI efforts, see page 29 or visit **go.solution-tree.com/rti** to access *How Districts Hinder or Promote the Development of RTI*, a self-evaluation tool for district leaders.

In the end, creating a culture of collective responsibility is difficult, challenging, uncomfortable work. It takes leadership, persistence, hard work, and courage. But it can be done, and must be done, if we want to meet our moral responsibility to the students we serve. As Muhammad states, "When a school has a healthy culture, the professionals within it will seek the tools that they need to accomplish their goal of universal student achievement; they will give a school new life by overcoming the staff division that halts transformation" (2009, p. 16).

Activities and Tools Summary

Has your school created an effective school leadership team?

See *Building a School Leadership Team* (page 25).

Does your school have a culture of collective responsibility?

See *Creating Consensus for a Culture of Collective Responsibility* (page 27).

Has district leadership promoted or hindered RTI?

See *How Districts Hinder or Promote the Development of RTI* (page 29).

*Visit **go.solution-tree.com/rti** to download these activities and tools.*

Building a School Leadership Team

This activity is designed to help a principal or administrative team create an effective school leadership team.

First, list the names of the current members of what you might consider to be your guiding coalition. If no such group currently exists, list the potential members who come to mind.

Then consider the following personal characteristics that will impact your team's success. Write the name of each team member under any characteristic that applies (a person may be listed under more than one). Eliminate any person from your list who possesses none of these characteristics. Note that it is recommended that a member of each teacher team be on the leadership team. Does your team have the necessary balance?

Position Power	Expertise
Ask: Are enough key players on board so that those left out cannot easily block progress?	Ask: Are the various points of view—in terms of discipline, work experience, and so on—relevant to the task at hand adequately represented so that informed, intelligent decisions will be made?

Simplifying Response to Intervention © 2012 Solution Tree Press • solution-tree.com
Visit **go.solution-tree.com/rti** to download this page.

Credibility	Leadership
Ask: Does the group have enough people with good reputations that its recommendations and decisions will be taken seriously?	Ask: Does the group include enough proven leaders to be able to drive the change process?

Creating Consensus for a Culture of Collective Responsibility

A culture of collective responsibility is based on two fundamental beliefs:

1. The first assumption is that we, as educators, must accept responsibility to ensure high levels of learning for every child. While parental, societal, and economic forces impact student learning, the actions of the educators will ultimately determine each child's success in school.

2. The second assumption is that all students can learn at high levels. We define "high" levels of learning as "high school plus," meaning every child will graduate from high school with the skills and knowledge required to continue to learn. To compete in the global marketplace of the 21st century, students must continue to learn beyond high school, and there are many paths for that learning, including trade schools, internships, community colleges, and universities.

Discussing the following critical questions will assist a school leadership team in creating consensus for a culture of collective responsibility aligned with these beliefs.

1. **How will we provide a compelling case for change?** For someone to change, they first must see a compelling reason to change. In other words, one must show why there is a need to change. Raising test scores and/or meeting district/state/federal mandates hardly meets this goal. Instead, look to paint a picture of what adulthood will likely look like for students who don't succeed in school.

2. **What must we do differently?** Besides a compelling reason to change, one must also provide a "doable" plan. The noblest cause is useless if the changes required are seen as unrealistic. Staff members want a clear picture of exactly what changes are necessary to achieve learning for all students.

3. **How do we know these changes will work?** Having experienced the pendulum of school change for the past decades, many educators are skeptical of change processes. What evidence is available to demonstrate the validity of the recommended changes? (Besides the research quoted in *Simplifying Response to Intervention*, the website allthingsplc.info has dozens of schools and hundreds of pages of research validating the elements of professional learning communities [PLCs] and RTI.)

Simplifying Response to Intervention © 2012 Solution Tree Press • solution-tree.com
Visit **go.solution-tree.com/rti** to download this page.

4. **What concerns do we expect, especially from staff members traditionally against change?** The leadership team should brainstorm the concerns staff members will have regarding the recommended changes. What will be the leadership's response to these concerns?

5. **What is the best setting and/or structure for the conversation(s) needed to create consensus?** One of the leadership team's greatest leverage points is its ability to determine the location, structure, and timing of the conversation(s) to create staff consensus. All stakeholders must have a voice in the process, but not necessarily in the same meeting. Sometimes the feelings of the silent majority can be drowned out by the aggressive opinions of a loud minority resistant to change. Consider a series of meetings with teams, grade levels, or departments. Also, set clear norms for the meeting, as professional, respectful dialogue is essential.

6. **How will we know if we have reached consensus?** Remember, it does not take 100 percent approval to get started; it takes consensus. Consensus is reached when all stakeholders have had a say and the will of the group has emerged and is evident, even to those who disagree (DuFour, DuFour, Eaker, & Many, *Learning by Doing*, 2010). Consider how many key people will be needed to create the tipping point necessary for consensus.

In the end, true commitment comes when people see that the changes work. So the key is to build consensus, then get started doing the work. You will never get commitment until you start doing the work, but you cannot start until you get consensus.

How Districts Hinder or Promote the Development of RTI

Rate your district's progress on using professional change strategies to promote the development of response to intervention (RTI) practices on a scale of 1 (not at all successful) to 10 (highly successful).

1. Building a shared vision and leaders' capacity to support change:

   • Top administrators exhibit deep understanding of RTI.

   • Top administrators have developed a vision of RTI implementation.

   • Top administrators have engaged in a dialogue about RTI with school staff.

   1   2   3   4   5   6   7   8   9   10

   Specific examples:

2. Developing capacity to address individual student achievement gaps:

   • Top administration has articulated the shift from teaching to learning.

   • Top administration has articulated the shift from coverage to mastery.

   • Top administration has "given permission" to cover less, learn more.

   • Top administration controls outside pressures of accountability.

   1   2   3   4   5   6   7   8   9   10

   Specific examples:

3. Developing a web of knowledge resources for RTI:

   • Top administration has attempted to build shared knowledge, rather than relied on regulations.

- Top administration has gone beyond mere identification of RTI specialists through common training.

1   2   3   4   5   6   7   8   9   10

Specific examples:

4. Establishing mutual accountability among professionals:

- Teachers feel accountable to district or state.
- Teachers feel accountable to each other.
- Teachers feel more accountable for results on their formative assessments than state tests.

1   2   3   4   5   6   7   8   9   10

Specific examples:

Additional Notes

Adapted from J. E. Talbert (2010), "Professional Learning Communities at the Crossroads: How Systems Hinder or Engender Change," in M. Fullan, A. Hargreaves, & A. Lieberman (Eds.), Second International Handbook of Educational Change. *Dordrecht, Netherlands: Springer Press.*

Building Structures for Collaboration

Fulfilling the obligations of collective responsibility requires more than the belief that all students can learn at high levels—it also requires collaborative structures and tools to achieve this goal.

Let us go back to what it takes for all kids to learn:

Targeted Instruction + Time = Learning

What is the likelihood that an individual teacher can target every lesson to meet the individual learning needs of each child in every class? Can a teacher teach to every child's learning style in the same lesson? Can a teacher give every student unlimited time to learn each standard? Obviously not. There is no way an individual teacher has all the time, all the skills, and all the knowledge necessary to meet the individual needs of every child. Applying the formula for learning as an individual is nearly impossible. But collectively, the combined knowledge and skills of an entire staff *can* meet the learning needs of every child. Teachers must move beyond viewing students as "my kids" and "your kids" and instead regard all the students as "our kids." This need for a *collective* effort is why we believe that RTI must be built upon professional learning community practices; the only way a school staff can achieve the mission of learning for all students is by working together (DuFour et al., 2010).

Creating Teams, Not Groups

Collaborative teams form the engine that drives a school's RTI efforts. By *team*, we do not mean groups that assemble for traditional grade-level and department meetings, nor do we mean protocol-driven gatekeeper groups that meet only to identify students for special education testing. The act of meeting together does not define a group of people as a team. Committed educators have long been meeting in an effort to assist students in need. At times, they have been successful, but they rarely work as teams. Groups meet together, and often have the same goals as a team. But after the meeting, group members go back to their classrooms and work in isolation. The individuals in the group "parallel play": they do the same work side by side, giving the appearance of a coordinated effort, but in reality having very little impact on each other's efforts.

Conversely, members of a true team "work *interdependently* to achieve *common* goals for which members are mutually accountable" (DuFour et al., 2010, p. 3, emphasis in the original). The common goals uniting team members are shared learning outcomes for their students, and all team members take collective responsibility to ensure that all students succeed. The team's collaboration stretches beyond coordinating curriculum and assessments, and impacts what goes on in each team member's classroom. What they achieve collectively is far greater than what they can achieve individually. Members of a true team gain so much from each other that they could not imagine doing their job without their teammates. These are the characteristics of true teams, and they represent the standard whenever "teams" are discussed in this book.

Essential RTI Teams

The inverted RTI pyramid (fig. 3.1) shows how a school can create collaborative structures that support collective responsibility and drive RTI implementation. Two types of teams are required: teacher teams and schoolwide teams. While both types of teams share mutual accountability for student learning, each has specific responsibilities in core instruction and interventions.

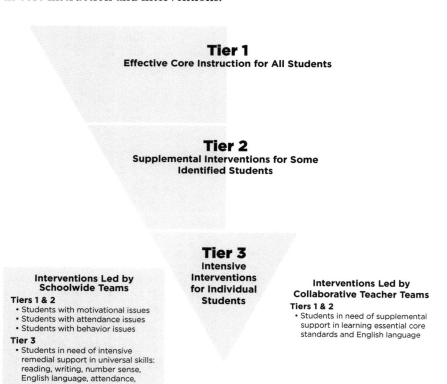

Figure 3.1: Team responsibilities in the inverted RTI pyramid.

Collaborative Teacher Teams

Collaborative teacher teams are teams comprised of educators who share curriculum and thus take collective responsibility for students learning their common essential learning outcomes. Most often, these are teachers who teach the same grade level, subject, and/or course. The responsibilities of each teacher team in the RTI process are as follows:

- Clearly define essential student learning outcomes
- Provide effective Tier 1 core instruction
- Assess student learning and the effectiveness of instruction
- Identify students in need of additional time and support
- Take primary responsibility for Tier 2 supplemental interventions for students who have failed to master the team's identified essential standards

There are fair and logical reasons why a collaborative team of teachers should be responsible for taking the lead in ensuring that every student learns the essential standards of their course and/or grade level:

- **They are highly trained and credentialed in the subject.** Who on campus is better trained to design core instruction and supplemental interventions for students struggling in pre-algebra than the teachers who possess a degree in mathematics, are credentialed in the subject, and have experience teaching pre-algebra?
- **They know the content best.** Through the concentrated instruction process that will be described in chapter 4, teacher teams will take primary responsibility for identifying the essential standards in their grade, subject, or course; determining the level of rigor expected of all students; identifying the prerequisite skills and knowledge needed for success on these standards; arranging the standards into a logical scope and sequence; unwrapping the essential standards into learning targets (subskills); and determining how best to assess student learning on each learning target. No one on campus is likely to know these specific learning outcomes better than the team of teachers who have gone through this process.
- **They have the assessment data.** These teachers identified the best way to assess each learning target, selected or created the assessment, administered it, graded it, and know which students have not demonstrated mastery of each essential standard. No one on campus is likely to have a better understanding or more timely access to this critical information.
- **They know their students best.** These teachers see the students daily in their subject and/or grade level. They know which students struggled during core instruction, which students may have been absent on key days of instruction, which students demonstrated difficulty focusing. No one on staff is likely to know each student's ability and difficulties in a subject better than the educators who teach the students every day.

- **It is why they were hired.** Is it unfair or unreasonable to ask a team of U.S. history teachers to take the lead in making sure that students learn U.S. history? That is why these individuals were hired. It is the first priority of their job description and most likely their passion. If these teachers do not take the lead in ensuring students learn U.S. history, who should?

We are not suggesting that it is solely the job of each teacher collaborative team to ensure that every student learns their essential content, or that other schoolwide resources should not be used to support teacher teams with core instruction, intervention determination, and/or supplemental interventions to support their students in need of help. The point is this: who is going to take the *lead*? When it comes to students learning essential grade-level standards for a particular subject and/or grade level, the teachers who teach that content should be empowered to both design Tier 1 core instruction and lead the school's response when students require additional instruction to achieve these critical learning outcomes.

Teacher Team Structures

When creating collaborative teacher teams, there are many effective teaming structures. They include the following:

- **Grade-level teams.** Grade-level teams are composed of teachers who teach the same grade and thus share common grade-level essential standards. This team structure usually works best at the elementary level, as elementary teachers are usually responsible for multiple subjects, including language arts, mathematics, science, and social studies.

- **Subject/course-specific teams.** Subject/course-specific teams unite teachers who teach the same subject and/or course of study. Examples of this team structure (most common at the secondary level) include biology, chemistry, and physics teams.

- **Vertical teams.** Vertical teams share common learning outcomes that are developed across consecutive years of school. Examples include a K–2 primary team at the elementary level or a high school language arts team at the secondary level. While the grade-level standards are not identical from kindergarten to second grade, essential skills such as phonemic awareness and number sense are held in common and developed across all three grades, with increasing rigor over time. Likewise, a ninth- through twelfth-grade language arts team does not share identical content standards, but does share essential skills such as persuasive writing or analytical reading. Vertical teams can also ensure that prerequisite skills are taught in sequence (using the *Essential Standards Chart*, a tool we'll explore in chapter 4). This team structure often works best at smaller schools, where there may only be one teacher who teaches a particular grade level, subject, or course.

- **Interdisciplinary teams.** Interdisciplinary teams are composed of teachers who teach different subjects, but share common students. When it comes to identifying students in need of additional help, determining interventions, and providing coordinated academic and behavior support across a student's instructional day, interdisciplinary teams have many benefits.

Unfortunately, there is also a significant drawback to this team structure—teachers on an interdisciplinary team do not usually share common curriculum. We described earlier that some of the essential responsibilities of a collaborative teacher team are identifying essential standards, providing effective core instruction, and assessing student learning on these standards. So, if a sixth-grade language arts teacher needs to identify essential sixth-grade language arts standards, determine effective ways to teach these standards, and create assessments to measure student learning of these standards, how beneficial will it be to have this teacher meet with sixth-grade science, math, and social studies teachers to achieve this goal? To accomplish these responsibilities, it would be best if the teacher met with fellow sixth-grade language arts teachers.

There are two ways a school can address this drawback to interdisciplinary teams. First, teachers can be on two teams—a subject-specific team and an interdisciplinary team. This structure would combine the best of both worlds—a teacher can be on a team that shares content and a team that shares kids. We have seen many schools use this dual-team model with powerful results. Unfortunately, this structure also requires twice as much weekly teacher collaboration time, which is not always feasible.

The second option is for interdisciplinary teams to identify common essential standards that are focused on skills, not subject-specific content. For example, an interdisciplinary team can focus on the college-ready skills recommended by David Conley (2007), including:

+ Analytical reading and discussion
+ Persuasive writing
+ Drawing inferences and conclusions from texts
+ Analyzing conflicting source documents
+ Supporting arguments with evidence
+ Solving complex problems with no obvious answer

These essential learning standards are not subject specific—instead, each teacher on the interdisciplinary team can use his or her unique subject content as the vehicle to teaching these higher-level thinking skills. The team can clearly define these common learning outcomes, discuss effective Tier 1 core instruction, develop common rubrics to assess these skills, and respond collectively when students need additional help. This approach can work especially well at smaller secondary schools.

While there are numerous ways to structure teacher collaborative teams, all these structures have one characteristic in common: if the purpose of a school's collaboration is to improve student learning, then team members must share student learning outcomes. Ronald Gallimore and his colleagues found that "to be successful, teams need to set and share goals to work on that are immediately applicable to their classrooms. Without such goals, teams will drift toward superficial discussions and truncated efforts" (Gallimore, Ermeling, Saunders, & Goldenberg, 2009). These common learning goals are what unite and focus the work of each teacher team. This focus on learning will ensure that the teacher teams are able to fulfill the vision of collective responsibility.

Schoolwide Teams

In contrast to teacher teams, which focus on the specific learning outcomes of a particular grade level, subject, or course, schoolwide teams are designed to coordinate a school's core instructional program and support resources across the entire building. To achieve this goal, we recommend two specific schoolwide teams: a school leadership team and a school intervention team.

School Leadership Team

As mentioned in the previous chapter, a school leadership team serves as the "guiding coalition" for the building. Comprised of representatives from each collaborative teacher team, administration, and classified and support staff, this team's primary responsibility is to unite and coordinate the school's collective efforts across grade levels, departments, and subjects. To achieve this goal, the school leadership team should specifically:

- Build consensus for the school's mission of collective responsibility
- Create a master schedule that provides sufficient time for team collaboration, core instruction, supplemental interventions, and intensive interventions
- Coordinate schoolwide human resources to best support core instruction and interventions, including the site counselor, psychologist, speech and language pathologist, special education teacher, librarian, health services, subject specialists, instructional aides, and other classified staff
- Allocate the school's fiscal resources to best support core instruction and interventions, including school categorical funding
- Assist with articulating essential learning outcomes across grade levels and subjects
- Lead the school's universal screening efforts to identify students in need of Tier 3 intensive interventions before they fail
- Lead the school's efforts at Tier 1 for schoolwide behavior expectations, including attendance policies and awards and recognitions (the team may create a separate behavior team to oversee these behavioral policies)
- Ensure that all students have access to grade-level core instruction
- Ensure that sufficient, effective resources are available to provide Tier 2 interventions for students in need of supplemental support in motivation, attendance, and behavior
- Ensure that sufficient, effective resources are available to provide Tier 3 interventions for students in need of intensive support in the universal skills of reading, writing, number sense, English language, motivation, attendance, and behavior
- Continually monitor schoolwide evidence of student learning

Without question, the leadership team has critically important responsibilities that greatly affect the entire school. This is why we stress that it is this team's job to lead— not to dictate. It should unite the school's staff toward their mission of collective responsibility and coordinate the school's limited resources to best achieve this goal.

For the team's leadership to be effective it must meet frequently; every other week is a realistic goal. A calendar of meeting dates should be set at the beginning of the year, and the time must be considered sacred for all involved.

School Intervention Team

While the school leadership team takes the broader, macro view of the school's efforts to ensure high levels of learning for every child, the primary responsibility of the school intervention team is to lead the school's focused micro view on the specific students in need of Tier 3 intensive support. Students in need of intensive support most often struggle due to:

- Significant weaknesses in the foundational skills of reading, writing, number sense, and/or English language
- Chronic and excessive absenteeism
- Severe behavior and/or motivational concerns
- Combinations of all these factors

Because the obstacles facing these students are often systemic and profound, meeting their needs will usually require multiple interventions, embedded in the instructional day and administered by highly trained professionals. It is unlikely that an individual teacher or teacher team will have the diverse expertise and resources to best diagnose the needs of a student needing this level of help, nor would a teacher team have the authority to assign the schoolwide resources (school psychologist, speech and language pathologist, counselor, specialists, and special education teacher) needed to provide intensive interventions.

The primary purpose of an intervention team is not to be the gatekeeper to special education testing; it is to focus intensely on the individual needs of a school's most at-risk students. Consequently, the primary responsibilities of the site intervention team are to:

- Determine the specific learning needs of each student in need of intensive support
- Diagnose the cause(s) of the student's struggles in Tier 1 and Tier 2
- Determine the most appropriate intervention(s) to address the student's needs
- Frequently monitor the student's progress to see if interventions are achieving the desired outcomes
- Revise the student's intervention(s) when they are not achieving the desired outcomes
- Determine when special education identification is appropriate

Because students in need of intensive support usually have multiple needs, it is important that the intervention team is comprised of site experts in the specific areas that cause students to struggle in school. When determining who should serve on this team, we suggest the following:

- **Principal.** We highly recommend that the principal participate on the intervention team and not delegate this responsibility. The principal is the school's instructional leader and has the most influence over schoolwide resources, as well as the ability to secure district resources when needed. This will also allow the principal to directly monitor the health of the school's Tier 1 and 2 programs. Participation on this team will be a significant time commitment, but what other job responsibility is more important for the instructional leader of the school than to actively support the students most in need?

- **Counselor.** Counselors are trained in child development and socioemotional needs. They often schedule student classes, which can be an important consideration when adjusting a student's core program. Counselors also often have knowledge of community resources that can support children and their families.

- **Psychologist.** Psychologists bring essential training in brain development, learning styles, learning disabilities, and appropriate accommodations. Additionally, they are trained in behavior interventions and often are responsible for writing behavior plans.

- **Speech and language pathologist.** The speech therapist is trained in language acquisition, speech and language development, and potential language impediments.

- **Nurse.** The nurse is trained to identify health-related issues that can affect students' success in school.

- **Special education teacher.** Special education teachers have specialized training and knowledge of strategies that can be appropriate for struggling students.

- **English language development specialist.** This specialist is trained in the instructional needs of English learners.

- **Reading specialist.** A reading specialist is highly trained in the instructional practices of the critical skill of reading.

- **Librarian.** A credentialed librarian has tremendous knowledge of the instructional resources that are available to support various learning needs.

- **Community resource officer.** Many schools have staff that work as community liaisons. They are a vital link to community resources that can support families in need.

This list of suggested intervention team members is not all-inclusive. Additionally, we understand that not every school has all these positions on site. However, while a school may not have an official reading specialist, it likely has a faculty member highly trained in the area of reading; the school may not have an English language development specialist, but will likely have a staff member with significant training and/or experience in the field. The guiding principle is to assemble a diverse team of experts who can address the many needs of at-risk students. Getting the right people together is the key to quality problem solving.

Like the school leadership team, the school intervention team must meet frequently. Weekly is recommended, with every other week being the minimum. A calendar of meeting dates should be set at the beginning of the year, and the time must be considered sacred for all involved.

Honesty and confidentiality are critical considerations for an effective intervention team. You may have noticed that parents and classroom teachers are not recommended as standing members of the school intervention team. We suggest that they be included *as needed*. During initial discussions regarding the causes of a student's difficulties, it can at times be difficult to be totally honest in front of the child's parent or classroom teacher. For example, it would be difficult to say, "The child may be struggling in core instruction because she has our school's most ineffective classroom teacher" or "The student shows signs of potential child abuse." Quality problem solving requires honest, frank, and sometimes difficult conversations—the type of conversations that are not always possible in a traditional parent/teacher conference setting.

Many schools have a similar team currently on site: the school's student study team (SST). The original concept of an SST was to ensure quality problem solving. In reality, however, the SST process at many schools is not focused on solving problems to help a child—instead, it is a mandatory step to qualify a student for special education testing. The team meets only as needed, so it often takes weeks to find a date when all the team members are available to meet. The meeting is usually paperwork driven and focused on completing the appropriate district forms. When the SST "plan" is complete, minimal monitoring of the plan takes place, and revisions are made sporadically at best. When the plan ultimately fails, the child is then referred for special education testing, which is often the desired outcome in the first place.

In the interest of using existing resources efficiently, a school that has an existing SST may decide to refocus the team's thinking and processes to be more effective for RTI purposes. If the team's work is aligned with the four essential principles of RTI and the characteristics and tasks of the school intervention team as we have described them here, the reinvented SST can serve in this problem-solving role.

Ensuring Team Effectiveness

Collaboration is not an innate skill. Considering that our traditional school system started with one-room schoolhouses, most schools have long-standing practices that are counterproductive to collaboration. For this reason, building the structures of collaboration must be deliberate and intentional.

Make Time for Collaboration

At its core, RTI is about creating a collective response when students need additional support, rather than leaving this response up to each individual teacher. This process is predicated on the staff having the time necessary to work together. When collaborative time is not embedded in the contract day, teachers are too often forced to make a choice between meeting the needs of their students at school and their children at home, or between making teaching their career and making it their entire life.

We have seen hundreds of examples of how schools have embedded collaborative time in the staff's contracted work time. The key criteria are: (1) it must be frequent, (2) it must be during a time that the faculty is paid to be on campus, and (3) it must be mandatory that every staff member participate. We have found that weekly team meetings are necessary for effective teacher collaborative teams. The meeting must also be of a duration that allows for meaningful work. Although powerful, targeted collaborative meetings can take place in forty-five to sixty minutes, we have rarely seen productive meetings occur in less than this amount of time. Finally, the meeting must be mandatory. Collaboration by invitation rarely works. Considering that the professional learning communities process is endorsed by virtually every national teacher professional association, it is difficult to understand why a teaching professional would desire or expect the *right* to work in isolation. More importantly, if a teacher is allowed to opt out of team collaboration, then that teacher's students will not benefit from the collective skills and expertise of the entire team. If the purpose of collective responsibility is to ensure that all students learn at high levels, then allowing any teacher to work in isolation would be unacceptable.

Occasionally, we encounter schools that claim to be stumped in their efforts to find the time necessary for collaboration. We find this perplexing, as the average teacher is paid to be on campus six to seven hours a day, totaling thirty to forty hours a week. Is it really impossible to carve out forty minutes of meeting time in a thirty-five-hour work week? More often than not, the problem is that the school is trying to find "extra" time, while keeping the current schedule unaltered. Very few schools have extra time in their schedule—that is, time that is currently unallocated to any particular purpose. For this reason, the task is not to find time for collaboration, but rather to *make* collaborative time a priority.

To illustrate this point, we offer this analogy. Imagine you visited your doctor and were told, "Your test results are in, and you are severely diabetic. You must begin taking daily insulin shots—without them, you could die." What is the likelihood that you would respond, "But doctor, you don't understand. I'm so busy; I don't have time to take insulin"? Not likely. Instead, you would probably take out your calendar, pencil in the insulin shots, and then build everything else around it. This is what schools must do to create collaborative time: make it the highest priority, pencil it into the schedule, then build everything else around it. Chapter 6 will address scheduling in more depth. For ideas from model collaborative schools, we recommend visiting the website allthingsplc.info.

Set Team Norms

We cannot overemphasize the importance of setting team norms—or collective commitments—to guide professional behavior while collaborating. True collaboration often requires staff members to have difficult conversations, and educators are passionate about their beliefs. People can feel vulnerable discussing the best ways to meet the needs of students or the current reality of what is not working. For this reason, teams must set collective commitments regarding how they are going to act with each other, such as starting and ending meetings on time, coming prepared, and sharing the workload equally. These norms are so important that they are not merely recorded in a notebook and never looked at again. Instead, they are reviewed at the start of team meetings and revised as needed. Unfortunately, some schools struggle with building a collaborative culture because personal conflicts stop the team from functioning efficiently. It would be truly tragic if meeting the needs of students became impossible simply because the adults in the building cannot treat each other professionally.

Use Simple, Effective Forms to Guide Their Work

Schools and districts should develop a set of forms that guide teams in the process of assisting students. Forms should allow flexibility and problem solving while also helping teams ask the right questions and complete their work efficiently. Earlier we made the point that schools and districts should not turn their efforts into paper trails of Byzantine complexity. Forms and documentation alone are not going to help students, and ill-designed forms can delay when students receive support.

The following statements describe attributes of effective forms:

- **They help drive the process.** Busy educators benefit from simple, clear forms that direct them to ask the right questions and monitor the right data.
- **They are consistent.** We believe that school teams are in the best position to determine the necessary elements of their documentation process. Consistency of forms within a school will facilitate horizontal and vertical collaboration.
- **They provide space for specific data entry.** Certain data are more valuable than other data. Efficient forms allow ease of entry and analysis of critical data.
- **They use checkboxes whenever possible.** Instead of asking teachers to write a narrative that describes the strengths and needs of a student, create a list of characteristics, and allow educators to check those that apply.
- **They invite the contributions of parents and students.** The voices of parents and students are invaluable. Instead of sending them forms to complete on their own, talk with them in person or on the phone, and ask questions that will yield the types of information that can contribute to gains in student performance.
- **They save the most diagnostic and in-depth analysis for teams.** When problem solving occurs—and that is the most important part of the RTI process—teams should collaboratively analyze challenges and determine interventions. Asking a teacher to conduct an analysis on her own is inefficient and illogical. The teacher has already provided all the support she can; that is the reason she is seeking additional assistance from the team. Conduct analysis with the teacher *and* the team.
- **They explicitly detail what, when, and who.** Effective forms will record the student's history of performance and current level of performance, and will identify goals for future performance by a specific date. The needs of the student are as precisely described as possible given the diagnoses conducted up to this point. Precise information about the interventions to be provided are solicited—exactly what the intervention entails, when it will be provided, who will provide it, when and how progress will be monitored, and by whom. Of course, the form should also prompt the team to decide when it will next meet to ensure that the student is responding to the intervention and, if not, to increase the intensity of support.

Again, forms are not the most important part of ensuring the success of collective responsibility. However, poorly designed and used forms can greatly inhibit the success of RTI teams and the success of students. Good forms are communication tools that help intervention happen more quickly and more effectively.

See page 43 or visit **go.solution-tree.com/rti** to download *Team Foundations*, a recording tool to prompt teams to select members, identify norms, determine how norm violations will be addressed, plan team meeting time, and set team goals.

Closing Thoughts

Our discussion here of the critical components of effective collaboration is intended as an overview of the process. To dig deeper into PLC practices and structures for collaboration, we highly recommend the book *Learning by Doing* (DuFour et al., 2010). We consider this book the "PLC encyclopedia," as it goes in depth into every aspect of the PLC process and provides the tools necessary to support these outcomes.

Finally, we offer a warning: when an organization first starts to collaborate to ensure collective responsibility, the work will seem harder than before, and the collective results of the organization will often dip. Jerald Jellison (2006) defines this natural result of the change process as the "J" curve. When an organization implements change, the members will naturally be better at their old way of doing things than the new way. Team members have built competency with the old way, while the new approach requires a set of new skills that must be developed. Consequently, any organization implementing this kind of change should expect a dip in effectiveness.

The good news is that as the members of the organization gain proficiency in the new skills, performance improves, and the organization experiences far greater results than what they gained by their previous practices. We have seen too many schools and districts abandon collaborative practices because they did not experience immediate results. Schools and districts must expect this temporary dip and push through it to reap the benefits of these powerful new processes.

Collective responsibility focuses a school's collective efforts on one purpose: student learning. It creates the culture and collaborative structures necessary for RTI to work. Once a school has accepted responsibility for high levels of learning for every child, the next essential consideration is determining exactly *what* every student must learn to "learn at high levels"—in other words, we must answer the question, where do we need to go?

Activities and Tools Summary

Have your school teams addressed the foundational issues needed to be effective?

See *Team Foundations* (page 43).

Visit **go.solution-tree.com/rti** *to download this tool.*

Team Foundations

Team Members:

Our Norms:

We commit to reviewing these norms at every meeting, revising them as needed, and holding each other accountable for following them.

When Norms Are Broken, We Will:

Our Meeting Schedule:

Date: Time: Place:

Teams work toward common goals. Our goals to improve student learning are:

Specific **M**easurable **A**ttainable **R**esults-oriented **T**ime-bound

Simplifying Response to Intervention © 2012 Solution Tree Press • solution-tree.com
Visit **go.solution-tree.com/rti** to download this page.

Concentrated Instruction: Where Do We Need to Go?

Concentrated instruction: A systematic process of identifying essential knowledge and skills that all students must master to learn at high levels, and determining the specific learning needs for each child to get there. Thinking is guided by the question, Where do we need to go?

Once a school has created a sense of collective responsibility to ensure that all students learn at high levels, the next step is to engage its teachers in a dialogue to help answer the question, if all students are to learn, exactly what is it they must learn?

After synthesizing more than 800 meta-analyses involving many millions of students, John Hattie (2009) identified six "signposts" that point toward excellence in education. One of these signposts from his book *Visible Learning* reads as follows:

> Teachers need to know the learning intentions and success criteria of their lessons, know how well they are attaining these criteria, and know where to go next in light of the criteria of: "Where are you going?" "How are you going?" and "Where to next?" (Hattie, 2009, p. 239)

In terms of concentrated instruction, Where are you going? is synonymous with Where are *we*, as a team of teachers, going with this unit of instruction? Answering this question well is critical to the successful implementation of response to intervention. Without engaging teachers in a collaborative process to clarify exactly what knowledge and skills are essential for students to master, schools will become overwhelmed by attempting to provide interventions for everything in the curriculum.

This chapter will describe a realistic protocol that collaborative teacher teams can use to plan a team teaching–assessing cycle. In this protocol, teams (1) define the knowledge and skills that every student must master in order to be successful in school and in life (that is, Tier 1 core instruction), (2) plan when and how the team will provide additional time and support to those who need it (Tier 1 and Tier 2 interventions), (3) and create common formative assessments that will be used to monitor how well the core instructional program is working for each student. Chapter

5 will address the assessment cycle in depth, and chapter 6 will address how to select interventions; this chapter focuses on identifying and clarifying what all students must learn.

The inverted pyramid in figure 4.1 was introduced in chapter 1 as a way of thinking about who is responsible for various components of a system that helps every student experience success. In this chapter we will focus on the upper right portion of the pyramid—on effective core instruction for all students and the interventions provided by collaborative teacher teams as a part of that core instruction. We call this approach to Tier 1 "core and more."

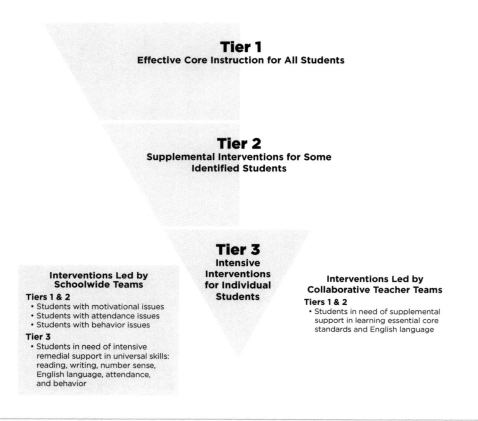

Figure 4.1: Team responsibilities in the inverted RTI pyramid.

A Focus on Coverage

In the United States, each state has attempted to define what all students must learn, and as a result many American schools and districts have abdicated their responsibility to define essential learnings to the state. Unfortunately, in their well-intentioned attempts to create academic content standards, states have identified far more than can possibly be learned in the amount of time available to teachers. After studying and quantifying this problem at McREL (Mid-continent Research for Education and

Learning), Marzano came to the following conclusion: "To cover all of this content, you would have to change schooling from K–12 to K–22. The sheer number of standards is the biggest impediment to implementing standards" (in Scherer, 2001, p. 15).

The process used to create state content standards might help shed some light on this problem. James Popham (2005) describes the process as one of convening subject-matter specialists and asking them to identify what is significant and important about their subject. This typically results in a document that concludes that almost *everything* about their subject is important. Popham adds, "These committees seem bent on identifying skills that they fervently wish students would possess. Regrettably, the resultant litanies of committee-chosen content standards tend to resemble curricular wish lists rather than realistic targets" (2005).

In too many schools, facing an overwhelming amount of content that they must cover, teachers pick and choose the standards they believe will be most beneficial to their students—or even worse, the standards they like to teach. In other schools, realizing that this haphazard approach to determining what students must learn may negatively impact student performance on high-stakes tests, teachers frantically attempt to cover all of the standards equally—even if this means that many students can never truly understand what they are learning or demonstrate mastery of a standard. *When everything is important, nothing is.* Both of these approaches are disastrous for student learning.

A Focus on Learning

In his book *Accountability for Learning*, Doug Reeves asserts a compelling alternative vision:

> We can wait for policymakers to develop holistic accountability plans, or we can be proactive in exceeding the requirements of prevailing accountability systems. If teachers systematically examine their professional practice and their impact on student achievement, the results of such reflective analysis will finally transform educational accountability from a destructive and unedifying mess to a constructive and transformative force in education. (Reeves, 2004, p. 6)

Rather than frantically trying to cover everything in the textbook, or treating every standard with the same sense of urgency, teacher teams must be given the time and training to clarify exactly what every student must master. This philosophy, in part, led McKinsey and Company (Barber & Mourshed, 2007) to identify the Singapore school system as one of the best in the world, based primarily on results from the Programme for International School Assessment, which directly compares the quality of education across systems and countries. Rather than identifying an impossible number of standards, the Singapore Ministry of Education adopted "Teach Less, Learn More" as its framework.

Effective core instruction cannot merely cover what is on the state test or plow through the pages of a textbook. In attempting to frame this discussion of "learning more" for educators, Rick DuFour, Becky DuFour, and Bob Eaker have repeatedly suggested that every collaborative teacher team ask and answer the following four questions:

1. What is it we want our students to learn?
2. How will we know if each student is learning each of the essential skills, concepts, knowledge, and dispositions that we have deemed most essential?
3. How will we respond when some of our students do not learn?
4. How will we enrich and extend the learning for students who are already proficient? (DuFour et al., 2010)

It is difficult, if not impossible, for schools to attempt to answer questions 2, 3, and 4 if they have not sufficiently answered the first question. Schools that attempt to build an intervention program before they have clearly identified what is essential for all students to learn are placing the cart before the horse. Therefore, we advocate that teacher teams work together to establish what, exactly, Tier 1 instruction must include for each student to succeed in school and life.

Identifying Essential Skills and Knowledge

Reeves (2002) has offered one set of criteria that teachers might use to distinguish between what is nice and what is essential for students to know:

- **Endurance**—Will this standard provide students with knowledge and skills that are valuable beyond a single test date?
- **Leverage**—Will it provide knowledge and skills that are valuable in multiple disciplines?
- **Readiness**—Will it provide students with knowledge and skills essential for success in the next grade or level of instruction?

Larry Ainsworth (2003) proposes a similar set of questions: what do your students need for success—in school (this year, next year, and so on), in life, and on state tests? Ainsworth suggests that consideration of state test items might be *part* of the discussion about what is essential for all students to learn, but is not the only consideration.

In 2009, governors and state commissioners of education from forty-eight states, two territories, and the District of Columbia committed to developing a common core of state standards for English language arts and mathematics for grades K–12. At the time of publication, forty-two states and territories and the District of Columbia have voluntarily adopted the standards (Common Core State Standards Initiative, 2010). The Common Core State Standards provide yet another resource to schools attempting to define what is essential for all students to learn. Questions that schools might want to ask include: How do the Common Core State Standards compare to the district's "power standards" or to the collaborative team's identification of what is essential for all students to learn? How does the scaffolding of skills in the common core compare to the results of previously held vertical conversations between teachers in a building or across buildings?

While the Common Core State Standards have attempted, among other things, to lessen the amount of content, they continue to challenge schools to choose between coverage and mastery. As Richard DuFour and Robert Marzano note, "At the fourth-grade level alone the common core includes forty-three standards. . . . When one considers the fact that a busy fourth-grade teacher has only thirty-six weeks and 180 days in the school year, the task of teaching forty-three standards appears daunting if not impossible" (DuFour & Marzano, 2011, p. 93).

Collaborative teams of grade-level or course-alike teachers should discuss, debate, and dialogue about which standards are essential, using all of the resources and criteria just mentioned. As they grapple with these issues, teams should refer to copies of their state content standards, district power standards, the Common Core State Standards, and released test items from state tests, as well as the blueprints for their state tests. The discussion about which standards are most important should not occur in a vacuum. Teams need not begin with a completely blank piece of paper, but should refer to these documents as they attempt to answer the question, What is it we want our students to learn?

We are often asked, who should determine what is essential for all students to learn, the district or teams of teachers? The answer is both! In creating a list of power standards, it is important for the district to understand that without some process that involves teacher teams at each school site, there is likely to be a huge gap between the intended curriculum established by the district and the implemented curriculum taught when teachers shut the doors to their classrooms (Marzano, 2003). It is also important to understand, however, that in choosing essential standards, teachers are not advocating the elimination of certain standards; they are simply "prioritizing the standards and indicators rather than regarding all of them as being equal in importance" (Ainsworth, 2003, p. 6).

Get Beyond the List

Teachers sometimes conceptualize the task of identifying what is essential for all students to learn as making a list, or even worse, as placing checkmarks by or highlighting those standards they deem to be essential. In order to understand the standards at a deep level, the discussion must result in more than checkmarks on a page. The dialogue needs to ensure that team members (1) are interpreting the standard in the same way, (2) have agreement on the level of rigor and what might constitute proficiency, and (3) have identified the prerequisite skills and knowledge necessary for students to be successful in mastering the new standard. Even if we assume that the Common Core State Standards represent the "perfect" answer for every school, for example, simply handing those standards to teachers and telling them to "go forth and teach them" does not guarantee that teachers will interpret them in the same way. Teachers must be involved in a process that helps them to understand essential learnings in a similar way. Participation in this kind of process also helps to ensure that teachers will have greater agreement on the importance of each standard and the pacing of instruction around that standard, both of which facilitate the creation of common assessments by the collaborative team.

Equally important is that this kind of process creates ownership. When teammates engage in this kind of deep, professional discussion, they feel they are helping every student to learn what they have deemed to be essential, as opposed to simply getting students ready to take a test created by a group of faceless, nameless testmakers. This kind of internal ownership is highly desirable and directly supports the development of collective responsibility, as opposed to adherence to a more centralized accountability in which teachers attempt to prepare students based upon what others consider to be important. According to Joan Talbert, "Centralized accountability systems can work against the development of mutual teacher accountability. Their emphasis on near-term gains in test scores pushes a pace of change that undermines the development of PLCs" (Talbert, 2010, p. 560). In a PLC, a team of professional teachers says to its members, "*We* determined that all students must learn these standards; therefore, *we* must take responsibility when some students don't learn."

Rewrite the Standard Into Teacher-Friendly, Student-Friendly Language

Rather than create a list of state or district standards with checkmarks placed next to certain standards, we recommend that schools engage teachers in a process and dialogue utilizing the form in figure 4.2 (page 51).

Describe the Standard

In the first column, teams should not simply indicate the number of the standard. Listing *Algebra I Standard 3.1.2* does not reveal much about the standard itself. Simply copying down the wording of the standard as expressed in the state document also does little to ensure that individual teachers are interpreting the standard in a similar fashion. We recommend that teams discuss the standard and together reword it into teacher-friendly and student-friendly language that helps to clarify what the standard actually means, as in figure 4.3.

Description of Standard
Students understand and use the rules of exponents.

Figure 4.3: Description of standard in student-friendly language.

Define Rigor

Next, teacher teams need to grapple with what level of rigor would represent proficiency on this standard. Even if teachers have discussed and clarified what the

What Is It We Expect Students to Learn?

Grade:	Subject:	Semester:		Team Members:	
Description of Standard	**Example of Rigor**	**Prerequisite Skills**	**When Taught?**	**Common Summative Assessment**	**Extension Standards**
What is the essential standard to be learned? Describe in student-friendly vocabulary.	What does proficient student work look like? Provide an example and/or description.	What prior knowledge, skills, and/or vocabulary are needed for a student to master this standard?	When will this standard be taught?	What assessment(s) will be used to measure student mastery?	What will we do when students have already learned this standard?

Figure 4.2: Essential standards chart.

continued ↓

Essential Standards Criteria (Reeves, 2002, p. 54)

1. **Endurance:** Will this standard provide students with knowledge and skills that are valuable beyond a single test date?

2. **Leverage:** Will it provide knowledge and skills that are valuable in multiple disciplines?

3. **Readiness:** Will it provide students with knowledge and skills essential for success in the next grade/level of instruction?

For a reproducible version of this tool, visit **go.solution-tree.com/rti** *or see page 72.*

standard actually means, this does not ensure that each teacher will expect the same level of rigor. After examining released state test items, benchmark assessments, and other indicators, teams should come to agreement on what students will be able to do as a result of mastering this standard. Figure 4.4 shows an example of rigor for the standard in question. In other instances, the team might say, "See the attached rubric" or "See the attached anchor paper."

Example of Rigor
Simplify: $5x^3y^7$ $10xy^9$

Figure 4.4: Example of rigor for this standard.

Identify Prerequisite Skills

Next, teacher teams should discuss what prior knowledge and skills are necessary for students to learn the standard at the level they have defined as proficient (fig. 4.5).

Prerequisite Skills
Multiplying monomials and polynomials

Figure 4.5: Prerequisite knowledge and skills needed for success on the standard.

As we will discuss in chapter 5 on convergent assessment, at the beginning of each school year, or even each unit of instruction, a screening process should take place to identify those students lacking the prerequisite skills identified as necessary for success in the upcoming unit(s). This kind of universal screening (some might even call it a pretest) is directly aligned to those standards the team has determined as essential and should result in an immediate intervention for the identified students. Since the remediation will need to occur as soon as the unit begins, teachers must prepare strategies for remediation during unit planning.

Moreover, imagine the impact on student learning if this intervention were timed to take place *before* initial instruction begins! In our current example, the algebra I team would provide those students who did not demonstrate proficiency in multiplying monomials and polynomials with intervention *before* the unit on understanding and using the rules of exponents begins. This would also be done in such a way as to not pull these students out of core instruction.

Agree on Pacing and Common Assessment

To plan for intervention in this way, team members must also discuss the pacing of their instruction. In this example, the algebra I team decided to introduce the unit on exponents in February, thus allowing students lacking the necessary prior skills to use the entire month of January to master the prerequisite skills.

At this point in the process, teacher teams might also determine their summative assessment for the unit of instruction. In this case, the team felt confident that the textbook's end-of-chapter test was well constructed and well aligned to their instruction (see fig. 4.6).

When Taught?	Common Summative Assessment
February	Chapter 4

Figure 4.6: Common assessment and pacing.

Different terms have been used to describe the process outlined here. Larry Ainsworth (2003) and Doug Reeves (2002) refer to *power standards*, Jay McTighe and Grant Wiggins (2004) to *identifying desired results*, Robert Marzano (2007) to a *guaranteed and viable curriculum*, and John Hattie (2009) to the question, Where are we going? Whatever terms a school uses, it must engage teacher teams in an ongoing process that leads to deeper understanding of what they want all students to learn.

Identify Extension Standards

While the collaborative team is determining what is essential for all students to learn, we believe that some consideration should be given, in advance, to how the team might provide meaningful enrichment and extension for those students who demonstrate that they have already mastered these same standards. Rather than beginning the instructional cycle and then discovering (and teams are probably not surprised) that some students already know the materials, why not identify what might truly provide an extension to these students' learning rather than simply assigning them busywork? Just as teachers must plan to provide immediate remediation to students who lack prior skills, so too should they plan to provide immediate enrichment to students who have already mastered the standard. This can be done in several ways. Teachers can make the actual content more rigorous; make the process or activities in which the students engage more rigorous; or make the culminating product, which applies what students have learned, more rigorous (Tomlinson, 2000).

Plan for Extra Time and Support

After clarifying what all students must learn, defining the level of rigor, identifying the prior skills needed for success, and agreeing on the instructional pace and summative assessment for the unit, teacher teams should next develop a general plan for remediation, intervention, and enrichment.

No matter how well we teach a unit, it is likely that some students will not be prepared for the instruction and will require some additional help around prerequisite skills (remediation). In addition, some students, although they possess the prior skills needed, might still struggle with the learning and require some additional time and support (intervention). Finally, other students will breeze through the unit because they have already mastered the material, and they will require some enrichment and extension. Rather than reacting to these scenarios as they occur, teacher teams should proactively prepare for each of these eventualities as part of their overall plan for the trimester, quarter, or semester.

Unwrap the Standards Into Learning Targets

Decades ago, it might have been sufficient to describe what students will learn in school as "reading, 'riting and 'rithmetic." While the three Rs are still important, they alone are vastly insufficient in defining what students must learn.

Once a teacher team has determined the essential standards for the trimester, quarter, or semester, it's time to drill down deeper into all of the component parts that provide the underpinning for a standard. This can be a time-consuming process, and for this reason we recommend that teams first complete the *Essential Standards Chart* (page 72) for a unit, trimester, or quarter of instruction. Then, as time permits, teams should drill deeper into two or three essential standards. We recommend that teams do not spend the entire school year drilling deeper until they have reached initial agreement on what is essential. We can't wait an entire school year to impact student learning. Each year, a team can drill deeper into more of what has been determined to be essential until a detailed plan has been developed.

Beyond simply rewording the standard into teacher-friendly, student-friendly language, teachers need to tightly align these standards with their curriculum, instruction, and assessment. This process of alignment is described by many different terms: *unwrapping* the standards, *unraveling* the standards, *unpacking* the standards, or *deconstructing* the standards, to name a few. All of these approaches have one end in mind: to make the process of using standards more manageable and to ensure that teachers understand and interpret the standards in the same way. For the purpose of consistency, we use the term *unwrapping* to describe this process.

Some standards are discrete and describe a specific target: "Students count, read, and write whole numbers up to 100" (California Content Standards, Number Sense Standard 1.1; California Department of Education, 2000). However, other standards encapsulate many learning targets: "Students know plant and animal cells contain many thousands of different genes and typically have two copies of every gene. The two copies (or alleles) of the gene may or may not be identical, and one may be dominant in determining the phenotype while the other is recessive" (California Content Standards, Life Science—Genetics, Standard 2d; California Department of Education, 2000). It is especially important to unwrap a standard such as the latter example to identify and describe everything that students must know and be able to do. These statements of intended learning for students are called *learning targets*.

Once a standard has been unwrapped into a number of learning targets, teachers can build their assessments at the target level, rather than attempting to assess an entire standard. A general guideline to increase the reliability of such assessments is to use three to five questions or "prompts" per learning target (Prometric Services, 2011).

Many helpful books exist that can guide teacher teams in how to unwrap their essential standards; we will not attempt to do so in this book. However, we do want to emphasize the importance of this process to RTI, because outlining specific learning targets early on helps us to better respond later when students don't learn, by addressing the causes of student struggles rather than the symptoms. Focusing interventions based upon discrete learning targets (not the entire standard) will be discussed at length in chapter 6.

Imagine the following scenario. A teacher is asked to work with a group of students who have failed to learn Life Science Standard 2d: "Students know plant and animal cells contain many thousands of different genes and typically have two copies of every gene. The two copies (or alleles) of the gene may or may not be identical, and one may be dominant in determining the phenotype while the other is recessive" (California Content Standards, Life Science—Genetics, Standard 2d; California Department of Education, 2000). The only data the teacher has is that all of these students have failed this standard. Knowing only that broad information, the teacher is likely to start from the beginning of the unit and reteach the whole standard to the entire group of students. But the fact that the students failed is a *symptom*, not a diagnosis. Have they failed because they don't understand what an allele is? Because they don't understand why alleles are found in pairs? Because they don't understand which cells do not have pairs of alleles? If the middle school science team had unwrapped Life Science Standard 2d into these discrete learning targets *before* the lesson, when some students struggled later, the teacher could have gathered information about each student's learning relative to each target and grouped the students for intervention based on the precise *cause* of their struggles.

This need to measure precise progress and offer targeted interventions is why unwrapping essential standards is so critical to the successful implementation of RTI.

Building Common Formative Assessments

Now that the collaborative teacher team has identified which standards are essential for all students to master and has unwrapped some or all of those standards into learning targets, the team is ready to build common formative assessments to help teachers answer the question, Where are we now? and to help students answer, Where am I now? These assessments, linked to individual learning targets rather than an entire standard, allow the collaborative team to focus on causes rather than symptoms when students struggle.

Formative assessment is intended to generate feedback that can be used to improve and accelerate student learning (Sadler, 1998). When teachers use formative assessment in this way, students can learn in six to seven months what will normally take an entire school year to learn (Leahy, Lyon, Thompson, & Wiliam, 2005). Using formative assessment, teachers can:

- Determine what standards students already know and how well they know them
- Decide what changes in instruction to make in order to help each student be successful
- Create lessons appropriate to the needs of students
- Group students for intervention and enrichment
- Inform students of their own progress in order for them to set goals

There is great flexibility in terms of what this looks like; as Guskey notes, "Formative assessments can vary in form and length depending upon the grade level and subject matter. They can be short quizzes, written assignments, oral presentations, skill demonstrations, or performances. In essence, formative assessments are any device teachers use to gather evidence of student learning" (Guskey, 2010, p. 55).

While individual teachers are constantly gathering this kind of evidence in their own classrooms, collaborative teams of teachers plan frequent, *common* formative assessments as part of their instructional cycle, and use this information to respond collectively to the needs of *all* their students. Formative assessments are considered common when student learning is "assessed using the same instrument or process and according to the same criteria" (DuFour et al., 2010, p. 63).

Using formative assessments to improve both the teaching of the collaborative team and the learning of students is hardly a new idea. Decades ago, Benjamin Bloom (1971) described a similar process called *mastery learning*. Bloom asserted that all students could master learning at high levels if they were given additional time and support, and that this additional time and support was guided by what he referred to as "corrective feedback." This corrective feedback, valuable to both individual students and the collaborative team, is provided through the information gleaned from a team's common formative assessments.

Assessments should be conducted in such a way that students feel that assessments are being done "with" them and "for" them, rather than "to" them. Assessment authority Rick Stiggins describes the need to include students in the process of examining assessment data in the following way:

> But professional learning communities cannot be merely about teachers making decisions based on common assessment data. Students must be partners in the community, too. Assessment must encourage and support them in their pursuit of excellence. (Stiggins, 2007a, p. 61)

Research continues to demonstrate that this approach has exceptionally positive effects on student learning (Hattie, 2009). In fact, in a meta-analysis published in 1990, Kulik, Kulik, and Bangert-Drowns found that mastery learning programs improved student performance by nearly one-half of one standard deviation, especially for low-achieving students, leading them to conclude:

> Few educational treatments of any sort were consistently associated with achievement effects as large as those produced by mastery learning. . . . In

evaluation after evaluation, mastery programs have produced impressive gains. (Kulik et al., 1990, p. 292)

This takes us full circle back to the formula for learning we discussed in chapter 1:

Targeted Instruction + Time = Learning

This formula is really nothing more than Bloom's mastery learning process with a slightly modified vocabulary. Tom Guskey states it this way: "If teachers could provide the necessary time and appropriate learning conditions, nearly all students could reach a high level of achievement" (Guskey, 2010, p. 53).

Again, at this stage, collaborative teacher teams should build assessments to assess narrow learning targets rather than the entire standard. Exactly how teams do that is beyond the scope of this book. Instead, we recommend that teams look to some of the following publications: *Balanced Assessment* (Burke, 2010); *Classroom Assessment for Student Learning* (Stiggins, Arter, Chappuis, & Chappuis, 2007); and *The Handbook of Formative Assessment* (Andrade & Cizek, 2010). We will also provide more information about common formative assessments in chapter 5.

We are often asked, "Where does intervention begin?" The answer is, of course, at Tier 1 as part of initial instruction, and that intervention cannot be done effectively without the information provided by common formative assessments to guide the process. Assessments do not merely mark the end of an instructional unit (summative assessment) but are used throughout the instructional process (formative assessment) to provide feedback—to students about where they are, as well as to the team about where to go next, with which group of students, and why. Common formative assessment data are used to identify not only students who need more time and support, but also students who are ready to participate in extension activities. The team's use of this information should not result in simply reteaching certain material "louder and slower" (Guskey, 2003). Instead, teachers should use new strategies, materials, and approaches that accommodate differences in student learning styles and needs (Sternberg, 1996). Discovering all of the necessary new strategies for high-quality corrective instruction and enrichment would no doubt be daunting for an individual teacher working alone, but a collaborative team of teachers can very effectively support one another in discussing and sharing such strategies.

A Protocol for Getting Started

Rather than incorporating some of the ideas explained thus far in this chapter as "random acts of improvement," schools will experience far greater success if they implement these ideas in a strategic and systematic way. We recommend the following protocol, based on our experiences in working with schools across North America:

1. Complete the *Essential Standards Chart* (page 72) for the first period of instruction (trimester, quarter, or semester).

2. Before the unit begins, identify how and when the team will identify and support students in need of remediation and enrichment. The *entire team* should reserve time for this additional time and support, not just each individual teacher.

3. As time permits, unwrap two or three of the essential standards into learning targets, starting with those that will first be introduced to students.

4. Build common assessments by identifying three to five questions for each of the learning targets identified.

5. Use the results from these common assessments to identify and monitor students needing more time and support with specific learning targets (focus on causes, not symptoms).

6. As time permits, unwrap the next two or three essential standards into additional learning targets, following up with those that will next be introduced to students.

7. Build common assessments by identifying three or four prompts for each of the additional learning targets identified.

8. Use the results from these common assessments to target students needing more time and support with specific targets. Use this same information to provide enrichment to those who have already mastered the learning targets.

9. Repeat this process for the second period of instruction (trimester, semester, and so on), beginning again with the *Essential Standards Chart.*

We do not want to make this protocol too time-consuming or overwhelming for teams, especially those just getting started. However, there is one very powerful, additional step that might be added as time permits and as teams gain confidence in the process: screening students for prerequisite skills. Using the information from the corresponding column of the *Essential Standards Chart,* teams could construct a very efficient assessment to identify those students without the prior skills necessary to be successful in mastering the new essential standard(s) identified by the team. Remember, the best intervention is prevention.

This is serious, powerful work, and it takes time to do it well. At the same time, as our colleague Anthony Muhammad (2009) argues, change must be doable—not overwhelming. In many schools we've seen, teacher teams are fully engaged in unwrapping standards and building common assessments. The only problem is that the entire school year becomes consumed by this important process, and very little is done to actually help struggling students during this year of "unwrapping."

For these reasons, we suggest that schools use a scaffolded approach and follow Stephen Covey's (1989) advice to "begin with the end in mind": student learning. To begin, teacher teams should use the first two or three collaborative meetings to complete the *Essential Standards Chart.* Once the framework has been created, this step may take even less time in subsequent years. After the general plan has been created, teams begin the work of unwrapping the standards two or three at a time, then building common assessments around the learning targets (subskills) they've identified, and finally using the assessment data to drive interventions. In this way, the process can start having an immediate impact on student learning. When the team revisits its plan in the following school year, teachers will have another opportunity to unwrap more essential standards, and with their increased competence and confidence, the process as a whole should go faster.

Implementing the Team Teaching– Assessing Cycle

Now that we have described the planning process, we'll examine how the process is implemented in classrooms. Figure 4.7 gives an overview of the cycle of teaching and assessing, as executed by teacher teams.

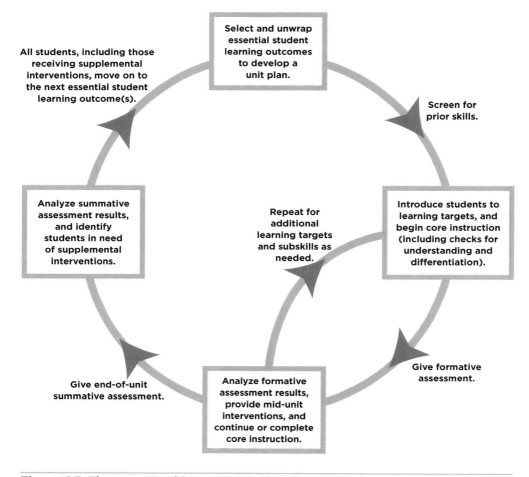

Figure 4.7: The team teaching–assessing cycle.

Depending on the complexity of the essential standard(s) selected by the teacher team for the current unit, the cycle may take several weeks or more to complete. For example, if a team unwraps a single standard to discover that there are eight separate learning targets associated with that standard, the team might decide to use the first week of the cycle to focus on only the first four learning targets. The second week would focus on the next two learning targets, and the third week of instruction might focus on the final two targets. In this example, the mini-cycle in the lower-right quadrant of figure 4.7 would rotate three times (once for each week's cluster of learning targets) before the team's common summative assessment is given. However, students who struggled on those formative assessments would receive ongoing additional time and support from the team during each week of the cycle. This is what we mean by calling Tier 1 core and more: while the core instruction cycle continues, students who need more time and support receive it. This "more" is possible because the team reserved additional instructional time to provide ongoing support at the beginning of the unit, rather than waiting for the summative assessment results to show, too late, that students have struggled.

See page 74 or visit **go.solution-tree.com/rti** to access the *Teaching Cycle Planning Calendar* to help teacher teams plan when they will introduce the learning target(s) to their students, use common formative assessment to assess student learning and measure teaching effectiveness, plan for interventions and extended learning during core instruction, and give a final common assessment.

But what happens when, despite the team's best efforts, some students still do not demonstrate mastery on the summative assessment? A new cycle begins as the team moves on to a new unit on new standards. Some students continue to need additional time and support, however, and they receive that support in addition to Tier 1 core instruction for the new unit (see fig. 4.8, page 62).

In figure 4.8, the bold outer circle represents Tier 1 core instruction for the *new* unit, for which *all* students will receive instruction. The second circle depicts Tier 2 intervention, and the small inner circle depicts Tier 3 intervention on the learning targets from the *previous* unit. Students who continue to need additional time and support are in the cycle for new instruction *and* in either the second or inner circle for intervention. This is a key point! Students should never miss Tier 1 core instruction in order to receive this additional time and support.

Additionally, note that lines connect the screening for prior skills to *either* Tier 2 or Tier 3 intervention. Remember, the best intervention is prevention! Once we have determined which students do not have the prerequisite skills to be successful in the unit, they are given additional time and support *before* or *as* that unit begins. If they lack the necessary skills, why wait for them to fail before giving them the help they need?

Shoring Up the Core

We repeatedly read that approximately 80 percent of students receiving a well-instructed, research-based curriculum should experience success as a result of initial core instruction in the classroom. We believe that understanding this often-quoted statistic is the key to implementing RTI. So many schools facing sanctions under NCLB immediately seek Tier 2 and Tier 3 interventions as the quick fix to their schools' problems. To these schools we say, "You don't have an intervention problem, you have a 'what you do all day long in the classroom' problem." If a strong core instructional program can account for up to 80 percent of students experiencing success, schools should place a majority of their efforts on strengthening their core instructional programs.

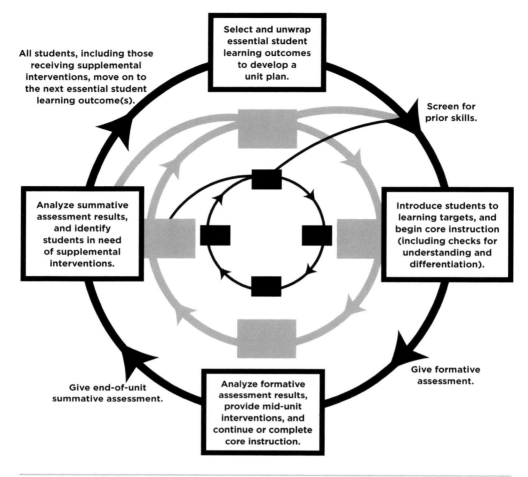

Figure 4.8: The team teaching–assessing cycle, including Tier 2 and Tier 3 interventions.

In addition to the process outlined in this chapter, we believe it is also important to clarify what is meant by the frequently used term *fidelity*. We often hear it used in reference to learning, but while fidelity is important, it must become fidelity to standards and learning instead of fidelity to programs. The programs will still be our primary, or even our sole, resource, but we must more intelligently and professionally use these resources to shore up the core instructional program.

Most major publishers' K–6 English language arts programs are chock-full of *stuff*. There are dozens of units per grade level and, for each unit, dozens of activities and worksheets. In addition to these materials, three or four additional worksheets per lesson are available as ancillary materials. In the area of reading comprehension alone, each grade level's materials introduce students to up to six comprehension strategies and twenty comprehension skills. This abundance of materials can present problems. Some programs even provide entire workbooks full of interventions and/or enrichments, often overwhelming the classroom teacher with choices.

Further complicating the effective use of these programs is that state standards specify the use of certain skills and strategies—usually no more than six or seven in a given grade level. Meanwhile, publishers' programs present more than twenty distinct comprehension skills, and yet a careful analysis reveals that those skills can actually be sorted into four or five *major* skills, as many are closely related. Teaching students to apply these skills and strategies in the sequence and manner prescribed by the publisher may not be the most diagnostic and successful approach.

Is there another option? We propose that two simple steps would make our core instruction in the area of reading comprehension skills (and any other curricular area) more successful for students. First, educators, as a collective community of learners, should examine their publisher-provided resources to identify which are standards-based and which are not. Think of these resources as tools, not scripts. Lesson and unit planning should be informed and determined by the standards. Second, data on specific students' strengths and needs should also inform lesson and unit planning. In short, we do not support blind adherence to a group of materials designed without any specific group of students in mind.

Further, while many textbooks are organized and sequenced logically, teachers may choose to reorder units, chapters, and lessons to better serve student needs and to combine separate areas of the text that refer to the same standard or sets of standards. Standards and student needs, not textbooks, should drive our instruction. Teachers (and students) may more deeply engage with standards if they can rearrange lessons when creating curriculum pacing guides such as the *Essential Standards Chart* introduced earlier in this chapter.

Teachers committed to providing a solid core experience will take advantage of instructional days that are freed by focusing only on standards-based lessons rather than plowing through the textbook. These additional instructional days can be spent on content with which students have more difficulty. In all content areas, the way we use our curricular resources can be focused and improved to ensure that students' first exposure to learning is as thorough and successful as possible.

Concentrated instruction is not the result of purchasing new materials, although wonderful new materials are increasingly available. It is not the result of districts creating lists of power standards and handing them to teachers without allowing time for the teachers to debate, clarify, and ultimately to own what is essential for each student to master. Nor is it accomplished by perseverating on last year's NCLB data or last trimester's benchmark assessment data. It is achieved when time is given to each collaborative teacher team to define, with certainty, where they are now and where they are going, and then to use that information to answer the question, Where to next—for each student in our care, and for us as a team?

Concentrated Instruction and Behavior Systems

Behavior has a profound impact on a student's ability to learn at school, and instructional interventions are not the only method by which schools can substantially improve student learning. One study of at-risk youth in Philadelphia City Schools found that sixth-graders with poor behavior (those earning an unsatisfactory final behavior mark) have a one in four chance of making it to twelfth grade on time (Neild & Balfanz, 2010). In fact, if the cause of poor achievement is related to student motivation, attendance, and behavior, schools that initiate instructional improvements and interventions may be treating the symptoms without addressing the real underlying ailment.

To achieve success for every student, schools and classrooms must be safe, predictable places in which high expectations are the norm, all types of adults and children are welcome, and respect is modeled by all adults and expected of all students. Positive behavior must be rewarded, and undesirable behavior must immediately, consistently, and constructively be redirected. Effective RTI models apply the same four essential guiding principles, use the same tiered system of supports, and answer the same critical questions of learning for behavior as for academics.

Schools that commit to initiating and sustaining a system of behavioral supports will experience increased student learning (Sugai & Horner, 2002). A school's core instruction in behavior should result in at least 80 percent of students being able to articulate what is expected of them, because these behaviors have been taught, actively supervised, practiced, and acknowledged. These Tier 1 behavioral supports should also result in at least 80 percent of the students responding to the high behavioral expectations as a result of the supports put in place to prevent problems before they occur.

Ensuring timely, systematic, successful, and certain access to behavioral supports falls to the schoolwide leadership team, as the inverted RTI pyramid indicates (see fig. 4.9). Alternatively, the school leadership team may choose to create a special schoolwide behavior team to take lead responsibility. Regardless of which approach a school takes, the team ensures that all staff assume collective responsibility for the success of all students and concentrates instruction on specific behavioral expectations. This is a particularly important point with behavior; students are proficient at taking advantage of staff's inconsistencies. The team then guides the convergent assessments that help the schools appropriately identify and respond to the behavioral needs of groups and individuals.

Behavior concerns fall into two categories:

1. **Academic misbehaviors** include behavior such as not paying attention, not completing assignments, missing class, using poor study habits, and so on. Often they are signs of lack of motivation, lack of knowledge of the "rules of school," or attendance problems. In our work with schools, we sometimes hear educators refer to attendance as a social rather than academic misbehavior, but we consider it an academic behavior since it has such immediate academic consequences.

2. **Social misbehaviors** include behaviors such as acting out, using inappropriate language, or engaging in physical confrontations. These behaviors are

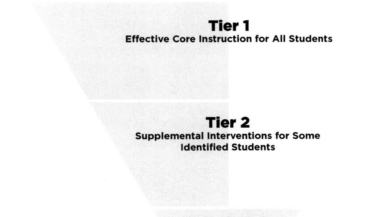

Tier 1
Effective Core Instruction for All Students

Tier 2
Supplemental Interventions for Some Identified Students

Tier 3
Intensive Interventions for Individual Students

Interventions Led by Schoolwide Teams
Tiers 1 & 2
- Students with motivational issues
- Students with attendance issues
- Students with behavior issues

Tier 3
- Students in need of intensive remedial support in universal skills: reading, writing, number sense, English language, attendance, and behavior

Interventions Led by Collaborative Teacher Teams
Tiers 1 & 2
- Students in need of supplemental support in learning essential core standards and English language

Figure 4.9: Team responsibilities in the inverted RTI pyramid.

qualitatively different from academic misbehaviors; academic misbehaviors may appear as acts of omission aimed at avoiding a task or situation, while social misbehaviors may appear as acts of commission aimed at getting attention (Kohn, 1996).

While these behaviors can appear different, they both can occur in combination with other difficulties, they both are often symptomatic of other deficiencies, and we believe they will both best be ameliorated through explicit instruction and preventative measures. We must proactively prepare and equip all students to succeed in all aspects of schooling, and we owe it to students to fully and explicitly explain our expectations for their behavior—behavior that will contribute to the climate for high levels of learning.

In terms of concentrated instruction, what essential learning outcomes do we want for students in the area of behavior? Generally, we want students to self-regulate and self-monitor. While we recognize and accept responsibility for explicitly teaching students to behave in ways that support high levels of learning, our ultimate goal is for them to independently and spontaneously practice positive behaviors. Let's examine concentrated instruction for each type of behavior.

Academic Misbehaviors

Research on the connection between motivation, engagement, and self-regulatory strategies has shown that highly engaged learners contribute greatly toward a scholarly and productive school climate (McCann & Turner, 2004). To be optimally successful, students must be authentically engaged in their learning and intrinsically motivated. In schools with many intentional nonlearners (students with engagement or motivation issues), a focus on academic instruction may not even be the first or most important initiative. While such schools may otherwise have effective practices in place, if students are not encouraged to set goals, to reflect on their own thinking and effort, and to persist—if schools do not foster environments in which students regulate and engage with their own learning—students will not reach their full potential.

When it is confirmed that neither a lack of quality instruction nor a lack of skills is the cause of poor academic performance, it can likely be attributed to inadequate self-regulatory skills. Students may lack specific self-regulatory skills such as:

- **Time management.** Students are more successful when they can control the amount of time they spend on tasks. Time management includes such subskills as planning, allocating time for tasks, setting goals, monitoring, organizing, scheduling, and prioritizing.
- **Organization.** Students are more successful when their desks, paper, assignments, and binders are carefully organized.
- **Note taking.** Students are more successful when they understand how to take notes, both in terms of determining *what* to note and how to structure notes.
- **Goal setting.** Students are more successful when they can set long-term goals and understand how to set short-term goals that will lead to achieving long-term goals. The other self-regulatory skills are tools to achieve those goals.
- **Self-motivation.** Students are more successful when they are consistently and highly engaged—that is, when they are intrinsically motivated. Intrinsic motivation comes not from external rewards such as grades, but rather from the pleasure of working on a task or the sense of satisfaction in completing it.

These strategies have rarely if ever been explicitly taught in schools. The vast majority of students either learn these strategies implicitly (by reflecting on their success or through their parents) or not at all. When students exhibit behavioral difficulties and lack of self-regulation is suspected as the cause, the school should explicitly teach or reteach students how to behave in a scholarly manner that will lead to success.

Schools that make a commitment to teaching all students the behavioral rules of school embrace the idea that the best intervention is prevention. To provide concentrated instruction on academic behaviors to improve engagement, motivation, and students' use of self-regulatory strategies, schools should do the following:

1. **Explicitly teach and reinforce self-regulatory strategies.** Effective schools make instruction on tasks and academic behaviors a central role in each classroom. Students need to learn successful ways of organizing

binders, taking notes, and setting short- and long-term goals. In concentrated instruction for RTI, instruction on self-regulatory practices is universal and reinforced throughout the year.

2. **Assign high-quality tasks for students to complete.** When tasks are meaningful to students, and students understand the significance of tasks to their lives and to key content, the likelihood of them successfully self-regulating increases. When staff know what interests students and make tasks relevant, they can establish meaning and purpose for assignments, in turn encouraging students to motivate *themselves*.

3. **Praise and encourage effort to support a growth mindset.** Lack of self-motivation is one of the trickiest student problems that teachers face. In too many classrooms, students are passively compliant at best. These students may lack intrinsic motivation because they have not been encouraged to attribute their success or failure to their own effort. Instead, they hold what is called a fixed mindset about their own intelligence; they believe they just aren't "smart" (Dweck, 2006). Effective schools help students see the connection between effort and achievement.

4. **Emphasize the importance of regular attendance.** The extent to which we measure and track student attendance will signal to staff, students, and families the importance of attendance. If you believe that the correlation between high rates of attendance and achievement is high (and most of us do), then make this belief publicly known, create attendance competitions between classes and grade levels, and celebrate high attendance rates. Furthermore, emphasize the importance of attendance by proactively reaching out to families with students who had attendance challenges the year before. We possess these data; if the problem is predictable, it's preventable. Make a before-the-school-year phone call that positively communicates your excitement for the coming year. Ask about the student's summer and whether there is anything that the school can do to help him or her prepare for a successful year. If absences occur during the first few weeks of school, reach out again with more vigor, and ensure that the school is providing access to any supports and resources that will lead to improved attendance.

5. **Build positive relationships between adults and students.** Students who feel connected to adults at school are more authentically involved in their learning (Osterman, 2000).

The schoolwide intervention team responsible for behavior can brainstorm specific commitments and practices to embed for each of these areas. Chapter 5 will discuss how to screen and assess students for academic misbehaviors.

Social Misbehaviors

When it comes to social misbehaviors, prevention—systematic, schoolwide prevention—is essential. We recommend that supports be provided through a schoolwide system of behavioral supports such as Positive Behavior Interventions and Supports (see http://pbis.org). Empirical studies of systems of behavioral support have found that behavior supports are most successful in creating positive learning environments when they are efficient, relevant, and sustainably managed (Zins & Ponti, 1990). The goals of implementing a system of behavioral supports within schools include improving climates within classrooms and schools so that optimal learning can occur; decreasing adults' reactive behavior management practices; coordinating academic and behavioral supports; and improving supports for students with complex behavioral challenges (Sugai & Horner, 2002).

Like academic systems of intervention, behavioral supports must be systematic. All staff must accept responsibility for actively supervising all students, and all stakeholders must be consistently committed to establishing high social, cultural, and behavioral expectations. Appropriate behaviors must be clearly defined, explicitly taught, and modeled by adults at all times. Positive, desired behaviors must be acknowledged, both verbally and with small, agreed-upon tokens. Problem behaviors must be immediately and consistently corrected. Instead of unintentionally egging students on or "pushing students' buttons," staff must patiently precorrect and remind when they see that students are at risk of misbehaving. Data must be continuously collected and analyzed so that informed adjustments can be made. A flexible continuum of supports for students with stubborn behavioral challenges must be developed and consistently nurtured. Finally, staff must be willing to reflect upon their instruction; engaging, well-designed instruction fosters positive behavior.

Concentrating instruction in the area of social behavior means taking collective responsibility for student behavior and committing to explicit, consistent modeling and reinforcement of agreed-upon expectations. The school leadership team, or a designated behavior team, should take the following actions.

1. **Clearly define behavior as a responsibility of the schoolwide team.** The schoolwide team should gather information from stakeholders who are representative of the demographics of school and community, including:
   + Staff members who often voice opinions about student behavior
   + Experts and novice staff in the area of effective behavior management
   + Students and parents

   The team will be the primary initial and ongoing group responsible for managing the system of behavioral supports. On a monthly basis, the team should present and analyze data with the entire staff, asking for feedback and following up on questions and concerns, and should plan on conducting annual self-assessments and be prepared to propose changes to the staff.

2. **Identify expectations and desired behaviors.** The next task is to identify key topics that represent high expectations for student behavior. These topics are brief, are stated positively, and complement high levels of academic achievement. A common list of topics is:
   + Be respectful of self, others, and property.
   + Be responsible and prepared.
   + Be ready to follow directions.

Or the topics may be stated more briefly, such as:

+ Respect
+ Responsibility
+ Readiness

The team describes how each of the topics will be observed in selected, key locations across the school campus. These locations may include common areas, such as classrooms, lunch areas, libraries, and restrooms, particularly if there is concern among stakeholders that certain locations require special attention. Next, the team specifies three to five observable behaviors that would represent each of the key expectations in each of the settings. For example, given the key expectations and the sample settings listed earlier, the team would describe what it would look like if students were respectful, responsible, and ready in classrooms, the lunch area, the library, and in restrooms.

A clever way to approach this topic is to first ask staff to brainstorm all the negative, naughty ways in which students are not respectful, not responsible, and not ready in each of the selected settings. Once this therapeutic activity has been completed, the team challenges staff to think differently: to thoughtfully describe what it would look like if students displayed positive behaviors.

3. **Teach desired behaviors.** The next step is to explicitly teach and model for students the specific behaviors they will be expected to exhibit. Desired behaviors should be taught in the same manner as academic skills. Schools often create a matrix that lists positive behaviors in each of the settings that the team has selected for each of the different key expectations (such as respect, responsibility, and readiness). A *Sample Behavior Expectations Matrix* is included at the end of this chapter (page 76). This matrix should be widely publicized, displayed, and explained. The positive behaviors are also prominently displayed in each of the specific school settings that are indicated on the matrix. For example, some of the ways in which students show respect, responsibility, and readiness in the library are displayed on a large poster near the library entrance.

Without the firm and consistent commitment of every adult on campus, the implementation of a system of behavioral supports will not yield results. Teachers also need to expect the same high level of behavior in their classrooms. While teachers' individual styles and personalities are important aspects of classroom life that should be preserved, classroom management practices and procedures should be based on a schoolwide plan. Consensus must be reached on the fundamental expectations for student behavior in classrooms. Each classroom should display prompts, reminders, and the matrix of behavior expectations. All classroom teachers must teach schoolwide behavior expectations in typical classroom contexts and routines, and provide a consistent interpretation of these expectations in doing so.

Convergent assessment and systems of supports in the area of behavior will be addressed in subsequent chapters.

District Responsibilities for Concentrated Instruction

While concentrated instruction in behavior and academics is the responsibility of the school staff, the district can play a role in supporting their efforts.

District leadership, especially in those districts with a number of schools in program improvement status, often focuses on heroic efforts to remediate students several years behind in reading or math skills without considering why so many students have failed to learn as a result of initial instruction. This reactive approach, while understandable, does little to proactively prevent the problem from recurring. Research indicates that problems frequently exist on a classwide basis rather than an individual level (VanDerHeyden & Burns, 2005; VanDerHeyden, Witt, & Gilbertson, 2007). If 80 percent of children can become successful as a result of first, best instruction (Batsche et al., 2005), shouldn't district leadership devote 80 percent of its efforts toward improving Tier 1 concentrated instruction, rather than focusing most of its time, energy, and resources on "plugging holes in the dike"?

As noted earlier, we are constantly confronted with situations in which district leadership may give lip service to the work of RTI, while simultaneously reinforcing the need for schools to "get the scores up now, or else." Consequently, schools often seek out quick fixes that will result in a sudden bump in test scores rather than investing in the long-term work of developing and using a variety of student assessments and data to identify individual learning gaps, designing interventions to address identified gaps in student learning, and using student achievement data to evaluate and refine their interventions. These quick fixes include such educationally bankrupt ideas as using practice tests that prepare students to regurgitate answers without understanding; focusing only on the "bubble" students while abandoning those far below basic; and encouraging teachers to cover everything that will be tested rather than working for mastery of essential standards.

District leadership sends another mixed message when it develops a district pacing guide without communicating to teachers that it is a *guide*, not a law. Pacing guides are about coverage of content, not about concentrated instruction, and certainly not about mastery. If district leadership feels strongly about the issuance of a pacing guide, it must also communicate that this guide is advice, and that schools will enjoy some degree of defined autonomy (Marzano & Waters, 2009) when considering how to give students more time and support when they are not successful.

District leadership can help to promote concentrated instruction by carefully controlling outside pressures and messages that tend to push schools and teachers back toward coverage rather than toward mastery, and by reinforcing the message that less is more. When collaborative teams of teachers jointly assess the performance of their students—using disaggregated test data, formative assessments, student work, and simple checks for understanding—they are able to more effectively target interventions to meet each student's learning needs. They learn from their interventions what works and what needs to be changed. District leadership must be careful not to discourage schools and teachers from making the long-term commitment to change represented by RTI by focusing on only short-term gains on high-stakes state tests.

Joan Talbert put it this way:

> Federal and state accountability systems enforce a view of teaching as implementing a set curriculum according to a pacing guide. Districts are forced to adopt "best curricular programs," and low-performing districts place pressure on teachers to implement them with "fidelity" in their class-rooms. This silver-bullet approach detracts from a view of teaching as involving judgments and a vision of PLCs as analyzing student learning and crafting ways to address performance gaps. (Talbert, 2010, p. 558)

Collaborative teams of teachers need to have laser-like clarity about where they are going. They need to filter out all distractions and focus on each individual student's mastery of what has been determined to be essential. Once developed by the team, the essential learnings should be shared with students in order to engage them in their own learning as much as possible. Instruction and assessment are inextricably linked and, when done well, are really part of one process. As soon as the journey of learning begins, we must not only know *where* we are going, but must also constantly be aware of *how* we are going in order to make mid-unit adjustments—by providing intervention and extension. It is also useful to know where students are before the journey even begins, because not all students start the grade level or course in the same place. Some begin well behind the "starting line" and need a boost from the very beginning of the year. These processes will be discussed in the next chapter, "Convergent Assessment."

Activities and Tools Summary

Has each teacher team clearly identified what they expect all students to learn?

See the *Essential Standards Chart* (page 72).

Has each teacher team planned a Tier 1 instruction and assessment cycle for essential standards?

See the *Teaching Cycle Planning Calendar* (page 74).

Has the schoolwide intervention team defined and communicated the expectations for positive behaviors in specific areas and at specific times in the school?

See the *Sample Behavior Expectations Matrix* (page 76).

*Visit **go.solution-tree.com/rti** to download these activities and tools.*

Essential Standards Chart

What Is It We Expect Students to Learn?					
Grade:	Subject:	Semester:	Team Members:		
Description of Standard	**Example of Rigor**	**Prerequisite Skills**	**When Taught?**	**Common Summative Assessment**	**Extension Standards**
What is the essential standard to be learned? Describe in student-friendly vocabulary.	What does proficient student work look like? Provide an example and/or description.	What prior knowledge, skills, and/or vocabulary are needed for a student to master this standard?	When will this standard be taught?	What assessment(s) will be used to measure student mastery?	What will we do when students have already learned this standard?

Working in collaborative teams, examine all relevant documents, common core standards, state standards, and district power standards, and then apply the criteria of endurance, leverage, and readiness to determine which standards are essential for all students to master. Remember, less is more. For each standard selected, complete the remaining columns. Complete this chart by the second or third week of each instructional period (semester).

page 2 of 2

Teaching Cycle Planning Calendar

Essential standard(s) that **all** students must learn:

Learning targets to be shared with students:

Use the planning calendar to schedule the following:

1. When will we start the unit of study? How will we share the learning target(s) with the students? When will each target be introduced?

2. When will our team meeting(s) during the unit of study be held? When are intervention/extension times available?

3. When are good points during the unit of study to collect evidence of student learning? How and when will we give common formative assessment(s)?

4. When will we collectively analyze the common formative assessment data?

5. When will we reteach students who do not demonstrate mastery of the learning targets on the common formative assessment(s)?

6. When and how will we provide extension and enrichment to those who demonstrate mastery on the common formative assessment(s)?

7. When will we give the end-of-unit common assessment?

Monday	Tuesday	Wednesday	Thursday	Friday

Simplifying Response to Intervention © 2012 Solution Tree Press • solution-tree.com
Visit **go.solution-tree.com/rti** to download this page.

Sample Behavior Expectations Matrix

	Everywhere and All the Time	Recess	Library	Walkways	Restrooms	Lines	Computer Lab	Lunch Area
Respect	Respect school and personal property. Follow adult directions. Display good manners. Use appropriate language.	Follow adult directions. Include others in games. Be a good sport. Kick balls only on grass.	Use quiet voice. Use sticks properly. Sit properly; push in chairs. Walk in library.	Use quiet voice. Follow adult directions.	Use quiet voice. Respect the privacy of others. Keep clean.	Use quiet voice. Walk quietly in a line to class.	Line up on ramp in single file.	Use a quiet voice. Display good table manners. Keep hands behind back while waiting your turn in line.
Responsibility	Walk at all times. Put forth best effort. Sit and play in designated areas.	Use equipment properly. Follow game rules. Use restroom and drinking fountain. Walk on blacktop.	Enter only with adults. Return books on time.	Walk. Use quiet voice. Walk with hands behind back.	Flush. Wash your hands.	Sit or kneel. Walk with hands behind back. Hold ball with two hands.	Finish work before free time.	Clean up your own mess. Walk to and from lunch tables.
Readiness	Be on time. Have all materials.	Follow freeze procedures. Walk to line. End all games at first bell.	Follow checkout rules.	Walk directly to where you're going on sidewalks.	Use during recesses.	Watch for your teacher.	Walk to the nearest computer around the perimeter.	Stay seated at the tables and on the line until dismissed.

Convergent Assessment: Where Are We Now?

Convergent assessment: *An ongoing process of collectively analyzing targeted evidence to determine the specific learning needs of each child and the effectiveness of the instruction the child receives in meeting these needs. Thinking is guided by the question, Where are we now?*

Once a school has created a collaborative culture focused on collective responsibility for student learning and identified the learning goals all children must reach to be successful in school and in life, it should next gather the evidence necessary to determine where each child is in his or her learning relative to the goal. This evidence, gathered through convergent assessment, answers the question, Where are we now?

Convergent assessment ensures that interventions and enrichments are both timely and targeted. Instruction must target specific skills or knowledge in a timely sequence that proceeds toward a known learning destination. If we don't know exactly where each student is and what he or she needs to succeed, our interventions and enrichments will be well-intentioned "shotgun blasts" of strategies aimed at a plethora of skills in hopes that something will "hit."

Students should receive interventions and enrichments systematically, regardless of which teacher they have. Systematic support starts with a frequent, timely process designed to *identify* students in need of additional time and support: universal screening. But identification is not enough. After identification, the school must *determine* the specific needs of each child and match those needs to the appropriate instruction and interventions. Because the consequences of failure are so great, a school must then *monitor* each student's progress in each intervention. If assessment data demonstrate that an intervention is not producing the intended growth, then the school should *revise* the support to better target the student's specific needs; if the support works, the school should *extend* the student's learning to even higher levels (see fig. 5.1, page 78).

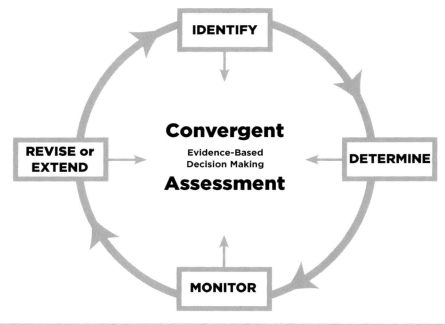

Figure 5.1: The convergent assessment cycle.

This chapter will explore how schools gather evidence of student learning using a systematic, timely, and reliable process.

Identifying Students Through Universal Screening

The best intervention is prevention. Imagine what could happen if rather than waiting for students to struggle and fail, we could determine, before instruction, which students lacked the prerequisite skills and knowledge to be successful. We could prevent many of the problems students face as they attempt to learn new material.

How do we identify those students who lack many or most of the skills needed for success in a particular class or grade level? Experienced teachers can probably informally identify students who desperately need more time and support by the end of the first week of school! But the *formal* process to identify students needing more time and support has become known as universal screening. The primary purpose of universal screening is to identify, as early in the school year as possible, those students who, without intensive Tier 3 intervention, are at risk of failing.

To better demonstrate the concept of universal screening, consider an analogy from the medical field. When a person is feeling sick and goes to the doctor, an assistant will often take the person's temperature and blood pressure before the patient meets with the doctor. If the temperature is 101 degrees, the patient will wait in turn to see the physician. But what if the person's temperature is 105 degrees? The patient gets to "jump the line" and will receive help immediately, because the screening points to such a serious level of illness that treatment cannot wait—the patient could die in the waiting room.

A temperature reading is a basic medical test that can indicate a serious problem quickly, but it alone is certainly not enough information for the doctor to determine the *cause* of the illness—additional diagnostic tests will be needed. Similarly, in RTI, universal screening is a quick surveying process intended to identify students most in need of assistance—not to diagnose their precise learning needs. Some screeners do provide more accurate information, but most do not. As James McMillan writes, "Benchmark assessments are formal, structured tests that typically do not provide the level of detail needed for appropriate instructional correctives" (2007, pp. 2–3). Schools should evaluate whether their universal screening tools help to identify students for differentiated instruction and/or intervention *and* determine their placement. A tool that only identifies students is perfectly acceptable; this simply means that the team has selected a time-efficient and cost-effective way of identifying students needing more support. More time-intensive and costly diagnostic assessments can then be delivered to a smaller group of students.

Understand Screening Approaches

As described earlier in this book, we believe that many of the responsibilities associated with RTI should be assigned to one of two teams: the collaborative teacher team or the schoolwide intervention team. The responsibilities for universal screening might also be divided between these two teams. The schoolwide intervention team can conduct broad universal screening, and collaborative teacher teams can create their own tools to screen for skills, knowledge, and vocabulary that have been identified as prerequisites to achieving mastery of the essential standards selected by the team. A third possibility for universal screening is benchmark assessments developed and administered by the district.

School Leadership Team Screening

We believe that the school's leadership team is best suited to conduct universal screening at the beginning of the school year to identify those students needing Tier 3 interventions in reading, writing, number sense, and English-language development. Additionally, we believe that the leadership team should identify those students for whom attendance and behavior have been problems in the past, and attempt to intervene early in the school year before these issues become problems again. In this section we will discuss how the leadership team might identify students needing immediate Tier 3 support in reading, writing, and number sense using one or a combination of three approaches: a universal screening tool created by an outside entity; a district-created benchmark assessment; or a screener created by a collaborative teacher team. In subsequent chapters, we will discuss how the schoolwide team might also identify students needing English language development.

Reading

Reading is the single most important skill a child must acquire. Without reading skill, success in school—and in life—is nearly impossible. A student's reading skills are the most accurate indicator of whether he will drop out of high school, live in poverty, be incarcerated, or die prematurely (Rouse, 2005; Ysseldyke, Algozzine, & Thurlow, 1992). It is estimated that up to 80 percent of students identified as having a specific learning disability do not have a disability at all—they simply never mastered the ability to read (Baird, 2008).

Reading is the language of learning. Consider for a moment how you would feel if you lived in a country in which you could not decipher or comprehend the native language. You could not read street signs, menus, newspapers, or written directions. How would you appear to the natives? You might seem to have a low IQ or to be slow-minded or disabled. This is how students who can't read often appear to educators. They struggle in nearly every class because they cannot read the textbooks, comprehend test questions, or access critical information and skills.

Because reading is so essential to learning, proactive schools start each year with a universal screening that takes every student's "reading temperature" and identifies those in need of additional support. This screening, intended to identify students needing immediate Tier 3 support, is the responsibility of the school leadership team. Appropriate universal screening measures consist of brief assessments focused on target skills that are highly predictive of future outcomes (Jenkins, 2003). The testing instrument should be quick and simple to administer, as all students will be assessed. An excellent resource to review universal screeners produced by an outside entity is the website for the National Center for Response to Intervention (www.rti4success.org).

Remember, universal reading screeners are not designed to provide precise, detailed, diagnostic information. Their purpose is to identify students reading multiple grades below proficiency so these children can be provided intensive help immediately. Additional diagnostic assessments may then be used to determine each child's specific reading needs. The activity *Reading Domains, Skills, and Assessments* (page 111 or online at **go.solution-tree.com/rti**) can help a school's teacher teams and/or intervention team identify the needs and appropriate interventions for a student struggling with reading.

Writing

As students progress in school, their content knowledge in specific subjects is regularly assessed through the skill of writing. If students cannot express knowledge effectively through the written word, they are likely to struggle in most classes. Many students fail in core subjects such as science and history not because they do not understand the content but because they cannot write effectively about what they have learned.

Accordingly, the schoolwide team should universally screen for writing ability at the start of each year, with the goal of identifying students who are significantly below grade level. This could be accomplished by administering a short writing prompt—perhaps a thirty-minute timed writing—with the results analyzed quickly and holistically. Remember, the purpose of the data review is not to mark errors, but to identify students extremely at risk in writing. Think about it: how long does it take to determine that a student work sample is significantly below grade level? Seconds.

This information is then used to provide these struggling writers with immediate, intensive Tier 3 writing support, as well as to notify their content/grade-level teachers that these students may need reasonable assessment accommodations, such as the option of oral exams, to fairly assess their content knowledge.

Number Sense

Number sense is an intuitive understanding of numbers, their magnitude, relationships, and how they are affected by operations. It is more than just math skills; it represents a "feel" for numbers, sequencing, and mathematical logic. Number sense is needed for more than math. Try understanding the periodic table of elements, interpreting a timeline in history, or determining heart rate in physical education without number sense. Number sense can greatly influence a student's success across many subjects and classes. For this reason, the intervention team should screen all students for number sense at the beginning of each school year.

English Language Development

Annual screening for English learners is typically mandated by state law. Depending on the school's EL population, these assessments may be given to a few students, most students, or anywhere in between. Thus, the administration of these tests is organized, supported, and perhaps administered by school leadership team. While these assessments do provide student scores in reading, writing, listening, and speaking, the lack of timeliness with which the data are reported back to schools often prevents teachers from using that information. Fortunately, there are other brief screeners that can provide immediate feedback regarding the current levels and needs of English learners, such as the Express Placement by EL Achieve (found at http://elachieve.org).

How should schools use these screeners? Content mastery and language mastery are not identical. Students may be ready to process new learning, but language may be inhibiting their ability to learn. Students may possess knowledge of content but lack the language knowledge to demonstrate their mastery. Screening data can help schools determine the most qualified teachers and the best settings in which students will learn at the very highest levels. Screening data will also help schools determine which students should receive targeted language supports for beginning, intermediate, and advanced learners. We do not lower expectations for English learners; knowledge of a language other than English is not indicative of a deficiency. We simply ensure that English learners receive the targeted language supports that they need to succeed.

Collaborative Teacher Team Screening

Many of the mastery learning models stress the importance of administering a quick and targeted preassessment to all students before beginning instruction to determine if they have the prerequisite knowledge and skills for the upcoming unit (Guskey, 2010). The PLC team of grade-level or course-alike teachers should be primarily responsible for screening those skills and knowledge (reading, writing, number sense, and in certain instances, the academic vocabulary required by their English learners) directly related to the mastery of the essential standards they have selected. Using the *Essential Standards Chart* (page 72), the teacher teams have already determined what is essential for all students to learn, the level of rigor that represents mastery, and what prerequisite skills are necessary. They are thus best positioned to administer and analyze these kinds of highly specific screening measures.

Once teams have identified essential standards, it sometimes makes more sense for those teams to create preassessment screening tools highly aligned to their essential standards than to rely on a broad universal screener administered by the schoolwide team, which could be far less aligned and thus far less useful. This is especially true in middle and high schools. Some universal screening tools, such as the *Dynamic Indicators of Basic Early Literacy Skills* (DIBELS), are commonly used by many elementary schools regardless of what they have identified as essential for all students to master because the skills measured are so ubiquitous (letter naming fluency, initial sound fluency, phoneme segmentation, and so on). However, as the grade levels progress upward, school teams increasingly need to align their universal screening with those content standards they have determined are essential.

District-Created Benchmark Screening

A third possibility (in addition to a screener produced by an outside entity and team-created screeners) exists in the form of district-created benchmark assessments. While district benchmark assessments can inform policy and decision making at the both the school and district levels, a similar concern arises around the issue of alignment. If schools are given some autonomy to determine what is essential for all students to learn, and then to develop assessments to determine if they have indeed learned, it is important that there be an ongoing effort to bring the district benchmark assessment into alignment with these teacher-created, teacher-owned assessments.

In *Power Standards*, Larry Ainsworth (2003) describes an alignment process he attributes to Douglas Reeves—the accordion model, in which the dialogue to align teacher-created assessments with district benchmarks expands and contracts like a bellows, expanding to include input from across the district and contracting to a core group of district representatives who make decisions. First, representatives from schools bring drafts of their essential standards to an initial district meeting (bellows in). The participants in this meeting incorporate the collective input from the various school sites into a revised version of the district essential or power standards and send this document out to the school sites for review by all teachers (bellows out). After offering feedback and revisions, the schools return their modified essential standards to the district (bellows in). Revisions and suggestions from the schools are incorporated into the final draft and distributed to all sites. The district benchmark assessment is then aligned to the new district benchmark standards. In this way, school teams can still experience some degree of autonomy and ownership by aligning district benchmark assessments with their ongoing discussion regarding what is essential for every student to learn.

Select a Screening Method and Clarify Responsibilities

Beginning in upper elementary school and continuing on into middle and high schools, we would recommend either of the following approaches to universal screening:

1. **Use a benchmark assessment designed by the district or an outside entity, but filter out any items that are not directly aligned with the essential standards selected by the team.** Focus on the information that directly relates to the prerequisite skills and knowledge that students will need to master those essential standards; if and when time permits, review other information from the screener that might be valuable but not directly linked to what has been determined to be essential.

2. **Alternatively, empower teacher teams to create their own universal screening tools that are completely aligned with what they have determined to be essential.** Again, a team of middle or high school teachers that has spent a good amount of time determining what is essential for students to learn, the level of rigor representing mastery, and the prerequisite skills directly linked to those essential standards is probably very well positioned to create a screening tool that will tell them which students need more time and support before initial instruction begins.

The value of universal screenings tied to specific learning targets becomes evident in planning. Suppose, for example, that a math team knows that the unit on solving quadratic formulas by factoring (an essential learning target) will begin in February. If the team provides additional time and support in January to those students who have not yet mastered factoring (as indicated by this specific kind of universal screening), the team will *prevent* many struggles and help more students succeed as a result of the Tier 1 instructional program. Screening information, when tightly aligned to essential skills and knowledge, will help teams to better understand how to create differentiated instruction for the learning success of all students (Tomlinson & McTighe, 2006).

The school leadership team and collaborative teacher teams should define who will be responsible for conducting the screening and when the screening will take place. See page 113 or visit **go.solution-tree.com/rti** to access the *Universal Screening Planning Guide* to guide teams through this discussion.

Some schools, in order not to overwhelm teachers new to RTI and universal screening, may want to implement universal screening conducted by the intervention team only, using either screeners produced by an outside entity or unaligned district benchmark assessments. However, once a universal screening process is in place, we strongly recommend that collaborative teams begin utilizing a preassessment of prerequisite skills before each unit, so they can build those skills with students as needed, before the unit begins. Research supports the potential benefit of this kind of preteaching (Deshler & Schumaker, 1993; Guskey, 2010; Leyton, 1983). Remember, the best intervention is *prevention*!

Interpret Data

In addition to helping schools to identify and determine the placement of students in need of more time and support, universal screening can also help to monitor the effectiveness of Tier 1 core instruction. Consider the universal screening data from a curriculum-based measure (CBM) shown in figure 5.2.

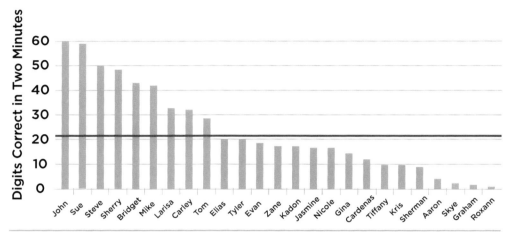

Figure 5.2: Third-grade math: Addition and subtraction of digits 0–18.

Rather than evaluate problems as right or wrong, CBMs are used to "audit" overall skill development. This is why they make good universal screeners. In this case, we learn how many digits students can compute correctly in two minutes. The horizontal black bar represents the level of proficiency this team has determined necessary for students to be successful in third grade (that is, they need to be able to correctly compute 20 digits in two minutes at the beginning of the year). We can use these data not only to *identify* those students needing more time and support, but also to question why one-half of the students entering grade 3 lack the prerequisite mathematical fluency to be successful in mastering third-grade math. Further diagnostic testing would be required to determine the causes of this lack of fluency with numbers. In other words, we know the students are "sick," but we do not yet know why.

In this case, based on the number of students who are not succeeding at Tier 1, we would advise the school, "You don't have an intervention problem, you have a 'what you do all day long' problem that must be analyzed and changed." Research demonstrates that the first step in identifying individual students with significant learning difficulties is to rule out the effect of a classwide problem (VanDerHeyden & Burns, 2005; VanDerHeyden, Witt, & Naquin, 2003). Universal screening can be used both to identify individual students who should receive additional time and support at the start of the school year to prevent difficulties *and* to identify schoolwide or classwide problems.

Misunderstandings About Universal Screening

Universal screening is one of the most misunderstood and misapplied aspects of RTI. Too often, universal screening processes are designed and implemented from a rigid, protocol-driven point of view without considering the realities and demands of schools and classroom teachers. Let's examine some of these misunderstandings.

Universal Screening Must Be a Test

Without question, the use of research-based universal screening tests is an accurate way to identify students significantly below grade level. However, in some cases, administering these tests can be quite time-consuming and thus potentially delay initial instruction and early prevention for weeks until all students have been assessed. We commonly see situations in which it takes four to six weeks for schools to universally screen all students at the start of each year.

Can a school use other means, such as end-of-year assessment data, to identify returning at-risk students? Taking this approach would allow schools to begin intensive help for those students immediately, thus not losing weeks at the start of each school year administering universal screening tests that confirm what the school already knew. If the primary purpose of universal screening is to identify students in need of intensive support before they fail, then using valid, previous-year assessment data can sometimes be a timely, effective way to achieve this end. If schools choose this method of screening, it is strongly recommended that they follow up by monitoring identified students during the first four to six weeks of intervention to confirm their need for such placement (Compton, Fuchs, Fuchs, & Bryant, 2006).

We have worked with elementary schools that have used their traditional "pink and blue" card process to document each student's end-of-year achievement levels in universal skills. A teacher who taught a child all year is usually well qualified to identify that student's ability in the critical areas of reading, writing, and number sense. This information can then be used immediately by next year's teachers.

A proactive middle school administration can work with their "feeder" elementary school(s) to identify incoming students in need of intensive support. Similarly, high school counselors can work with their feeder middle school(s) to identify incoming extremely at-risk freshmen and proactively provide additional support. Support in the first year of high school is particularly important. According to research by Ruth Curran Neild, Robert Balfanz, and Liza Herzog:

> Ninth grade is a treacherous year for students, particularly those in large urban districts. Even students who were doing moderately well in the middle grades can be knocked off the path to graduation by the new academic demands and social pressures of high school. Among students who sent their first serious distress signal in 9th grade, those who earned fewer than two credits or attended school less than 70 percent of the time had at least a 75 percent chance of dropping out of school. Most of these students did not drop out immediately but attempted 9th grade courses for another one or two years before finally giving up on school altogether. (Neild, Balfanz, & Herzog, 2007, p. 30)

This is not to suggest that using the previous year's data for universal screening is perfect. Clearly, this process cannot identify intensively at-risk students who are new to a district. A screening process is still necessary at the start of the school year to identify the needs of these students. Additionally, there are benefits to starting each school year with an accurate picture of every student's proficiency level in essential skills. Teachers can use these data to plan initial instruction, create differentiated groups, and determine a baseline score from which to measure student growth on foundational skills throughout the year. These are worthwhile outcomes, but they are secondary benefits of universal screening. Achieving these additional benefits must be weighed against consuming the first weeks of school with baseline testing, delaying instruction until all the testing is finished, and delaying intensive support to the most at-risk students.

Universal Screening Tools Must Be Scientifically Research-Based and Nationally Normed

We recommend that schools use the most effective, proven assessment and intervention tools available. The more valid and reliable the data are, the more accurate our educational decisions for each student. Unfortunately, to date there are not scientifically research-based assessment tools available for all essential skills, all subjects, and all grade levels. Some of the tools we do have are cost prohibitive for some schools. In these cases, which is better: universal screening with a tool that is not nationally normed or no universal screening at all?

Let's consider again the purpose of universal screening: it is a quick process to screen for students who are significantly below grade level. In many cases, it does not take a finely tuned measurement tool to make these determinations. If a student does poorly on a universal screening tool, it is understood that the school will need to follow up with additional diagnostic assessments that will be more accurate and specific. As schools begin implementing RTI, we suggest that they neither spend months in the quest of the perfect universal screener nor delay universal screening because they cannot afford to purchase the best assessment tools. Just start! If staff determine that the current screening tools are not consistently valid and reliable, then consider other tools.

Universal Screening Must Be Administered Multiple Times a Year for All Students

In current practice, universal screening is administered with varying frequency across North America; some schools screen three times a year, others just once at the beginning of each year. Either method can be effective, but some additional steps should be undertaken if screening just once.

There are some tremendous benefits to universally screening all students multiple times a year. If a school starts the year by assessing every student in reading, then repeats this process at the midpoint and again at the end of the year, the data can be used to determine each student's growth in reading. For this reason, district-created benchmark assessments are often used as a universal screening tool because they are usually administered in the fall, winter, and spring to every child. The data can also be disaggregated to identify strengths and weakness in the school's core reading program. For example, if a majority of students entering the school year above grade level in reading show little growth over the subsequent screening assessments, that would be an important red flag that initial core instruction is not meeting the needs of students starting above grade level.

At the same time, many schools just starting to implement RTI can find universal screening of all students multiple times a year overwhelming. Again, we must keep our focus on the primary purpose of universal screening: to identify kids in need of intensive support before they fail. Measuring the growth of all students throughout the year is a valuable outcome. At the same time, if the screening process overwhelms staff, many teachers may resist giving universal screening tests at all—thus defeating their primary purpose. For some schools, starting with the universal screening at the beginning of each year is an acceptable first step.

Some fear students may not be accurately identified by an annual screening. As mentioned earlier, Compton et al. (2006) suggest that students identified through once-a-year screening should be monitored on a weekly basis for four to six weeks to confirm the status indicated by the universal screener. As a side benefit, the weekly assessments will also help to determine the placement of the student for intervention more accurately.

Tier 2 Interventions Must Be Administered Before Tier 3 Interventions

This is one of the most curious practices we see throughout North America. The primary purpose of universal screening is to identify students in need of intensive support, yet after identifying these kids, some schools delay placing students into Tier 3 interventions. These schools usually see RTI as a process to identify kids for special education, and their district guidelines often require that Tier 2 support be proven ineffective before Tier 3 support can be provided. In that case, why screen at all? By delaying intensive support, these schools are withholding lifesaving medicine. If it's unclear whether a child needs intensive help, it is prudent and appropriate to begin with supplemental support, but if there is clear and conclusive evidence that a student is educationally "hemorrhaging," then providing these students "aspirin" when they obviously need intensive care is misguided at best.

We suspect that RTI purists may cringe at some of our recommendations. In a perfect world, every school would start its RTI journey by utilizing research-based universal screening assessments and would administer these assessments to every student multiple times a year. In reality, teachers newly introduced to RTI often find these expectations overwhelming. These feelings usually cause teachers to resist RTI or take a compliance approach to the new demands and carry out universal screening with the attitude of just "getting it done" so they can get back to their teaching. This response is hardly surprising, as RTI is a seismic shift in school culture, structure, and practice.

In our experience, when teachers consider the cause noble and believe the goal is achievable, a vast majority will work tirelessly to help their kids. But if the cause is undistinguished or the goal unobtainable, then creating the collective vision and commitment needed to succeed is virtually impossible. We have found that most successful RTI schools start with reasonable, focused "baby steps." As teachers get more proficient at the process, a school can then begin to focus on the secondary benefits of universal screening. Making universal screening simple and practical is far better in the end for kids than being philosophically pure but ineffective in actual practice.

Determining Student Needs

After identifying those students in immediate need of additional time and support, the school must determine the specific needs of each child and then match these needs to the appropriate instruction and interventions.

Depending on the specificity of the universal screening tool used, further diagnostic assessments may or may not be needed in order to more accurately determine the cause of each student's struggles. Schools must grapple with the following issues:

1. If we use a very brief universal screening tool, we may not have enough information to adequately determine what each student needs. Therefore, we will have to follow up with those students identified as at risk by our universal screening tool with a more diagnostic assessment.

2. If we use a more detailed universal screening tool, it will take much longer to administer and score, but may give us enough information to determine each student's needs.

Diagnostic assessments are typically highly targeted on specific skills and produce results that are highly individualized (Pierangelo & Giuliani, 2006). Some widely used diagnostic assessments include, but are not limited to, the Diagnostic Reading Assessment (Scholastic Testing Service, Inc.), the Qualitative Reading Inventory (LITE), and KeyMath3 (Pearson). These kinds of diagnostic assessments are best used in conjunction with a brief, universal screening tool because they take a considerable amount of time to administer and score. Rather than administering them every year to every student, even to those who are achieving at an advanced level, use them more strategically to help determine the exact needs of students who have first been identified as at risk by a universal screener.

The information from universal screeners and diagnostic assessments should be combined with informal observational data from the collaborative team to determine how to best meet the needs of each student at risk. Accordingly, both the schoolwide intervention team (which is involved with the universal screening and diagnostic assessments) and the collaborative teacher team have an important role to play in determining how to best provide additional time and support to struggling students.

As previously stated in chapter 4, collaborative teacher teams should complete the *Essential Standards Chart* at the beginning of each trimester, quarter, semester, and so on. Once the team begins to receive information from universal screeners and diagnostic assessments, and as it collects its own data from working with struggling students in the classroom each day, we recommend that team members next begin to formulate a plan to provide additional time and support both to students who struggle and to those who demonstrate that they have already mastered essential standards. This plan is developed collaboratively by the team and is based on its sense of collective responsibility for all students.

Accordingly, the following questions should be posed at the beginning of instruction rather than waiting until the inevitable occurs:

- What structures and/or schedules currently exist that might support our plans for remediation, intervention, and extension?
- What resources exist that we might be able to use to support these efforts?
- Which members of our team will work with which group of students, and why?
- What have we been doing successfully that we could build upon?
- What evidence will we collect to help guide our answers to these questions?

Figure 5.3 shows a planning sheet, the *Proactive RTI Planning Form*, that teams may use to record their decisions.

Plan for Remediation	Plan for Intervention	Plan for Enrichment
Based on the prior skills needed, how will we determine which students need remediation before we begin initial instruction? Who will conduct the remediations? When?	After initial instruction and differentiation, what is our team's plan to provide additional time and support to those students who have not learned? Who will conduct the interventions? When?	After initial instruction and intervention, what is our team's plan to provide additional time and support to those who have learned? Who will conduct the enrichments? When?

Figure 5.3: Proactive RTI planning form.

For a reproducible version of this tool, visit **go.solution-tree.com/rti** *or see page 115.*

Acknowledging that some students will need help with prior skills, some will need additional time and support, and some will easily master the content is an important step in the realigned thinking of a team that focuses on learning instead of teaching. Examples of flexible structures or schedules that provide extra time for this kind of support will be discussed in chapter 6.

Monitoring Student Progress

After a school has *identified* students in need of extra help and *determined* the correct intervention to meet the child's need(s), the school must *monitor* each student's progress. Consider for a moment the name of this process: response to intervention. At the foundation of RTI is a belief that, as educators, we will make instructional decisions for students based on how they respond to our efforts. If an intervention is working, it confirms that the child's diagnosis is correct, the "medicine" is appropriate, and the child is on track for a full recovery. But if the child is not responding to our interventions, then it means either the diagnosis is incorrect or we have selected the wrong medicine. Accurate and timely assessment data are essential to make this type of determination.

This is the purpose of convergent assessment: an ongoing process of collectively analyzing evidence to target the specific learning needs of each child and determine the effectiveness of the instruction the child receives in meeting these needs. Both collaborative teacher teams and the schoolwide intervention team work together to measure student learning and evaluate a school's instructional effectiveness.

In order to monitor how students are responding to interventions, we recommend a cyclical process similar to the teaching–assessing cycle discussed in chapter 4 (see fig. 5.4). Just as teachers monitor student response to initial instruction, so do they monitor student response to intervention.

The formative and summative assessments identified in the instructional plan are progress-monitoring tools. The data provided from these assessments are vital in determining if the intervention has worked or if more intensive help is needed.

This information is even more powerful when students are engaged in the intervention process. When students understand why they are in an intervention, what learning outcome(s) they must master, and how they are doing toward meeting the goal, they are much more likely to hit the target. Progress monitoring should not only guide a teacher's instruction, it should be used to help the learner take ownership of his or her learning.

Of all the elements of RTI, we have seen schools struggle with progress monitoring more than any other aspect. There are two primary reasons for this. For many schools, the difficulty is not an assessment problem, but a targeting problem. Many schools offer only broad interventions: they place all students who are failing math in the same intervention, but because their needs are all different, the teacher in charge of the intervention is unsure how to monitor progress on those diverse needs. In contrast, if a group of students is assigned help with multiplying exponents, the teacher knows exactly what to monitor: the ability to multiply exponents.

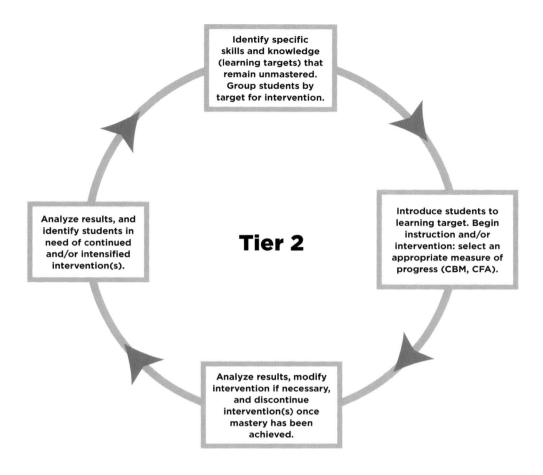

Figure 5.4: Progress monitoring at Tier 2.

The second reason so many schools struggle with progress monitoring is because they create overly demanding, oppressive RTI documentation processes. As discussed in chapter 3, the documentation process of RTI can help guide thinking by prompting the right questions, promoting communication, coordinating efforts across intervention providers, and collecting vital information needed to make informed decisions about a student. When paperwork is used for these purposes, it can be a powerful tool.

Unfortunately, too many schools and districts view paperwork from an exclusively legal perspective. Because special education is such a litigious process, and RTI is now the legal process used to qualify students for special education, many states and districts have created RTI paperwork that is equivalent to an IEP (individualized education plan) for every child who receives an intervention. When RTI is implemented successfully, only a small fraction of the students receiving interventions will ultimately be recommended for special education identification—yet the school documents every student as if all of them are on this track. The ongoing formative and summative assessment practices described in this book provide valuable data and documentation that can and should be used if and when a student is referred for special education identification. But adding additional layers of forms, duplicate documentation, and paperwork unfairly burdens classroom teachers, takes resources away from helping kids, and leads to an RTI model focused more on compliance than helping students. Ultimately, the best way to stay legal is to ensure that all students learn.

In order to simplify this important process and make it less overwhelming to teachers, we will discuss three methods of effectively monitoring student response to intervention: formative assessments, common formative assessments, and curriculum-based measures.

Formative Assessment

Again, once we have screened to identify students who need help from the very inception of the school year, instruction begins, and then we have an emerging and continuing need to find out which students are learning those things we determined to be essential—to *monitor* their progress. The sequence of identifying a learning target(s), assessing a student's current level of mastery of this target, and then working to address any distance between the two captures the very essence of formative assessment.

Formative assessment is not a test but a process, in which "teachers adjust their ongoing instructional activities or students adjust the procedures they're currently using to try to learn whatever they're trying to learn" (Popham, 2008, p. 6). The State Collaborative on Assessment and Student Standards (SCASS) defines it this way:

> Formative assessment is a process used by teachers and students during instruction that provides feedback to adjust ongoing teaching and learning to improve students' achievement of intended instructional outcomes. (Council of Chief State Officers, n.d.)

More recently, Dylan Wiliam has offered this definition:

> An assessment functions formatively to the extent that evidence about student achievement is elicited, interpreted, and used by teachers, learners, or their peers to make decisions about the next steps in instruction that are likely to be better, or better founded, than the decisions they would have made in absence of that evidence. (2011, p. 43)

Note that in these definitions, formative assessment is used by both teachers and students, and takes place *as part of instruction.* It provides valuable feedback about student progress toward a learning target to both teachers and students, who then make adjustments to improve that progress. For teacher teams, these adjustments take the form of instructional interventions, both small and large, ranging from core instruction to intensive Tier 3 support. Teachers use formative assessment to learn which students did or did not respond to initial instruction at Tier 1, as well as which students did or did not respond to further intervention efforts at Tier 2.

Common Formative Assessments

A second and very significant method for monitoring student progress and response to intervention is the use of common formative assessments by a team of teachers. While individual teachers are constantly gathering this kind of evidence in their own classrooms, collaborative teams of teachers plan frequent, *common* formative assessments as part of their instructional cycle, and use this information to respond collectively to the needs of *all* their students. These assessments are considered common when student learning is assessed "using the same instrument or process and according to the same criteria" (DuFour et al., 2010, p. 63). Common formative assessments provide a point of comparison by showing the results from varying methods of instruction; this professional comparison is important since RTI is meant to be administered by trained professionals. Common formative assessments provide the basis for grouping students by need, thus increasing the capacity of individual teachers to address all student needs. Again, the team of grade-level or course-alike teachers who have participated in the discussion of what is essential for all students to learn and what level of rigor represents mastery is best positioned to devise the common formative assessments (CFAs) that will help both the teachers and the students to understand where they are in the learning. The *Common Assessment Team Protocol* (page 117 or **go.solution-tree .com/rti**) can help a teacher team analyze common assessment to guide interventions and extension.

Target Causes, Not Symptoms

Teacher teams can better serve the needs of all students, and students receive even more useful feedback, when the common formative assessment is focused on the *individual learning targets* that underpin an essential standard. The more thoroughly a team unwraps an essential standard into individual learning targets (as discussed in chapter 4), the better, more specific, and more diagnostic the evidence gathered will be. After all, "the first step in any kind of assessment is being clear about what it is that you want to know about" (Brookhart & Moss, 2009, p. 24). What we want to know is the *cause* of the student's struggle, not the symptom.

Consider the set of data in table 5.1.

Table 5.1: Sample Student Data Set

Student	Number Correct	Percentage Correct
Student 1	30	100%
Student 2	29	96%
Student 3	13	43%
Student 4	30	100%
Student 5	19	63%
Student 6	30	100%
Student 7	27	90%
Student 8	28	93%
Student 9	25	83%
Student 10	25	83%
Average	25.6	85.1%

If a teacher team had established that 80 percent correct represented proficiency on this assessment, then two students in particular deserve immediate attention: Student 3 and Student 5. In most traditional grading systems, we would say that these students had failed and are in need of intervention. All we know, however, is that they failed; we don't know *why*.

Grades and test scores are only symptoms of a student's struggles. A student might fail a test for a multiplicity of reasons (Stiggins, 2007a). And yet, another piece of data that is often used to "target" interventions is the student's score on last year's high-stakes state test. "Far below basic" is a symptom; it does not tell us exactly why a student scored far below basic. Despite this, many intervention classrooms across North America today are full of students who have failed an assessment or a class and/ or scored far below basic on the state assessment. Look in these classrooms, and you will find beleaguered teachers trying to discover *why* their students failed or scored far below basic.

Teachers need to know why a student failed to provide a targeted intervention. The more targeted the intervention, the more successful the outcome. Effective assessments, then, provide data on specific causes of student struggles, and they do that by assessing specific learning targets. Unwrapping standards into learning targets *before instruction* helps us to better understand *after instruction* exactly what the students didn't understand (the why) that caused them to fail the test (the symptom).

Many standards, especially as the grades progress, are rather complex and represent more than a single point of knowledge or a single skill. In table 5.2, a single standard was unwrapped into five discrete learning targets (LT 2a, 2b, and so on), and each target was assessed with five to six questions.

Table 5.2: Expanded Student Data Set

Student	Number Correct	Percentage Correct	LT 2a	LT 2b	LT 2c	LT 2d	LT 2e
Student 1	30	100%	100%	100%	100%	100%	100%
Student 2	29	96%	83%	100%	100%	100%	100%
Student 3	13	43%	100%	100%	33%	50%	100%
Student 4	30	100%	100%	100%	100%	100%	100%
Student 5	19	63%	100%	100%	17%	0%	100%
Student 6	30	100%	100%	100%	100%	100%	100%
Student 7	27	90%	100%	100%	100%	100%	50%
Student 8	28	93%	100%	100%	83%	83%	100%
Student 9	25	83%	100%	100%	100%	17%	100%
Student 10	25	83%	100%	83%	83%	100%	50%

These kinds of targeted questions are also known as *subskill mastery measures* (SMMs) that assess smaller domains of learning (learning targets) based on the team's predetermined criteria for mastery (Fuchs & Deno, 1991). SMMs give teachers the information necessary to target which exact knowledge, skill, or point of reasoning needs reinforcement. These kinds of assessments have been supported in the research (Burns, 2004; Burns, 2007; Burns, Tucker, Frame, Foley, & Hauser, 2000; Gravois & Gickling, 2002).

With this kind of information, we can begin to address the underlying *causes* of Student 3's and Student 5's struggles with this standard. Both students who failed the assessment completely mastered learning targets 2a, 2b, and 2e. They both need additional time and support with learning targets 2c and 2d. With this kind of information, teacher teams can target their interventions student by student, skill by skill.

This level of specificity allows the team to target the intervention and also to monitor how the student responds to the intervention. In other words, common formative assessments built from SMMs can be used to assess how students respond to the initial instruction (Tier 1), and can also be used to monitor the progress of students receiving additional time and support (Tier 2).

Collaborative teams can make two or three sets of questions: one set to monitor how students are responding to initial instruction, and an additional set or two (slightly altered versions of the same questions that measure the same target) to monitor how students are responding to intervention at Tier 2. While this intervention is delivered by one of the teachers on the team, other teachers can help students who struggled with learning targets 2a, 2b, or 2e.

Curriculum-Based Measurement

While focusing on discrete learning targets or subskills is a great improvement over simply knowing a student has failed the test, it is difficult to use this approach to measure the change in student performance over an extended period of time (a trimester or quarter) in the acquisition of certain skills directly related to the ability to read or to compute. A third method for monitoring student progress over time and how students are responding to intervention that is more effective at that task is curriculum-based measurement (CBM).

Curriculum-based measures are especially useful when monitoring early literacy measures such as letter naming fluency, letter sound fluency, nonsense word fluency, and phonemic segmenting and blending tasks; mathematics measures such as math fact fluency; early numeracy measures such as quantity array, quantity discrimination, and number identification; and written expression such as correct word sequences. In other words, upper-grade elementary teachers and/or middle and high school teachers will generally not find much utility in monitoring students using CBMs, unless they are working with students who have not yet mastered these skills associated with primary grades. Conversely, first-grade teachers wishing to monitor student growth over time in such skills as phonemic segmenting and blending may find much greater utility in using CBMs rather than CFAs because this is what CBMs are designed to measure.

Most CBMs are efficient, accurate, and, best of all, inexpensive or free! CBMs allow teachers to monitor student response to initial instruction and to intervention on an ongoing, frequent basis (Deno, 1985; Deno, Marston, Shinn, & Tindal, 1983; Deno, Mirkin, & Chiang, 1982). They are quick and easy to administer and are sensitive to short-term gains in skills.

Revising or Extending Support

Using formative assessments in this way, teachers can monitor the effectiveness of Tier 1 core instruction and determine where students "are" relative to where they are "going." If the evidence demonstrates that a student is not meeting the intended outcome of the Tier 1 instruction, the collaborative teacher team *revises* the support and provides more intensive and targeted assistance. In the rare instance that a student does not respond to supplemental and intensive support, the schoolwide intervention team carefully considers whether special education identification is justified, appropriate, and necessary to meet the student's needs.

Once a student reaches grade-level expectations, the same flexible time and resources used to provide supplemental and intensive support to struggling students are used to *extend* students to even higher levels of achievement. In their book *Integrating Differentiated Instruction and Understanding by Design*, Tomlinson and McTighe (2006) suggest that teachers need first to establish essential standards for student achievement and then to design many paths of instruction to enable all learners to be successful. To reach *extended* learning standards, Tomlinson and McTighe encourage teachers to differentiate for students through the following design elements: content (what students learn and the representative materials); process (activities through which students make sense of key ideas using the essential skills); product (how students demonstrate and extend what they understand and can do as a result of a span of learning); and learning environment (the classroom conditions that set the tone and expectations of learning).

Convergent Assessment and Behavior Systems

In addition to using convergent assessment to determine student learning needs, we must also gather the evidence necessary to determine where each child is in his or her learning relative to behavior goals. This evidence answers the question, Where are we now? Recall that convergent assessment ensures that interventions and enrichments are both timely and targeted. In the areas of motivation, behavior, and attendance, an informed, proactive approach is of supreme importance.

Identifying Students Through Universal Screening

Universal screening plays an important role in identifying behavioral issues before they become huge problems for both the student and the school. By effectively screening students to identify who may be at risk for behavioral challenges, supports can be preventative.

Academic Misbehaviors

Schools should universally screen at the start of each year to identify students with past excessive absenteeism and should be proactive in supporting these students as the new year begins. We can quite often anticipate those who may have difficulties with attendance, much in the way as we can anticipate students who may have difficulties with academics.

This screening process can be as simple as using the school's student data management system to query for students with a significant number of absences from the previous year or, for new students, contacting feeder schools to query for attendance data. The school can then meet with the students and their parents prior to the school year, identify the causes of the child's attendance problem, and create a plan to address these concerns. These students should also be put on a watch list that triggers the school attendance clerk to notify the proper person each time one of these students is absent.

It's also possible to screen for engagement and motivation issues. An understanding of Schlechty's (2001, 2002) five types of student responses to school tasks is a starting place for schools committed to fostering students' engagement. By assessing students against Schlechty's five types of engagement, schools can identify students in need of support and can even determine the intensity and type of support needed. When schools reassess students later in the school year against the five types of engagement, they can monitor progress and determine next steps. The five types are:

1. **Authentic engagement.** The process and completion of tasks have clear meaning and immediate value; that is, a student would read a book because of a personal interest in a subject.

2. **Ritual engagement.** The process and completion of tasks have little meaning or immediate value; that is, a student would read a book only to finish an assignment.

3. **Passive compliance.** Tasks are completed to avoid a negative consequence; that is, a student would locate only the minimum amount of information to finish an assignment.

4. **Retreatism.** A student disengages from a task, and does not attempt to comply, but does not disrupt others; that is, a student neither reads nor researches nor attempts the assignment.

5. **Rebellion.** A student refuses to attempt the task, disrupts others, or attempts to substitute tasks of greater interest.

Teachers can brainstorm with the schoolwide intervention team to create a process for screening students to identify those most in need of support.

Given that we intend for some academic behaviors to be self-regulated, it is entirely appropriate to involve students directly in the screening, diagnosing, and monitoring of these issues. Schools can use a survey such as the simple *Self-Regulatory Assessment Tool* (page 117, or online at **go.solution-tree.com/rti**) we've created.

Social Misbehaviors

The *Student Risk Screening Scale* (SRSS) (Drummond, 1994) is an efficient, effective behavioral screening tool. A copy of the SRSS is included at the end of this chapter (page 118).

Staff members may complete the screen three times a year; the initial completion of the screen may be six weeks into the year, so that staff can become more familiar with the students. The midyear and end-of-the-year screens can be used to monitor student progress, to identify students whose behaviors may have begun to change, and to identify students for whom staff will create opportunities for success at the beginning of the following year.

The SRSS uses a four-point scale to objectively assess observable characteristics. Once this screen has been completed, the data can be analyzed in the same manner as academic data. Scores for students can be summed to identify those most at risk, and individual ratings can be analyzed to begin to diagnose targeted interventions. Moreover, the average scores for each characteristic can be compared to determine relative areas of need within classes, grade levels, or schools. Staff might also discover that certain teachers have relatively low or high ratings. Conversations emerging from these analyses can help improve the Tier 1 behavioral supports across campuses. This screen, or other behavioral screens, can help proactively and preventively assist students and identify the types of behaviors with which groups of students may need assistance.

For schools that lack the time and expertise to immediately use this tool, there are some simple ways to begin identifying students in need of intensive behavioral support. Before the school year starts, the staff can screen for students who earned multiple suspensions, office referrals, and/or poor behavior grades from the previous year. Recommendations from the previous year's teachers can also be helpful.

The results of the SRSS should be analyzed and shared by the school intervention team with the entire staff to identify trends, successes, and needs. It is absolutely essential that administrators and other support staff respond to identified students as soon as possible and that the response is communicated to all stakeholders (including parents and students). Teachers become justifiably frustrated when follow-ups to the screening are delayed or the supports provided are not communicated properly.

Determining Student Needs

Just like when students struggle with academics, when they struggle with motivation, behavior, and attendance, it's important to target causes, not symptoms. In a schoolwide system of behavioral supports, the intervention team should conduct analyses to determine what may be leading to poor behaviors that negatively impact learning. Progress-monitoring tools, discussed in the next section, are also critical to determining student needs on an ongoing basis.

Before becoming too consumed with determining which behavioral interventions a student needs, remember: a student experiencing behavioral challenges will often have a history of academic failure. Therefore, when diagnosing the origins of behavioral difficulties, carefully examine any ways in which a student may be struggling or feeling academically frustrated. Perhaps the student does not truly understand a teacher's directions. Perhaps the student does not possess the skills to work cooperatively with others. Perhaps the student cannot read and comprehend the text. While supporting students behaviorally, remember to consider their academic needs as well, even if their academic needs are not immediately evident in the behaviors they are displaying.

Another caution: ensure that reputations and preconceptions do not unfairly label students. Instead, gather data and evidence to guide decision making, and identify which students need additional support. Sometimes, these data do not match our preconceived notions based on student (or family) reputation.

Academic Misbehaviors

As noted earlier, for students with attendance issues, conversations with parents to determine the cause are critical. We have also created a *Self-Regulatory Problem-Solving Tool* (page 119 or **go.solution-tree.com/rti**) to help staff determine specific-regulatory skills that students may need to learn.

Social Misbehaviors

A sample flowchart that schools can use to complete theses analyses is the *Behavioral Analysis Protocol* (page 121 or **go.solution-tree.com/rti**). By following the steps described on the flowchart, schools can take definitive steps in helping to improve a student's behavior. This process of searching for antecedents (causes) can be informed by the same strategies used in the functional analyses performed by school psychologists. School psychologists may assist in informing these analyses as they are crucial to the schoolwide intervention team in helping to design preventative measures to change behaviors before more formal functional behavioral analyses are necessary.

Monitoring Behavioral Progress

An essential but often underdeveloped element of RTI is a system of tracking and monitoring behavioral data. Not only does this tracking and monitoring help us continue to identify new students in need and determine exactly what they need, it will also help us monitor the success of individual students and of the school in improving behaviors. By regularly reviewing data, schools can ensure that they are identifying all students in need, they can analyze the data to determine specific needs, and they can monitor whether students and groups of students are improving.

Academic Misbehaviors

We value what we measure, and when we regularly measure attendance rates, publicize them, set goals, and/or make it a competition (among classes or grade levels), we communicate to all stakeholders that attendance is important and that we'll be closely monitoring it. Look for trends in the data, and ask questions such as:

- Which students have low attendance rates?
- At what times of year is attendance lowest?
- Are there classrooms or grade levels with lower attendance?
- What motivates students to attend?
- Is there a connection between the quality, rigor, and relevance of instruction and attendance for certain students in certain classrooms or courses?

Social Misbehaviors

We recommend that behavior documentation forms (BDFs) are completed, submitted, and recorded for all behavioral incidents, minor and major. BDFs should not and will not, if well designed, take much time to complete (less than thirty seconds) or record (less than fifteen seconds), yet the information they yield is priceless. These BDFs can be thought of as referrals, except that while referrals are usually only completed and recorded for serious behavioral infractions, BDFs are completed for *all* infractions after an agreed-upon threshold has been reached (for example, after two warnings to stay on task).

BDFs can be managed efficiently. While the student information systems that schools and school districts use to store students' personal information, take attendance, and warehouse data sometimes allow for inputting behavioral data, our experiences suggest that they may not align to schools' needs and may not allow data to be easily graphed and analyzed.

Using BDFs will result in many more referrals or reports of behavior issues than in the past. This is a good thing, and it relates to holding students accountable for and monitoring performance for both minor and major infractions. There must be agreement on what represents a minor and a major infraction. This should be explained fully and followed consistently by all staff. Moreover, the staff must define the processes for responding to minor or major violations. Typically, documentation for minor violations will be delivered to the office sometime during the day, but students need not visit the office.

Using the information gleaned from these BDFs, the schoolwide intervention team and indeed the entire staff will be able to proactively respond to trends that emerge from the data. These trends may answer questions such as:

- Which students are earning the most BDFs?
- What types of misbehavior are on the rise?
- In what locations across campus are these misbehaviors occurring?
- At what times are these misbehaviors occurring?
- Are there grade levels or departments that seem to be having particular behavioral concerns?
- Are there teachers or other staff members who may need extra support?

Well-designed BDFs, like the *Sample Behavior Documentation Form* included on page 124 (and online at **go.solution-tree.com/rti**), will also provide initial information on why student behaviors may be occurring, beginning the diagnostic process of determining antecedents to misbehavior. A behavior documentation form allows a school to efficiently gather evidence about misbehaviors in order to make wise, proactive decisions regarding the school's response to the behavioral challenges of individuals and groups of students. The schoolwide team designs this form to match the behavioral expectations that the school has established. The form is designed to be efficient to complete and should match the student information system into which the data is entered.

A cost-effective, efficient, and web-based software program exists that helps schools collect and analyze behavioral data from BDFs. Called the School-Wide Information System (SWIS), the program prevents the collection and use of data on student misbehaviors from becoming burdensome. The SWIS program provides ready-made labels for different types of misbehavior. It may be in schools' best interest to utilize these same labels, instead of creating their own, since SWIS does not allow schools to edit labels. Therefore, schools are wise to use the labels identified in SWIS when creating behavior documentation forms (these labels are used on the *Sample Behavior Documentation Form* on page 124). All staff must understand what each label represents. For example, what types of misbehavior would be represented by *disrespect* or *inappropriate language*? Once they have agreed on descriptions of misbehavior, staff members must consistently utilize those descriptions when documenting misbehavior for subsequent data analyses to be valid.

The school leadership team, and eventually the entire staff, must agree upon the strict definitions of minor and major infractions. Procedures must also be developed for responding to violations of behavioral expectations and for processing the behavior documentation forms themselves. Our goal should be to ensure that students are in class, learning, to the maximum extent possible. To achieve this, we recommend that administrators do not send call slips to bring students to the office. Instead, we recommend that administrators walk the campus, visiting classes and speaking to students right outside the rooms. This has several advantages beyond the preservation of student instructional time. First, teachers feel supported because they see administrators dealing with behavioral situations in a timely manner. Second, other students see that the school takes behavioral infractions very seriously. Students are very aware when their peers misbehave; when they observe the commitment demonstrated by administrators visiting students in class, they will better understand the priorities and focus of the school. Lastly, when infractions involve more than one student, as is often the case in instances of bullying or other intrapersonal conflicts, and when the students involved in the conflict are in the same class, visiting these classes sends the message to all students involved that administrators are committed to following up on all situations. This follow-up serves as the first form of intervention.

Revising or Extending Support

We can predict that strategies that at first successfully support students with behavioral concerns may need to be revised a few weeks later; it's almost as if students develop an immunity. Let's not be surprised and blame the student or ourselves. Instead, when students no longer respond adequately to behavioral interventions, we should be prepared to alter the type of support, which may mean a different or more intensive strategy.

Behavioral supports can also be extended. When a school feels justifiably proud that student behaviors have improved, the schoolwide team may determine that the expectations should increase and/or that the focus should change. For example, for schools that have improved student behavior in the classroom from disruptive to passively compliant, an extended goal may be to support students in becoming authentically engaged in their learning. Strategies such as SLANT (Sit up, Lean forward, Ask questions, Nod your head, Track the teacher with your eyes) and randomly selecting students when questioning can improve student engagement.

We have now described concentrated instruction and convergent assessment as it relates to behavior; in the next chapter, we will outline a process by which schools can develop effective systems of behavioral supports that ensures all students are guaranteed social and academic success.

District Responsibilities for Convergent Assessment

"What gets measured gets done"—this often-quoted saying by management guru Peter Drucker (1954) has great implications for district leadership relative to RTI. If collective accountability for the learning of each student shifts to the site and team level, what should district leadership monitor and measure to ensure that teams are effective and students are learning? What does convergent assessment look like for district leadership?

The following material has been adapted from an article by Edward Shapiro and Nathan Clemens (2009) from Lehigh University. Shapiro and Clemens suggest four measures that district leadership should monitor for systemwide evaluation of RTI: tier placement across benchmark periods, rate of improvement across benchmark measures, movement between tiers, and movement within tiers. *Convergent Assessment at the District Level* (page 125 or **go.solution-tree.com/rti**) provides an example of how schools and district leadership can begin to capture and evaluate these data.

Monitor Tier Placement Across Benchmark Periods

District leadership should carefully monitor the percentage of students scoring at the proficient, below basic, and far below basic levels across benchmark periods on universal screening measures. If an RTI model is successful, it should move more students toward proficiency as a result of Tier 1 instruction, and away from Tier 2 and Tier 3 interventions. This kind of movement over time indicates how well a particular school's RTI model is working compared to other schools.

For example, 60 percent of School A's students were successful as a result of only Tier 1 in the fall (40 percent in Tiers 2 and 3). By spring, 85 percent were successful with only Tier 1 support (15 percent in Tiers 2 and 3). At School B, 65 percent of students were successful as a result of only Tier 1 in the fall (35 percent in Tiers 2 and 3). By spring, 60 percent of the students at School B were successful with only Tier 1 support (40 percent in Tiers 2 and 3). This might cause district leadership to compare the efficacy of the instruction, assessment, and intervention practices at these two schools. On the surface, these practices seem to be creating greater student success at School A than at School B.

In the example in figure 5.5, oral reading fluency (ORF) was used to place and monitor third-grade students relative to their tier placement. Oral reading fluency has been recognized as a key indicator of overall reading achievement (Fuchs, Fuchs, Hosp, & Jenkins, 2001).

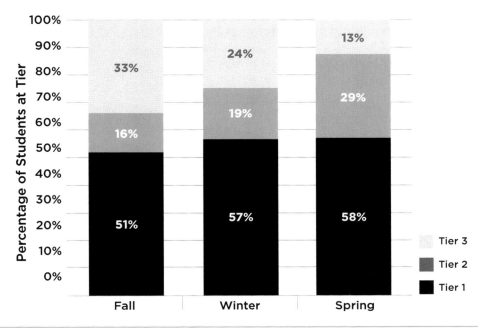

Figure 5.5: Third-grade tier placement, according to oral reading fluency scores.

As a measurement of oral reading fluency, the percentage of students who succeeded after only Tier 1 instruction improved from 51 percent in fall to 58 percent in spring. In this particular year, the percentage of students requiring Tier 3 intervention fell from 33 percent in fall to 13 percent at the end of the spring. Increasing numbers of students succeeding at Tier 1 combined with decreasing numbers of students at Tier 3 should be viewed by district leadership as a desirable outcome and evidence that the RTI model at this particular school is having the desired impact.

Beginning around grade 3, it is important for schools to look for additional measures beyond ORF when attempting to make decisions about overall reading comprehension (Catts, Hogan, & Adolf, 2005). Figure 5.6 (page 104) shows the risk levels (proficient/advanced = Tier 1, basic = Tier 2, below basic = Tier 3) on a benchmark measure of reading comprehension. This additional measure was given to the same group of third-grade students reported on in figure 5.5.

The data in figure 5.6 reflect more students scoring as low risk (needing Tier 1 instruction only) on the measure of reading comprehension than on the ORF measure. For example, in the spring, the data collected from the ORF measure in figure 5.5 show 29 percent of students at some risk (needing Tier 2 intervention). By contrast, data collected from the reading comprehension measure from figure 5.6 show 8.6 percent of students at some risk (Tier 2). Comparing figures 5.5 and 5.6 shows, then, that assessing proficiency based on ORF alone might have overidentified students who are at risk.

Using multiple measures can really improve decision making, especially for students in grade 3 and beyond. Shapiro, Solari, and Petscher (2008) and Clemens and Shapiro (2008) demonstrated that better decisions regarding individual students can be made

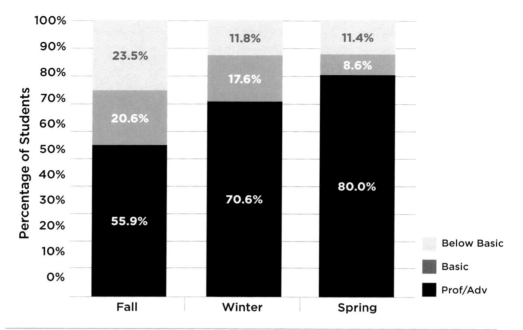

Figure 5.6: Third-grade risk levels, according to benchmarked reading comprehension scores.

when considering other reading comprehension data in addition to ORF. The fact that ORF begins to lose accuracy relative to older elementary and middle school students (Catts et al., 2005; Silberglitt, Burns, Madyun, & Lali, 2006) underscores the importance of using multiple measures to make inferences or decisions about students or about schools.

Change in the percentage of students in tiers across benchmark periods is one key indicator of the impact of RTI. Ideally, most students succeed as a result of only Tier 1 instruction. The proposed targets of 80 percent showing success as a result of only Tier 1 instruction, 15 percent requiring Tier 2 intervention, and 5 percent falling within an at-risk category that requires intensive Tier 3 interventions (per Batsche et al., 2005) are similar to the recommendations from School-Wide Positive Behavior Support (Walker et al., 1996). However, districts that have a student population that is highly transient or in which the majority of students have risk factors that impact educational achievement may find it difficult to achieve 80 percent success at Tier 1. In those cases, district leadership should still monitor the percentage of students successful as a result of Tier 1 instruction alone and hold their schools and themselves accountable to increase that percentage over time.

Monitor Rate of Improvement (ROI) Across Benchmark Measures

A second way to see if RTI models are working is to look at the overall ROI of students between benchmark periods. Universal screening measures, often collected at three points in time as benchmark measures, provide data that show how student achievement is changing over time. These data can be aggregated for an entire grade, school, or district. For example, Good, Simmons, & Kame'enui (2001) identified the predicted benchmark scores in reading at each point in the universal screening cycle (fall, winter, and spring) that would indicate with 90 percent probability a student's success in the subsequent year using *DIBELS*. AIMSweb® has also created a large normative database across multiple districts that offers data indicating the rate of improvement observed across students starting within different percentile ranks. Additionally, the Measures of Academic Progress® (Northwest Evaluation Association, n.d.) provide growth over time metrics for students by quartile. These are but a few examples of assessments that are intended to measure growth over time.

Using the ROI of typically performing students as a benchmark, districts can compare the ROI of students across a grade, a school, or even the district to determine how their students are performing compared to those in the national normative databases. Table 5.3 offers an example of grade 2 students in two different elementary schools implementing RTI. The average words read correctly (WRC) scores for students in the fall, winter, and spring of the school year are displayed, along with the average ROI of each group based on these scores compared to the ROI expected of students meeting the *DIBELS* benchmarks across the school year.

Table 5.3: Grade 2 Student Rate of Improvement (ROI) Compared to *DIBELS* Benchmarks

	Fall	Winter	Spring	Growth Rate (ROI)
DIBELS Benchmark	44.0	68.0	90.0	1.4 WRC/week
School 1	48.0	75.4	95.2	1.4 WRC/week
School 2	47.6	77.6	99.3	1.5 WRC/week

As table 5.3 shows, the second-grade students in School 1 achieved average scores in the fall, winter, and spring that were slightly higher than the targeted *DIBELS* benchmarks for those points in time during the year, but they demonstrated an average growth rate (ROI) that was only equal to the benchmark rate of growth. Students in School 2 showed a similar starting point to School 1 at the fall of the year but grew at a faster rate.

Analyzing the ROI of students across the tiers provides an index of the rate at which a group of students is progressing, and comparing that rate to normative or expected ROIs allows district leaders to determine whether students are progressing at rates close to what is expected of students at a given grade level. When a group of students is observed to demonstrate an ROI that exceeds the norm, it can be taken as evidence that the school's current RTI efforts are succeeding in helping all students experience success. This type of analysis can bring tremendous encouragement to schools with historically low-performing student populations. While those schools may not immediately see large numbers of students moving to lower tiers, they can celebrate the fact that their students' learning is growing at a rate that eventually will result in more average distribution across the tiers.

While useful to analyze the impacts of RTI implementation on groups of students, however, this kind of analysis should not be applied to individual students. Three data points are simply not enough to draw conclusions about individual students, or to predict a trend. Aggregating these data across an entire grade level or district greatly increases their usefulness and accuracy. Another important factor when analyzing and comparing school growth data is the baseline data (Silberglitt & Hintze, 2007). Schools with very low scores at the beginning of the school year simply have more room to grow, and this should be factored into the analysis of ROI by district leadership.

Monitor Movement Between Tiers

One sign of an effective RTI model is that students receiving Tier 2 or Tier 3 interventions are moved back to Tier 1 or Tier 2 as the school year progresses. Similarly, students who are struggling may need more intensive interventions and might be moved up to Tier 2 or Tier 3 interventions. When more students are moving to less-intensive interventions than those moving to more-intensive interventions, we may conclude that the RTI model is working. Conversely, when more students are consistently moving toward more intensive interventions, it would suggest that the RTI model be re-examined, especially as it relates to first, best instruction at Tier 1. Obviously, if a school experiences a sudden and dramatic change in demographics, conclusions relative to movement between tiers would need to be modified in consideration of this new variable.

Figure 5.7 shows the impact of tier movement across four schools implementing similar RTI models. Each school had three defined tiers of intervention, with each tier providing increasingly frequent and targeted interventions. The schools assigned students to tiers on the basis of universal screening. Progress monitoring was collected for students at Tier 2 every other week and once a week at Tier 3. Meeting monthly as grade-level teams, and quarterly as schoolwide data analysis teams, the school staff looked at student progress and made changes in intervention groups as well as tier assignment. Aggregated across grades and across schools, the data reflect that across the year, 36 percent of students moved to less-intensive tiers (that is, from Tier 3 to 2 or Tier 2 to 1), and 20 percent moved to more-intensive instructional tiers (from Tier 1 to 2 or Tier 2 to 3). As shown in figure 5.7, there was a net gain of 16 percent of students moving to less-intensive tiers compared to more-intensive tiers. Again, this adds another dimension of evaluation of the impact of the RTI model.

Monitor Movement Within Tiers

Finally, the progress of students receiving Tier 2 or Tier 3 interventions should be monitored to provide ongoing information about how students are responding to the interventions. Although there is no hard and fast rule regarding how often progress monitoring should occur, its frequency should be related to the intensity of the intervention. For example, students in Tier 2 should be assessed no less than every two weeks, while students in Tier 3 should receive at least weekly progress monitoring. In part, progress-monitoring data should indicate the rate of improvement (ROI) for each student receiving interventions. In turn, this ROI is analyzed to see if the student is responding to the intervention in positive ways that would result in the student being returned to Tier 1 instruction.

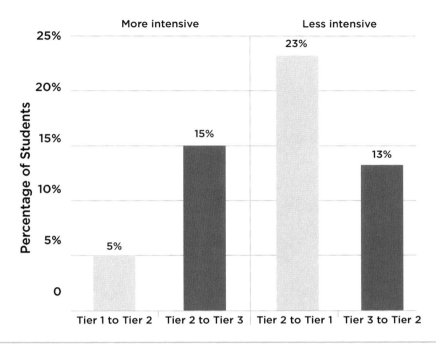

Figure 5.7: Tier movement aggregated across four schools implementing similar RTI models.

Given that all students assigned to Tier 2 and Tier 3 are by definition starting out below benchmark levels, and that the goal is to close that achievement gap, all of these students should have an individual targeted rate of progress that exceeds the rate expected of typical-performing students. For example, a second-grade student, Chris, who achieves the benchmark level performance on an ORF measure at the beginning, middle, and end of the year, would be expected to go from 60 words correct per minute (wcpm) to 110 by the end of the year. Assuming a 36-week school year, Chris would have a ROI of 1.39 wcpm per week ($110 - 60 = 50 \div 36 = 1.39$). Consider a second student, Sam, identified as in need of Tier 2 instruction with a fall ORF score of 50. Setting the goal for Sam to reach the benchmark level of 110 wcpm by the end of the year would mean that his targeted ROI would be 1.67 wcpm per week ($110 - 50 = 60 \div 36 = 1.67$). In other words, Sam needs to improve *faster* than a typically performing student (Chris) to close the gap toward the benchmark goal.

Students assigned to supplemental instruction should remain in that instructional program until a clear trend can be established through their progress-monitoring data. It has been recommended that a minimum of ten data points be collected before evaluating a trend (Good & Shinn, 1990). If progress-monitoring data are being collected every two weeks, at a minimum, students might remain in tiered instruction for eight to twelve weeks. Remember, we do not ever advocate one-size-fits-all solutions. The average number of weeks calculated in each case should be balanced by the input of the professionals. However, taking a generalized look across students assigned to tiered instruction, one can aggregate the attained ROI for each student to better determine the degree to which the students are "beating" the typical ROI as well as their own personal targeted ROIs. Looking across grades, schools, or districts, one can get another indication of the degree to which an RTI model is working.

Figure 5.8 analyzes data from an elementary school that had been implementing an RTI model. First-grade students were measured for nonsense word frequency (NWF), and older students for ORF; total number of students in intervention is noted as *n* = 6 for first grade, *n* = 9 for second, and so on.

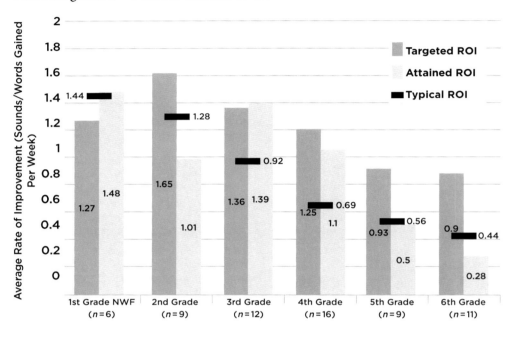

Figure 5.8: Sample rate of improvement data comparison.

Looking at grade 3 for ORF, one can see that the targeted ROI for the twelve students in tiered intervention was 1.36 wcpm/week. The actual ROI for these same students was 1.39 wcpm/week. Typically performing third-grade students in Tier 1 instruction (who started at or above the grade-level expectations) would achieve an ROI of 0.92 (see the black bar in the figure). These data indicate that in this third-grade sample, students in tiered intervention demonstrated an ROI that met the average targeted ROI and exceeded the ROI observed in typically performing students. This information suggests that the third-grade tiered intervention was successful in helping them to close the gap.

In second grade, however, the average ROI was well below both the targeted ROI and the typical ROI. The tiered intervention being delivered at this grade level needs to be re-examined and improved. Students receiving Tier 2 or Tier 3 interventions should be improving on pace to reach the same goals achieved by students in lower tiers.

At some schools with especially challenging achievement gaps, catching up may take more than a single year. Nonetheless, students who start out with a deficit must make *more* progress than those who start further ahead. This is why it is critical to consider rate of improvement when evaluating RTI models at individual school sites.

One Size Does Not Fit All

Many schools have overly complicated the gathering and recording of evidence to help guide their intervention efforts, thereby paralyzing their already overwhelmed teachers. Other schools have simply purchased a program that may have little direct connection or alignment to those standards they want all students to master. Why would we assume that one program would work equally well for all students? The following quote, while directed at intervention programs, could be applied to assessment programs that are merely purchased and handed to teachers as well:

> None of the intervention [assessment] programs were equally effective for all of the children studied. There may be individual characteristics of children that predispose them to more or less success with a particular program. Research examining this possibility is underway, but it's already clear that we need to move away from the "one size fits all" mentality and apply continuous assessment approaches that evaluate how well an instructional program is working with particular youngsters. (Lyon et al., 2001, p. 277)

The solution to helping all students achieve success doesn't come in a box. It comes when collaborative teams gather *ongoing*, detailed information, as part of instruction, to effectively identify students who need additional time and support in their current grade-level curriculum. Through the use of these data, teachers can identify exactly which students have not mastered specific essential standards; determine the specific needs of each child, subsequently matching each student's need to the appropriate instruction and intervention; and monitor the student's response. In other words, assessment data must describe student progress *by the student, by the standard, by the learning target.*

Convergent assessment is thus an ongoing process of collectively analyzing evidence to target the specific learning needs of each child and determine the effectiveness of the instruction the child receives in meeting these needs. For too many years, traditional assessment has merely been used to generate a grade to be placed into the teacher's gradebook and, ultimately, to sort students to find the "college material." As DuFour and Marzano (2011) proclaim, "The assessment process . . . is not used simply to *prove* what a student has learned, but to *improve* that learning" (p. 140, emphasis in the original).

In the next chapter, we will examine interventions in detail. We will define what an intervention is and is not, examine the characteristics of effective interventions, and discuss how to make time for interventions during the regular school day.

Activities and Tools Summary

Does your school have a protocol for determining the needs of a struggling reader?

See *Reading Domains, Skills, and Assessments* (page 111).

Does your school have a plan to identify students in need of intensive help *before* they fail?

See the *Universal Screening Planning Guide* (page 113).

Does your school have a protocol for planning for intervention, remediation, and enrichment?

See the *Proactive RTI Planning Form* (page 115).

Does your school have a simple protocol to help teacher teams analyze common formative assessment data?

See the *Common Assessment Team Protocol* (page 116).

Does your school have a protocol to assess whether a student can self-regulate his or her behavior?

See *Self-Regulatory Assessment Tool* (page 117).

Does your school have a tool to universally screen for students in need of intensive behavior support?

See the *Student Risk Screening Scale* (page 118).

Does your school have a protocol to help plan interventions for a student who struggles with regulating his or her behavior?

See the *Self-Regulatory Problem-Solving Tool* (page 119).

Does your school have a protocol for analyzing a student's behavior and designing targeted behavior interventions?

See the *Behavioral Analysis Protocol* (page 121).

Does your school have a protocol for staff members to document an individual student's behavior?

See the *Sample Behavior Documentation Form* (page 124).

Does your district have a process for collecting and analyzing student assessment across the entire district?

See *Convergent Assessment at the District Level* (page 125).

Visit **go.solution-tree.com/rti** *to download these activities.*

Reading Domains, Skills, and Assessments

This table can help teams identify where in the literacy continuum a student's reading is breaking down. By starting from the top left and working down and then to the right, teams may be able to determine where to begin intervening with a student.

CORE assessments can be found at: www.corelearn.com

DIBELS assessments can be found at: dibels.uoregon.edu

QRI (*Qualitative Reading Inventory*, 5th edition) can be found at: www.pearsonhighered.com

easyCBM assessments can be found at: easycbm.com

	Phonemic Awareness (Phonological Awareness)	Phonics	Fluency	Vocabulary	Comprehension
Assessment Types Universal screening Progress monitoring Diagnostic	DIBELS Next (FSF & PSF) easyCBM CORE	DIBELS Next (LNF & NWF) CORE	DIBELS Next (ORF) CORE easyCBM	DIBELS Next (Daze) CORE	DIBELS Next (Daze) CORE QRI easyCBM
Skills Within Reading Domains Skills are developed from left to right and top to bottom.	Listen for sounds	Letter-sound correspondence	Accuracy	Word classification	Vocabulary
	Rhyming words	High-frequency words	Rate	Antonyms and synonyms	Concept development
	Initial sounds	Short vowels	Prosody	Affixes and roots	Background knowledge
	Words in sentences	Consonant blends		Multiple-meaning words	Academic language
	Syllables in words	Long vowels		Homophones and homographs	Genre
	Track and order phonemes	Vowel digraphs And diphthongs		Word learning strategies	Text structure
	Phoneme isolation	R-controlled		Word origins and derivatives	Comprehension skills
	Phoneme identification	Multisyllabic words		Figurative language and idioms	Comprehension strategies
	Phoneme comparison	Compound words			
	Phoneme blending	Contractions			
	Phoneme segmentation	Inflectional forms			
	Phoneme deletion				
	Phoneme addition				
	Phoneme substitution				

Adapted from M. Pippitt-Cervantes (n.d.), Building Blocks of Reading Proficiency Skills Needed to Read. (http://publicportal.ousd.k12.ca.us/19941011911361475o/blank /browse.asp?A=383&BMDRN=2000&BCOB=0&C=57721)

Universal Screening Planning Guide

Universal Skill	At-Risk Criteria What criteria will be used to determine whether a child is in need of intensive support?	Screening Process What screening assessment and/or process will be used to identify students in need of intensive support?	When When will the screening process take place?	Who Who will administer the screening?	Intensive Support Available What intensive intervention(s) will be used to accelerate student learning and support the identified student(s)?
Reading					
Writing					
Number sense					
English language					
Attendance					
Behavior					

Simplifying Response to Intervention © 2012 Solution Tree Press • solution-tree.com
Visit **go.solution-tree.com/rti** to download this page.

Universal Screening Planning Guide Protocol

This activity is designed to assist a leadership team plan for universal screening by creating a process to identify students in need of intensive support *before* they fail. Because the purpose is to provide preventive support, it is best if this activity is completed prior to the start of the school year.

For each universal skill, answer questions for each column:

1. **At-Risk Criteria.** At each grade level, what criteria will be used to determine whether a child is in need of intensive support? For example, in reading, an elementary school may determine that any student entering first grade without the ability to properly recognize all 26 letters (uppercase and lowercase) is extremely at risk in reading and will be considered for immediate, intensive support. At a high school, any student whose reading ability is two or more years below grade level (grade-level equivalent) could be considered for immediate, intensive support.

2. **Screening Process.** What screening assessment and/or process will be used to identify students in need of intensive support? The leadership team should identify the most effective, efficient, and timely process to gather the at-risk criteria data on each student.

3. **When.** When will the screening process take place? Obviously, if the purpose of universal screening is to provide preventive support, then this data should be collected either prior to the start of the school year or as early in the school year as possible. Finally, as new students will enroll in the school throughout the year, it is important to consider how these students can be screened during the enrollment process.

4. **Who.** Who will administer the screening? As the leadership team has representation from every teacher team, as well as responsibility for coordinating school support staff, this team is best positioned to organize the resources necessary.

5. **Intensive Support Available.** What intensive intervention(s) will be used to accelerate student learning and support the identified student(s)? There is no point in universal screening if there is no plan to provide these students extra support in their area(s) of need.

One final consideration: for a school new to universal screening, it may be overwhelming to begin universal screening in all six universal skills, at all grade levels, immediately. In this case, we recommend that the leadership team identify the universal skill (reading, writing, number sense, English language, attendance, behavior) that is currently the greatest area of need in their school. Start by focusing on this one. As the school builds skill and competence in this area, others can be added.

Proactive RTI Planning Form

Plan for Remediation	Plan for Intervention	Plan for Enrichment
Based on the prior skills needed, how will we determine which students need remediation before we begin initial instruction? Who will conduct the remediations? When?	After initial instruction and differentiation, what is our team's plan to provide additional time and support to those students who have not learned? Who will conduct the interventions? When?	After initial instruction and intervention, what is our team's plan to provide additional time and support to those who have learned? Who will conduct the enrichments? When?

Common Assessment Team Protocol

This protocol is designed to help a teacher team quickly and efficiently discuss a common assessment. If each teacher reviews his or her own assessment data prior to the team meeting, then the team should be able to collectively complete this activity within a typical team meeting of forty-five to sixty minutes.

1. Which specific students did not demonstrate mastery on which specific standards? (Respond by the student, by the standard)

2. Which instructional practices proved to be most effective?

3. What patterns can we identify from the student mistakes?

4. How can we improve this assessment?

5. What interventions are needed to provide failed students additional time and support?

6. How will we extend learning for students who have mastered the standard(s)?

Self-Regulatory Assessment Tool

Score each self-regulatory domain as follows:

1 — "This does not describe me." **2** — "This sometimes describes me." **3** — "This often describes me." **4** — "This always describes me."

Self-Regulatory Domains	Descriptors	Score
Metacognition Having knowledge and beliefs about thinking	I try to see how what I study applies to my everyday life. I try to make connections between what I am learning and what I already know. I try to relate what I am studying to my own experiences. I try to relate topics from one subject area to another.	
Self-Concept Seeing oneself as smart	I know I'll be successful in school. When I begin a test, I feel confident that I will do well. I feel prepared for tests and am very focused. I confidently answer all test questions to the best of my ability.	
Self-Monitoring Being able to plan and prepare	I am up-to-date in my class assignments. I compare class notes with other students to make sure my notes are complete. I review my notes before the next class. I test myself to be sure I know the material I have been studying.	
Motivation Being able to maintain interest	I love being in school. I study all subjects with the same enthusiasm. When work is difficult, I set short-term goals and persevere I spend time with friends and playing only after I finish my work.	
Strategy Using techniques for organization and memorization, including rehearsal and elaboration	I make drawings to help me understand what I am studying. I learn new words or ideas by thinking about a situation in which they occur. I translate what I am studying into my own words. When I study, I have a lot of strategies to learn the material.	
Volition Making the efforts needed to stay motivated	Even when studying seems boring, I keep working until I finish. When it comes to studying, I never wait until the last minute. When I study, I set aside a length of time and stick to it. I concentrate fully when studying.	

Adapted from M. McMahon & J. Luca (2001), Assessing Students' Self-Regulatory Skills. (www.ascilite.org.au/conferences/melbourne01/pdf/papers/mcmahonm.pdf)

Student Risk Screening Scale (SRSS)

To determine who may be at risk in the area of social behavior, please rate how often your students show each behavior using the following scale:

0 = Never   1 = Rarely   2 = Occasionally   3 = Frequently

Total scores range from 0 to 21, forming three risk categories: low (0 to 3), moderate (4 to 8), or high risk (9 or higher). Students, teachers, and/or categories with high scores may benefit from supplemental support.

Student Name	Stealing	Lying, Cheating, Sneaking	Behavior Problems	Peer Rejection	Low Academic Achievement	Negative Attitude	Aggressive Behaviors

Source: T. Drummond (1994), The Student Risk Screening Scale (SRSS). Grants Pass, OR: Josephine County Mental Health Program. Used with permission.

Self-Regulatory Problem-Solving Tool

Once you have identified areas of academic behavior in which students are at risk, use this tool to help students set goals.

Self-Regulatory Domains	Suggested Goals
Metacognition Having knowledge and beliefs about thinking	Connect new lessons and subjects to your life and to other subjects in school. Pause every few minutes to think about the ways you are learning.
Self-Concept Seeing oneself as smart	Set long-term goals and make short-term plans to reach them. Be aware of your attitude about school and your motivation for learning. Talk to an adult when you worry about school. Learn techniques for coping with worry so you can focus on a task.
Self-Monitoring Being able to plan and prepare	Learn about testing yourself to make sure you have learned. Learn specific ways to review what you are trying to learn. Learn how to monitor whether you understand what you are reading and learning. Learn how to prepare for classes.
Motivation Being able to maintain interest	Work on setting short-term goals for individual tasks and assignments. Learn techniques for self-discipline.
Strategy Using techniques for organization and memorization, including rehearsal and elaboration	Learn ways that you can help organize what you are trying to learn. Learn how to identify the most important information that you are trying to learn. Learn about study aids provided in textbooks. Learn how to create your own study aids. Learn how to prepare for tests and how to create a plan of attack for taking a test. Learn about different types of tests and test questions. Learn how to reason through to an answer.

Simplifying Response to Intervention © 2012 Solution Tree Press • solution-tree.com
Visit **go.solution-tree.com/rti** to download this page.

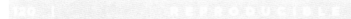

Self-Regulatory Domains	Suggested Goals
Volition Making the efforts needed to stay motivated	Learn how to create and follow a schedule.
	Learn how to deal with distractions, competing goals, and procrastination.
	Learn how to better concentrate.
	Learn to prioritize.

Adapted from M. McMahon & J. Luca (2001), Assessing Students' Self-Regulatory Skills. *(www.ascilite .org.au/conferences/melbourne01/pdf/papers/mcmahonm.pdf)*

Behavioral Analysis Protocol

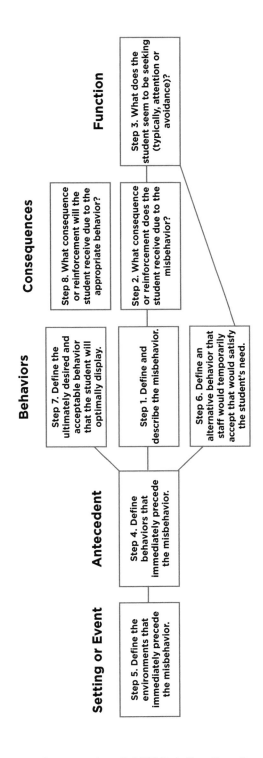

Function

Step 3. What does the student seem to be seeking (typically, attention or avoidance)?

Consequences

Step 8. What consequence or reinforcement will the student receive due to the appropriate behavior?

Step 2. What consequence or reinforcement does the student receive due to the misbehavior?

Behaviors

Step 7. Define the ultimately desired and acceptable behavior that the student will optimally display.

Step 1. Define and describe the misbehavior.

Step 6. Define an alternative behavior that staff would temporarily accept that would satisfy the student's need.

Antecedent

Step 4. Define behaviors that immediately precede the misbehavior.

Setting or Event

Step 5. Define the environments that immediately precede the misbehavior.

Simplifying Response to Intervention © 2012 Solution Tree Press • solution-tree.com
Visit **go.solution-tree.com/rti** to download this page.

Directions

A team can use this flowchart to help determine the causes of a student's misbehavior, and to help decide what types of behaviors would be accepted and preferred. We recommend that these steps be completed with, or at least communicated to, all stakeholders, including teachers, parents, and the student.

1. **Define and describe the misbehavior.** The team should describe the student's actions, words, and overall behavior as specifically as possible.

2. **What consequence or reinforcement does the student receive due to the misbehavior?** The team should detail what consequences the student has received as a result of the misbehavior.

3. **What does the student seem to be seeking (typically, attention or avoidance)?** Based on the team's responses in Steps 1 and 2, as well as other knowledge of the student, what need does the misbehavior seem to be meeting (what is the function or purpose of the behavior)?

4. **Define behaviors that immediately precede the misbehavior.** Based on observations of the student when he or she has exhibited this misbehavior, describe the student's actions, words, and overall behavior that occur before the unacceptable misbehavior as specifically as possible. This will help staff predict the misbehavior in the future and provide precorrections.

5. **Define the environments that immediately precede the misbehavior.** Where is the student, with whom is the student, what task is the student completing (or attempting to complete), and so on. This will further help staff predict the misbehavior and provide precorrections.

6. **Define an alternative behavior that staff would temporarily accept that would satisfy the student's need.** This will be an interim step; staff will "allow" a student to behave in a way that satisfies the "function" identified in Step 3 but that is also acceptable to staff. This behavior is not the ultimately desired behavior and will not be reinforced.

7. **Define the ultimately desired and acceptable behavior that the student will optimally display.** While Step 6 will be temporarily acceptable, the staff communicates, explains, and models the desired, acceptable behavior that will be ultimately expected.

page 2 of 3

8. **What consequence or reinforcement will the student receive due to the appropriate behavior?** Based on a discovery of items, objects, or activities that motivate the student (items, objects, or activities for which the student is willing to work), the staff determines positive reinforcers that the student will earn if the appropriate behavior identified in Step 7 is exhibited. The goal is to phase out these external reinforcers as soon as possible.

Here is an example of how a team might describe each step:

1. Brian pushes his supplies and papers off his desk and talks in an inappropriately loud voice when asked to work collaboratively with the members of his table team.

2. Brian receives verbal warnings and is sent to the back of the classroom or to the classroom next door if the acting out continues.

3. Brian seems to be seeking to avoid working on certain assignments or with certain students.

4. Brian fidgets in his seat, calls out off-task comments, gets out of his seat to sharpen a pencil (or throw a paper away), and/or begins "organizing" his desk or binder.

5. Brian seems to act out when asked to work collaboratively, particularly when the assignment involves reading and when team members have to work side by side to complete the task (in other words, each team member is not assigned a separate subtask). It occurs more in language arts and social studies than math and science, and more in the morning than the afternoon.

6. If Brian feels frustrated by the task or his classmates, he may either take a two-minute break at the computer or, if necessary, complete an alternative assignment.

7. The expectation, which will be modeled, is for Brian to join his team promptly to work; he cannot be the last member to join; he needs to listen and make positive comments (no put-downs or "complaining"); and he needs to successfully, cooperatively, and promptly complete his portion of the task.

8. Brian likes working on the computer. If he meets the expectation as described in Step 7, he will earn time on the classroom computer to play the math facts game during recess. The teacher, principal, Brian, and his mom will review the plan in three weeks to revise and/or set a higher expectation for Brian to meet before earning computer time.

Sample Behavior Documentation Form

Student name: _____

Staff: _____ Date: _____ Time: _____

Location: _____ classroom _____ walkway _____ library _____ restroom _____ playground _____ lunch area

Major:
_____ abusive/inappropriate language
_____ fighting/physical aggression
_____ defiance/disrespect/noncompliance
_____ lying/cheating
_____ harassment/bullying
_____ disruption
_____ truancy
_____ property damage
_____ forgery/theft
_____ use/possession of controlled substance/weapon

Minor:
_____ inappropriate language
_____ physical contact
_____ defiance/disrespect/noncompliance
_____ disruption

Follow-up action(s):
_____ no recess (_____ recess/days)
_____ conference with student
_____ parent contact
_____ privilege loss (_____)
_____ time in office
_____ in-house suspension (_____ days)
_____ out-of-school suspension (_____ days)
_____ other:

Comments:

Others involved:
_____ none
_____ staff
_____ teacher
_____ unknown
_____ peers (_____)

Motivation:
_____ obtain peer attention
_____ avoid task/activity
_____ don't know
_____ avoid peer
_____ obtain adult attention
_____ avoid adult
_____ obtain item/activity

Parent signature. Return to classroom teacher.

Parent signature: _____

Convergent Assessment at the District Level

School/District _____ Grade _____ School Year _____

1. What percentage of students is placed in Tier 1, Tier 2, or Tier 3 across benchmark periods?

	Fall	Winter	Spring	Improvement?		Comments
				F to W	W to S	
% at Tier 1				Yes ☐ No ☐	Yes ☐ No ☐	
% at Tier 2				Yes ☐ No ☐	Yes ☐ No ☐	
% at Tier 3				Yes ☐ No ☐	Yes ☐ No ☐	

2. What is the average ROI* for all students in a grade between two benchmark periods, and how does that ROI compare to normative growth rates and/or previously observed growth rates?

	Fall to Winter Avg. ROI	Winter to Spring Avg. ROI	Full-Year ROI	Comments
Grade _____				
Comparative Growth Rate _____	≥ Norm ☐ ≤ Norm ☐	≥ Norm ☐ ≤ Norm ☐	≥ Norm ☐ ≤ Norm ☐	

*ROI= (ending score – starting score) / # of weeks

3. How many students moved to a less or more intensive tier between benchmark periods?

Fall to Winter Analysis	# at Tier 1 in Winter	# at Tier 2 in Winter	# at Tier 3 in Winter	Summary	Comments
# of students at Tier 1 in fall: _____ # of students at Tier 2 in fall: _____ # of students at Tier 3 in fall: _____				% stayed at T1: _____ % dropped to T2/3: _____ % moved up to T1: _____ % dropped to T3: _____ % moved up to T1/2: _____ % stayed at T3: _____	

Winter to Spring Analysis	# at Tier 1 in Spring	# at Tier 2 in Spring	# at Tier 3 in Spring	Summary	Comments
# of students at Tier 1 in winter: _____ # of students at Tier 2 in winter: _____ # of students at Tier 3 in winter: _____				% stayed at T1: _____ % dropped to T2/3: _____ % moved up to T1: _____ % dropped to T3: _____ % moved up to T1/2: _____ % stayed at T3: _____	

Simplifying Response to Intervention © 2012 Solution Tree Press • solution-tree.com
Visit **go.solution-tree.com/rti** to download this page.

4. What is the average attained ROI on progress-monitoring measures for students in Tiers 2 and/or 3, and how does that ROI compare to the average targeted ROI for the same group?

	Fall to Winter				**Winter to Spring**		
	Avg. Targeted ROI	Avg. Attained ROI	Comments		Avg. Targeted ROI	Avg. Attained ROI	Comments
Tier 2 Students				Tier 2 Students			
Tier 3 Students				Tier 3 Students			

Simplifying Response to Intervention © 2012 Solution Tree Press • solution-tree.com
Visit **go.solution-tree.com/rti** to download this page.

CHAPTER 6

Creating a System of Interventions

Up to this point, we have focused our attention on the conditions necessary to ensure that most students succeed in initial Tier 1 core instruction. When a school creates a school culture focused on collective responsibility for student learning, ensures that every educator is part of a high-performing team, identifies the essential standards that all students must master, and frequently measures student learning and teaching effectiveness, a vast majority of the school's students are going to succeed. But our goal is not to have *most* students learn. If we want to achieve our mission of high levels of learning for *every* child, then we must be prepared with additional time and support for every student that demonstrates the need. Invariably, some students will need some extra help from time to time, while a few students will require a lot of extra help nearly every day. In other words, we must be prepared with a system of interventions designed to meet the unique needs of each child.

There are three critical considerations a school must address when creating an effective system of interventions. First, a school must build a toolbox of effective interventions. Students struggle at school for a multitude of reasons, so a school must be prepared with a variety of proven responses. Second, there must be time available during the school day to provide additional support without having students miss essential core instruction. Finally, there must be a systematic, timely, and reliable process to identify students in need of additional support. Without a foolproof identification process, some students will slip through the cracks. Failure to address these three critical components will place a school's RTI efforts on shaky ground and ultimately undermine the entire process. In this chapter, we'll examine how to create the toolbox and how to create flexible time during the school day for interventions.

What Is an Intervention?

Many schools and districts argue endlessly about the language used to define the words *intervention*, *strategy*, and *core instruction*. To bring clarity to the topic, an *intervention* is anything a school does, above and beyond what all students receive, that helps a child succeed in school. This additional support can be a practice, method, strategy, and/or program. The important consideration is this: if all kids at a school receive it, then it is part of Tier 1 core instruction and would not be considered an intervention. If a specific practice, method, strategy, or program *in addition* to core instruction is used on the child's behalf, it is considered an intervention. Interventions are not only actions directly in support of instruction. If a child demonstrates behaviors that interfere with the child's ability to learn and the school provides additional behavioral support, that is an intervention. Attendance support for a child with chronic absenteeism is an intervention. Medical support for a student with severe diabetes is an intervention.

A system of interventions can only be as effective as the individual interventions of which it is comprised. If a site builds a system of interventions with ineffective instructional programs and practices, all students will have certain access to what is not working.

Based on our work with hundreds of schools across North America, we see two primary reasons why many schools struggle with identifying effective interventions:

1. **The "more of the same" syndrome.** When we work with schools, we often have them list their current site interventions so we can assist with evaluating their effectiveness. A standard set of traditional "interventions" that have been used for years is listed first at practically every school: remedial support classes of varying types, study hall opportunities, summer school, retention, and special education. We then ask each school for evidence that these interventions are working—and are usually met with upturned palms and blank stares.

   We are not suggesting that highly effective summer school, special education, or study hall programs do not exist. A few do exist, but they are the exceptions. Research shows that the way most schools traditionally implement these programs is ineffective at best and detrimental to kids at the worst (Hattie, 2009). Our experiences as educators confirm this research. How many times have we seen a student below grade level in essential skills attend summer school, then return in the fall having significantly improved? Almost never. Instead, we often hear about how students in summer school "made up" a semester of English by attending three hours a day for six weeks. Did they master the essential learnings for the class, or simply jump through enough hoops to earn the credits? Nevertheless, most schools continue to utilize these ineffective responses.

   When it comes to interventions, giving at-risk kids more of what is not working is rarely the answer. Common sense would tell us this, yet many schools continue to build their system of interventions with practices that don't work, have never worked, and have no promise of getting better results next year.

2. **The "what program do we buy?" syndrome.** Many schools fall into the trap of searching for the Holy Grail of interventions—the perfect product to buy that will help all their struggling readers, writers, or math students. Wouldn't it be great if there were a single program a school could buy and every student would learn how to read? Every school would buy this program, and we would all be enjoying record student achievement!

Unfortunately, this product does not exist. At-risk readers don't all struggle for the same reason, so there is no one program that will address every child's unique needs. Some educational supply companies market their products as a cure-all; like most major corporations, their ultimate goal is to make a profit. If a company's claim sounds too good to be true, it probably is. There *are* some very good, scientifically research-based products available that can become powerful, targeted tools in a school's intervention repertoire—but there is no silver bullet. Ultimately, there is no "intervention-in-a-box" that can beat a highly effective teacher working with a targeted group of students. A school will get much better results if it spends less time searching for the Holy Grail and more time working in collaborative teacher teams to find the most effective teaching practices for its students.

Understanding the Characteristics of Effective Interventions

How, then, does a school build a toolbox of effective interventions? The key to success is in aligning interventions to the essential characteristics of effective interventions, which are:

- Research-based
- Directive
- Administered by trained professionals
- Targeted
- Timely

Let's examine what these characteristics mean in practice in real schools.

Research-Based

NCLB and IDEIA advocate the use of interventions based on "defensible research." The law sets the gold standard as "research that involves the application of rigorous, systematic, and objective procedures to obtain reliable and valid knowledge relevant to educational activities and programs" (IDEIA, 2004).

This scientific model of testing the reliability of specific interventions has proven to be problematic. Creating blind studies with carefully controlled conditions is extremely difficult in a school setting, as so many factors contribute to a child's success in school. By strictly applying the criteria of *scientifically research-based*, some districts have created lists of "approved" interventions that constitute the only programs that can be used by their schools, subsequently restricting a school's ability to creatively meet the individual needs of each child. We also know that, outside of primary reading, there are a limited number of scientifically research-based interventions for each subject and grade level. On the other hand, failure to measure the validity of a school's chosen intervention practices has created a situation wherein "too many schools have adopted programs based on hunches and anecdotes," according to Russ Whitehurst (Dahlkemper, 2003).

To help address this problem, we suggest a reasonable definition of research-based interventions: research-based interventions are instructional practices and programs for which there is credible evidence that the intervention can work and/or is working. In other words, a school should utilize interventions for which they can point to research that demonstrates a practice has a high likelihood of working or can provide student data that demonstrates the practice is working for a majority of students who have received the intervention.

For example, a significant body of research confirms that small-group tutoring tends to be a highly effective intervention (Denton, Anthony, Parker, & Hasbrouck, 2004; Gersten et al., 2007; Gunn, Smolkowski, Biglan, & Black, 2002; Vaughn, Wanzek, Linan-Thompson, & Murray, 2007). Based on this research, a secondary language arts team reviewing student assessment data on figurative language might decide to provide small-group tutoring to the students still struggling with the concept. While it is unlikely that a scientifically research-based study validates the use of small-group tutoring to specifically teach figurative language, there is a solid base of research to support trying the practice based on the success with the strategy in general.

As another example, suppose a team of fourth-grade teachers taught two-digit multiplication, each teacher using various instructional practices, then compared common assessment results after initial teaching (see table 6.1).

Table 6.1: Percentage of Fourth-Grade Students Demonstrating Proficiency in Two-Digit Multiplication

Teacher 1	Teacher 2	Teacher 3	Teacher 4
78%	67%	83%	97%

Based on these results, the team decided to try using Teacher 4's instructional strategy to reteach the standard to the students in need of additional help. Should this team be required to first find scientifically research-based evidence supporting Teacher 4's instructional method before using it with their students? That level of research is not necessary. The team already has evidence to support their decision, as their common assessment data serve as *action research* that demonstrates Teacher 4's method has a high likelihood of success. The team's assessment data prove the practice is working on their campus.

The problem is that many schools implement interventions that lack *any* evidence that they can work and/or are working. Take the traditional practice of retention. There is no research to suggest that retention is effective. John Hattie completed a meta-study on retention and found that if a child is retained once, the chance he or she will drop out of school doubles—retained twice, dropping out is virtually assured (Hattie, 2009). If a school decides to disregard this evidence, then the school can look to evidence in its district regarding students who have been retained. Are these students doing markedly better after being retained? Are a large majority of these students graduating from high school and continuing on to higher levels of learning? We suspect that few, if any, schools or districts in North America can produce evidence that retention is working for more than a rare handful of students.

If there is no research to suggest that an intervention can work, and no data to prove that it is working, how can any professional justify continuing the practice? As IDEIA rightly demands, our actions must be defensible.

Directive

Interventions *must* be mandatory. It is disingenuous for a school to claim that its mission is to ensure that all students learn at high levels, yet allow its students to choose failure. When help is optional, the students who are most likely to take advantage of this offer are the ones already succeeding at school, while the students least likely are those most at risk.

Making help invitational is rarely a problem at the elementary level. It is doubtful a second-grade teacher would say to the class, "If you need extra help in adding two-digit numbers, I am available at recess—come see me for help, if you want." Unfortunately, at the secondary level, it is all too common for students to be "offered the opportunity" for help. This practice of intervention by invitation is justified by a litany of misguided and illogical reasons, such as the following:

- **We are teaching the students responsibility.** Without question, student responsibility is a critical life skill. But if a school gives students the option to fail, is the school teaching responsibility, or merely punishing students for not already possessing the skill? By "offering" help, the school expects students to either have an intrinsic love of learning or to fully grasp the lifelong benefits or life-damaging consequences of not succeeding at school. This foresight would motivate students to forgo the short-term pleasures that youth enjoy, and instead delay their gratification and commit to the rigors of learning. How likely is it that the average high school student would go home after school and think: "I have a major test tomorrow in English, and the teacher has offered after-school help. But my friends have invited me to come over to play *Guitar Hero*. Let me make a T-chart and consider the short- and long-term consequences before I make my decision. If I fail the test, I will risk failing English, which is required to graduate. If I don't graduate, this will increase the chances that I will someday live on welfare, be incarcerated, and die young. Hmmm—I guess I better skip *Guitar Hero* today." Is this a fair and reasonable expectation? Research tells us that the average adolescent does not consistently make decisions based on long-term consequences and that adolescents often allow their emotions rather than decision-making processes to dictate their choices (Fischhoff, 1992; Fischhoff, Crowell, & Kipke, 1999; Ganzel, 1999).

  Most educators were very responsible students, so we should ask ourselves, "Were our efforts in high school motivated by an intrinsic love of learning or the long-term vision of how our studies would help us achieve our lifelong goals?" It is much more likely that we were motivated by positive recognitions at school and/or our parents giving immediate, short-term consequences at home. Schools that make interventions invitational are asking their students to possess a level of responsibility that many students are incapable of demonstrating consistently, all the while knowing that the students who choose poorly will most assuredly pay the price of lifelong failure for their decisions.

- **That's the real world.** Some schools claim that adults are not required to seek help, so requiring students to get help is enabling behavior that will not prepare children for the "real" world. This same logic results in classroom practices such as, "This assignment is due on Thursday. If you miss the deadline, you will receive a zero, and you cannot turn it in late or make it up. In the real world, you must meet deadlines." What if the assignment relates to an essential standard—a skill that has been deemed critical to a student's success in the course not just this year, but for years to come? Because the student will not be required to complete the assignment, or be given the opportunity to do the work for partial credit, the cost of this mistake becomes far reaching.

  As educators, we live and work in the real world. Honestly, how many adult rules are there in which there are no second chances? The list is pretty short. It is not unusual for a teacher to tell students that late work will not be accepted because that is the real world, yet that same teacher will miss a deadline to turn in required paperwork to the administration. If the teacher were given an equivalent lifelong consequence for missing a school paperwork deadline, the teacher would be fired for the error. If that happened in the real world, the teacher would say the consequence was unfair, unreasonable, and unjust—and the teacher would be right!

  This is not to say that adults do not pay a price for missing deadlines, or that students should not face consequences for poor choices. But the consequence should be fair, should allow students to make amends, and should not deny students the opportunity to learn. In the *real* world, adults expect nothing less.

- **It is the parents' job.** When kids do not show proper effort, many schools believe it is the parents' job to fix the problem. To some extent, this is true— parental responsibilities can have a significant impact on a child's success at school. Unfortunately, kids are not in the position to select their parents, nor do schools have much leverage on requiring parents to meet their parental responsibilities. In reality, when students are at school, the law considers the educators in loco parentis—in place of a parent. We have the responsibilities of a parent. If a child is in our care for thousands of hours over her K–12 education and does not develop the skills of responsibility, we need to take a hard look in the mirror.

- **You can't make a student do something.** Some schools feel that requiring students to do their schoolwork and attend interventions is futile, as educators do not have the ability to "make" kids do things. This perception is perplexing, as schools make students do things every day that they do not want to do. Does the average teenager want to get up early and be at school on time every morning? These same kids often sleep until noon when allowed on the weekends. Nevertheless, at virtually every school the vast majority of students arrive on time to class every day. Why? Because student expectations are clear, staff members consistently enforce these expectations, the administration supports the staff, and consequences happen quickly and consistently when students do not meet the expectation.

When schools ask, "How do we get students to attend interventions?" our response is, "How do you get them to first period? How do you get them back from recess or lunch? How do you get them to detention for violating a behavior rule at school?" It is no different. If a school *decides* that students will attend interventions and complete their work, and *takes actions* to teach, require, and monitor this outcome, students ultimately become more responsible. Educator Jamie Virga, considering the work of Albert Bandura (1993, 1997) puts it this way: "Individuals build their self-efficacy beliefs by successfully carrying out a challenging task at a high level. After you have an experience of mastery, when you are faced with a similar experience in the future, you will be able to draw on the past experience and have a powerful expectation that you will be successful" (Virga, 2010).

Ultimately, the question is, What is the best way to teach kids responsibility *and* ensure high levels of learning? For schools that believe teaching responsibility is best achieved by giving students the option to fail, we challenge them to show evidence that this practice is working at their school. Do the students who decide against getting help benefit from their error in judgment and make better choices due to their failure? Are the students who choose to disregard their homework and miss deadlines becoming more responsible? More likely, these students are missing assignment after assignment and failing class after class, semester after semester, year after year—all the while showing no newly gained initiative to seek out extra help.

There is no evidence to suggest that higher incidence of failure produces higher levels of responsibility and academic success. If there is no research showing that giving students the option to fail works, then how can a school continue this misguided approach? Interventions must be directive.

Administered by Trained Professionals

In the medical field, patients are assigned the help of medical professionals based on the severity of their illnesses and the expertise needed to address the problem. For example, someone suffering from the flu usually sees a nurse practitioner or family physician, while a cancer patient visits an oncologist. Effective learning interventions need to apply this same guiding principle. Douglas Reeves' research (2009) shows that one of a school's most effective learning strategies is to have highly trained teachers work with the students most at risk.

Unfortunately, the vast majority of schools do the exact opposite. According to the National Partnership for Teaching in At-Risk Schools, "Not only do the teachers of low-income students tend to be more poorly trained in the subject they teach, they also are far more likely to have significantly less teaching experience" (National Partnership for Teaching in At-Risk Schools, 2005). This is equivalent to sending patients with cold symptoms to the brain surgeon while assigning those with brain tumors to an intern.

This approach is justified at most schools by a cultural seniority system in which more tenured teachers "earn the right" to work with students who are high achieving, while new teachers must "pay their dues" with children who tend to be more low achieving. Often these practices are protected by teacher contract language that limits the ability of site administration to reassign teacher positions or revise a teacher's course or grade-level teaching assignment. School administrators sometimes support this seniority system because parents of the most successful students often complain if their child is assigned to an inexperienced teacher's class, while parents of at-risk students rarely voice this concern. Additionally, many schools have faced legal restraints to teacher assignments, as students must qualify to work with some school personnel. For example, traditional special education services were only available to students who qualified. This has forced schools to ask, What help does this student qualify for?

Because RTI allows schools to use site resources in more flexible, preventive ways, schools can now ask the more appropriate questions: What does this child need, and who on our staff is best trained to meet that need? Unless our most at-risk students have access to our most effective teachers, it is unlikely that any particular intervention strategy, practice, or program will prove effective.

Targeted

The more targeted the intervention, the more likely it will work. Most schools' interventions are ineffective because they are too broad in focus and rarely address a child's individual learning needs. For example:

- We consistently see schools offer interventions like study hall for all students with an F on their current report card. These students have earned Fs for a variety of reasons, yet one teacher is expected to address the numerous learning needs of the students in study hall.

- Schools often use universal screening data to place students in reading interventions, and then put all the kids who need intensive support in the same reading intervention. Will every student in the "red" group have the same difficulties in reading? There will surely be students who are weak in letter recognition, others who lack phonemic awareness and the ability to blend sounds into words, some who cannot recognize high-frequency sight words that have no phonemic pattern, and still others who may decode proficiently but cannot read fluently and comprehend what they are reading. All these students may score in the intensive range on a universal screening assessment, but they certainly do not have the same reading needs. It would be impossible for one teacher to meet all their needs in the same intervention period.

- Some schools place students in interventions based on prior-year state assessment results. For example, students who score below proficient on the state math assessment are automatically placed in a two-period math class. Again, it is highly unlikely that all the students scored poorly on the state assessment for the same reasons. What if a child's problem in math was due to high levels of distractibility—will two periods of math help the child become more focused? What if the problem was poor attendance—will two periods of math help the child attend school more frequently? It is much more likely that the child will just end up missing twice as much math the next year.

To target interventions effectively, we recommend that a school consider two criteria. First, a school must target interventions by the student, by the standard, and by the learning target. In other words, what specific essential skill or knowledge is the child lacking? It is not sufficient to say the child is struggling with algebra—with what part of algebra? It is not sufficient to even say the child is struggling with a particular algebra standard—with what part of the standard? Let's break it down to solving equations—with what part of solving equations? Exponents within an equation. Again, with what specific skill with exponents? Multiplying exponents. And at this point, a teacher now knows *exactly* what to reteach this child who is "struggling with algebra" during intervention time—multiplying exponents. And if a group of students share that need, we can group them together for reteaching.

This level of intervention specificity is why concentrated instruction is so vital. Unless a school has clearly identified the essential standards that every student must master, as well as unwrapped the standards into specific student learning targets, it would be nearly impossible to have the curricular focus and targeted assessment data necessary to target interventions to this level. In the end, a school needs to continually ask, What exactly do we want students to learn from this intervention? The more specific the answer, the more targeted the intervention, and the more likely you will hit the target.

Focusing efforts by the student, the standard, and the learning target is the first step in targeting interventions, but there is a second, equally important consideration: why didn't the student learn? We must address the cause of a student's struggles, not the symptoms. When a patient has a fever, the doctor understands that the fever is not the problem, but instead is a symptom of the patient's illness. If the doctor was only concerned with the patient's temperature, the doctor could put the patient in a bathtub of ice—but the minute the patient got out of the ice bath, the high temperature would probably return. To cure the patient, the doctor must address the cause of the problem, not just the symptoms.

Similarly, a school must address the cause of a student's difficulty in learning. Failing grades, poor test scores, disruptive behavior, and poor attendance are all symptoms. The key questions are: Why is this student failing a class? Why is this child demonstrating disruptive behavior? Why did this student fail the exam? Why is this student chronically absent?

To further demonstrate this level of targeting, consider this example. Using the math example given earlier, let's say a teacher team has identified seven students who are having difficulties with multiplying exponents. The team has grouped the kids together into the same intervention because they lack the same specific skill. That would be an excellent start. But if the school stopped there and did not dig deeper into why each student did not master the skill, what is likely to happen is this:

- Student 1 has solid prior knowledge and skills and has performed well in algebra all year—she just does not "get" the way her teacher taught multiplying exponents. She does not understand why she is being asked to add the exponents when the skill is called multiplying exponents. To address the cause of her problem, she needs to be taught the concept a different way.

- Student 2 is struggling with multiplying exponents because he still does not know how to multiply. He should have mastered the concept in third grade, but he didn't. To address the cause of his problem, he needs help in a prior, foundational skill.

- Student 3 has chronic absenteeism. She has no problem with learning when she is present for the lesson. Unfortunately, she sometimes misses multiple days a week. To address the cause of her problem, she needs help with attendance issues.

- Student 4 is an English learner. The cause of his problem is that he does not understand what the teacher is saying. Until he gets help in academic vocabulary needed to learn the concept, he will have difficulty learning how to multiply exponents.

- Student 5 is an unmotivated learner. She understood the concept in class, but she did not go home and practice the skill for homework. We know that homework is not designed to teach kids a concept, but instead to help make what they have learned permanent. Because she did not practice the skill, she forgot how to solve the problems on the test. To address the cause of her problem, she needs to be held accountable for doing her homework.

- Student 6 has significant behavior problems. He is constantly off task, in trouble, in time out, in the office, or suspended from school. He has the skills and knowledge to learn the new concept, if he could behave long enough to stay in class. To address the cause of his problem, he needs behavioral support.

- Student 7 suffers from ADD. When being taught how to multiply exponents, she was fine on the first two steps of the process, but then a bird flew by the window, which reminded her of the project she was painting in art class, and by the time she tuned back into the math lesson, the teacher was on the fourth step, and the student was lost. To address the cause of her problem, she needs classroom strategies that help her stay focused.

These seven students are not rare examples. Teachers know their faces in every school and most likely every classroom in North America right now. If these seven students are all placed in the same intervention session to reteach them how to multiply exponents, what is the likelihood that one teacher can effectively teach the skill a different way for Student 1, while she teaches the foundational skill of multiplication to Student 2, while she fixes an attendance problem with Student 3, while she teaches English to Student 4, while she gets Student 5 to get her work done, while she addresses the severe behavior issues of Student 6, all the while keeping the classroom environment disruption-free for Student 7? Even a masterful math teacher is probably not trained to deal with some of the causes affecting each child. No wonder teachers feel overwhelmed.

Instead of leaving each teacher to address all these issues in isolation, what if teams of teachers and school professionals discussed why each child was struggling and then grouped kids together by the skill *and* by the cause? Better yet, what if these groups were then taught by the staff member(s) best trained in each cause? A highly trained math teacher would be an excellent choice to help Student 1 or Student 2, while a school counselor may work with Student 3's absenteeism and take the lead with the school psychologist for creating a behavior plan for Student 6.

When a school can target interventions to this degree of specificity, that school can finally begin to achieve the mission of high levels of learning for every child.

Timely

An effective intervention program must respond promptly when students do not learn. At traditional schools, the monitoring of student progress usually takes place at the midpoint and end of each grading period. Educators provide quarterly and end-of-term report cards to students and their parents to mark a child's academic standing in each course of study.

This practice has two inherent problems. First, schools that merely *notify* parents of a student's failing progress are not providing an intervention; instead, they must delineate specific actions the school will undertake to provide the student additional support. Second, most grading period intervals represent 25–50 percent of the grading term. In that time, most struggling students can dig themselves into such a hole that it ends up being their grave.

To respond in a timely way, we recommend that a school identify students for extra help and/or have the ability to modify a student's interventions at least every three weeks. Recommendations to accomplish this goal will be described in the next chapter.

Aligning Interventions to All Characteristics of Effectiveness

To create a toolbox of essential interventions, a school must align each intervention it offers to *all* the essential characteristics of effective interventions: research-based, directive, administered by trained professionals, targeted, and timely. If even one essential characteristic is missing from a particular intervention, the likelihood of the intervention working is compromised. For example, a school could offer a math intervention that is research-based, administered by highly trained professionals, targeted to a specific learning target and cause, and is timely in response—but if the intervention is not directive, some students who need this help will choose not to attend. Or what if a specific reading intervention is research-based, directive, administered by trained professionals, and targeted? If the intervention is not timely, some students won't receive help until they have dropped significantly below grade level. All the effective traits of the intervention are useless to a student whose illness has become terminal by the time the treatment is prescribed.

We find that many schools are not getting the results they desire from their current interventions because their responses are misaligned to at least one of these essential characteristics. On the other hand, when schools evaluate each of their site interventions and align them to these essential characteristics, they can take interventions that are ineffective and make them highly successful. For example, we have visited districts that offer highly successful summer school programs that featured varied targeted offerings, use research-based instructional practices, are directed to specific students, and are taught by highly trained educators. Best of all, realigning the current intervention program to include all these traits usually does not require more money and more resources. Instead, it mostly takes a new way of thinking about interventions and a restructuring of current resources. A powerful activity, the *Intervention Evaluation and Alignment Chart* (page 153 or **go.solution-tree.com/rti**), can assist with this process.

Planning for Tiered Support

When creating a toolbox of intervention, besides aligning each intervention to the characteristics of effective interventions, a school must also consider how it can provide interventions that vary in intensity. Visually, this concept is captured in the tiers that comprise the RTI pyramid.

Tier 2 interventions are considered supplemental or "some" help. To use a medical analogy, sometimes a child gets an earache. If left unattended, this condition could become much more serious. But with some help from the right antibiotic, the child can be good as new in no time. In the medical field, this is a Tier 2 intervention. Likewise, at every school there are kids who need a little extra support to succeed in school. The "antibiotic" for one student may be a small-group tutoring opportunity with the teacher; for another, it could be a mandatory study hall to make up an assignment that was not completed; for another, it could be a targeted reward for demonstrating positive behavior in class. The key criterion is that it is "some" help beyond what is provided for all students in Tier 1 core instruction.

Whereas Tier 2 is "some" help, Tier 3 is "a lot" of help. To refer back to our medical analogy, students in need of Tier 3 help do not have an earache—they are hemorrhaging. Subsequently, providing an antibiotic will not be nearly enough to cure their condition; they need intensive care. Similarly, some students will need a lot of help to succeed at school. For some students, intensive help can be an intensive reading support class. For another student, it can be a daily study-skills class that helps the student organize and complete his homework, or a two-period math class that provides the student both access to grade-level curriculum and targeted remediation in prerequisite skills.

There are five characteristics that can define an intervention as more intensive:

1. **Frequency.** The more often a child receives a particular support, the more intensive the intervention.

2. **Duration.** The more time a student spends receiving a particular support, the more intensive the intervention.

3. **Ratio.** The smaller the teacher-to-student ratio, the more intensive the intervention.

4. **Targeting.** The more aligned a particular support is with the individual needs of a specific student, the more intensive the intervention.

5. **Training.** The more highly trained the staff member is in the student's area of need, the more intensive the intervention.

People often ask, "How long does a student remain in Tier 2?" The answer we offer is, again, that Tier 2 is "some" help. Tier 2 can be a single tutoring session, just as one doctor's visit can address some illnesses. In other cases, Tier 2 could take weeks, just as a person may wear a cast for weeks to heal a broken bone. Likewise, Tier 3 is "a lot" of help. A patient suffering from a ruptured appendix may be rushed into surgery, receiving extremely intensive medical care. If the surgery is successful, the patient is usually discharged from the hospital within days, and fully healed within a few weeks. Conversely, a patient requiring extensive knee surgery may need months of intensive physical rehabilitation to fully heal. Both conditions require intensive medical treatment, yet the length of time at this level of treatment will vary by the illness and by the patient's response to the treatment. Learning interventions are no different. We are concerned about schools or districts that set predetermined amounts of time to any tier in the RTI process. This approach is usually instituted when RTI is viewed as a way to qualify students for special education, with rigid protocols, paperwork, and timelines dictating the process to justify special education identification.

Considering our more liberal definitions of each tier as being "some" or "a lot" of help, one might wonder why we need tiers at all. Tiers in the RTI process are not intended to be a destination, a label, or a hoop to jump through to qualify a child for special education; they are to guide our thinking. A school's efforts to ensure that all students learn at high levels start with all students having access to grade-level curriculum and quality initial instruction—this is Tier 1. No matter how well a school differentiates core instruction, some students will need supplemental help after initial teaching—this is Tier 2. Other students will enter grade-level instruction with significant gaps in foundational skills and/or severe obstacles related to effort, attendance, and/or behavior. These students will need a lot of help to succeed—this is Tier 3.

It takes all three levels—all three ways of thinking—to meet the needs of all children. How this thinking is transformed into practice can and should look different from school to school, as the needs of each school are unique, the resources are different, and the strengths of each faculty vary. But the guiding principles are the same.

Making Time for Interventions

In addition to building a toolbox of effective, increasingly intensive interventions, a school must also create time during the school day for students to receive this help. Many schools try to find the time by extending the school day for interventions, offering extra help before school, at lunch, and after school. Unfortunately, this option has some inherent drawbacks. Most schools cannot require a student to come early or stay late, especially if the child is dependent on school transportation, must work to support the family, and/or is needed at home to help tend to younger siblings. Also, before- and after-school interventions usually extend beyond teacher contract hours, which in turn requires additional site funds to pay teachers a stipend for this work. When these funds are not available, schools often use less expensive options such as volunteers or classified staff to monitor the extended day programs. While volunteers and support staff can be helpful for some types of interventions, they often do not know the school's core curriculum, do not have access to the assessment data for each child, and do not possess the credentials or training to be highly effective in the areas they are tutoring.

This is not to suggest that all before- and after-school intervention programs are ineffective, but whatever a school offers during these times must also be offered during the school day for students who cannot come early or stay late. Ultimately, for interventions to work best, they must be offered during a time when teachers are paid to be there and students are required to be there.

Flexible Intervention Time at the Elementary Level

Creating flexible time at the elementary level is easier, as there is more flexibility in the master schedule, and a grade-level team can often alter its teaching schedule without affecting the other grades. Following are two suggestions for creating and using flexible time during the school day.

1. **Scheduled flex time.** At the start of each year, most grade-level teams sketch out a weekly plan for teaching the required subjects, "specials" times, recess, and lunch. The plan might look something like figure 6.1.

	Monday	Tuesday	Wednesday	Thursday	Friday
8:00–8:15	Calendar Time	Calendar Time	Calendar Time	Calendar Time	Calendar Time
8:15–10:00	Language Arts	Language Arts	Language Arts	Language Arts	Language Arts
10:00–10:20	Recess	Recess	Recess	Recess	Recess
10:20–11:45	Mathematics	Mathematics	Mathematics	Mathematics	Mathematics
11:45–12:30	Lunch/Recess	Lunch/Recess	Lunch/Recess	Lunch/Recess	Lunch/Recess
12:30–1:30	Science	Specials	Science	Specials	Health
1:30–2:45	Writers Workshop	Social Studies	Writers Workshop	Social Studies	Writers Workshop
2:45	Dismissal	Dismissal	Dismissal	Dismissal	Dismissal

Figure 6.1: Sample elementary schedule.

To create flexible time, the team can schedule intervention time into the weekly plan, as shown in figure 6.2 (page 144). While the way they use the time each week may vary, they have set the time aside to ensure that interventions can be provided without students missing new core instruction.

Some schools have taken this idea one step further and have scheduled flexible time across grade levels. For example, the primary grades (K–2) may schedule flexible time from 11:00 to 11:45. Instead of regrouping students based on age, they can be grouped by need. For example, there could be a second-grade student still struggling with subtracting single-digit numbers—a skill taught in first grade. This skill was recently taught as part of core instruction in first grade, and there are some first-grade students who need extra help on the same skill. Finally, a handful of kindergartners may have entered the school year already able to add single-digit numbers and are ready to learn subtraction. The prior skill for the second-grader, the core skill for the first-grader, and the enrichment skill for the kindergartner are all the same skill. Why have three different flexible groups, one at each grade level, all teaching the same skill?

2. **Push-in time.** Similar to the scheduled flex time, each grade level has been assigned a daily intervention/enrichment block of time. During this time, schoolwide resources "push into" this grade level, providing additional resources to target student needs. The push-in team may include special education staff, specialists, instructional aides, and administrators. These additional resources make it possible to provide greater differentiation during this flex time.

There is no one best way to create flexible time at the elementary level; we have seen many successful hybrids of these two approaches. The key in every case is that the school realized that all kids don't learn at the same speed. Making time a variable in the master schedule is required if a school wants all students to learn.

Flexible Intervention Time at the Secondary Level

At the secondary level, there are more obstacles to creating flexible time during the school day. It is difficult for a department or a grade level to create flexible time without affecting the entire school. Whereas a fourth-grade team can change the teaching schedule on any given day with minimal impact on the other grades, a secondary science department cannot decide to shorten classes on Fridays and create a flexible block of time to regroup and reteach kids who need extra help.

For this reason, secondary schools must create flexible time in the school's master schedule. This can usually be accomplished by shaving a couple of minutes off each class period and capturing minutes from transition times. By pooling these minutes together, the school can insert a flexible period of time in the master schedule for interventions and enrichment (visit **go.solution-tree.com/rti** for examples of schedules).

We want to caution secondary schools against one approach. We have seen many secondary schools create a tutorial period in their master schedules, but reap limited

	Monday	Tuesday	Wednesday	Thursday	Friday
	8:00–8:15 Calendar Time	8:00–8:15 Calendar Time	8:00–8:15 Calendar Time	8:00–8:15 Calendar Time	8:00–8:15 Calendar Time
	8:15–10:00 Language Arts	8:15–10:00 Language Arts	8:15–10:00 Language Arts	8:15–10:00 Language Arts	8:15–10:00 Language Arts
	10:00–10:20 Recess	10:00–10:20 Recess	10:00–10:20 Recess	10:00–10:20 Recess	10:00–10:20 Recess
	10:20–11:45 Mathematics	10:20–11:45 Mathematics	10:20–11:45 Mathematics	10:20–11:45 Mathematics	10:20–11:45 Mathematics
	11:45–12:30 Lunch/Recess	11:45–12:30 Lunch/Recess	11:45–12:30 Lunch/Recess	11:45–12:30 Lunch/Recess	11:45–12:30 Lunch/Recess
	12:30–1:15 Science	12:30–1:30 Specials	12:30–1:15 Science	12:30–1:30 Specials	12:30–1:15 Health
	1:15–2:15 Writers Workshop	1:30–2:45 Social Studies	1:15–2:15 Writers Workshop	1:30–2:45 Social Studies	1:15–2:15 Writers Workshop
	2:15–2:45 Flex Time		2:15–2:45 Flex Time		2:15–2:45 Flex Time
	2:45 Dismissal	2:45 Dismissal	2:45 Dismissal	2:45 Dismissal	2:45 Dismissal

Figure 6.2: Sample elementary schedule with intervention time.

results because they did not align this intervention time with the essential characteristics of an effective intervention. Like any intervention, tutorial periods can only be effective when they are research-based, directive, administered by trained professionals, timely, and targeted. For example, some schools create a mentor or tutorial period by either assigning students to a homeroom or extending a particular period (such as fifth period). In this structure, the student is supposed to get help from the homeroom or extended period teacher. But what if the student needs help in calculus AB, and the mentor or tutor is an art teacher? This hardly meets the criteria of interventions being taught by a highly trained professional in the child's area of need. Creating intervention time is challenging enough; be sure to use that time effectively.

Because creating flexible time at the secondary level requires revising the master schedule, it often takes staff consensus to create this level of change. At too many secondary schools, changing the master schedule is akin to reversing the rotation of the earth. We are starting to believe that when Moses came down from Mount Sinai, he brought more than the Ten Commandments—he also brought down the high school master schedule. The way many secondary educators fight to keep the master schedule unaltered, you would think God created it. We hear a multitude of excuses regarding why creating an intervention period during the school day is impossible:

- **It will take away from class time.** Creating a tutorial period for interventions is not losing instructional time—it is restructuring it. At most schools, a thirty-minute tutorial period for interventions can be created by shortening each class period only a few minutes per period. What can a teacher do with five minutes in class to reteach the students in need of additional help? Almost nothing. Conversely, what can a teacher do in thirty or forty minutes to help a targeted group of students? A lot!

- **It is not fair to the "advanced" kids.** Flexible time can be used for not only remediation and reteaching, but also for enrichment and extended learning. This flexible time can be used to help students in AP calculus as well as algebra I. At many high schools, when a student struggles in honors, advanced placement, and/or international baccalaureate curriculum, the approach of the school is not to provide extra help, but to assume that the child is not capable and remove her from the more rigorous coursework. We know that all students do not learn the same way or at the same speed; this universal truth applies to students in advanced physics just as it does a student in grade-level curriculum. For this reason, flexible time should not come at the cost of any student, as the very purpose of the time is to meet the individual needs of each child.

- **It is extra work for the teachers.** We cannot think of harder working professionals than teachers. At every campus, most faculty members work beyond their contract day for their students. They come early, stay late, and give up lunch to help kids. In reality, they *have* to do this, because there is rarely time designated in a teacher contract day to work with individual students. When a school creates flexible time during the teachers' contract day, it makes it possible for them to meet with individual kids without having to sacrifice their personal time.

As Rick and Becky DuFour state, "A school's schedule should be a tool to further priorities rather than an impediment to change. Your schedule is not a sacred document" (DuFour & DuFour, 2010, p. 6). Our traditional master schedule was perfect— to prepare kids for being adults in 1950 when the goal was teaching and not learning for all. Our world has changed. The question for every secondary school should not be, *Should* we build flexible time into our master schedule? Instead, the question must be, *How* will we build flexible time into our master schedule?

It is critical that teacher teams have ownership of the time. They should be the primary voice in how the time is used each week, which students are targeted, and what learning outcomes should be addressed.

Interventions and Behavior Systems

As we wrote in the preface, RTI's underlining premise is that schools should not delay providing help for struggling students until they fall far enough behind to qualify for special education, but instead should provide timely, targeted, systematic interventions to *all* students who demonstrate the need. This same thinking should be applied to behavior.

In chapter 4, we introduced the critical steps that the intervention team takes to design a system of concentrated instruction for behavior. We described that the team clearly identifies expectations and desired behaviors and the importance of explicitly teaching the desired behaviors. Chapter 5 identified how the team creates an efficient system for monitoring behavior; interventions that address both positive and negative reinforcement and remediation are addressed in this chapter.

We have introduced the critical steps that the school leadership team will oversee when organizing a system of behavioral supports. First, behavior is clearly defined as a responsibility of the school leadership team. Next, the team clearly identifies expectations and desired behaviors. Students are explicitly taught the desired behaviors, and the team creates an efficient system for monitoring behavior.

The most critical thing to understand about interventions for behavior is that in this area, we must think of our response as *support* instead of intervention. When trying to change behavior, the most effective approach is not intervening with negative behavior, but rather *reinforcing positive behavior*. Positive reinforcement and corrective, frequent, explicit feedback are how we change unwanted behaviors.

We have also argued earlier that misbehaviors have specific causes or antecedents. Supports must be tied to these causes. Some behaviors spring from lack of self-regulatory skills (in time management, organization, note taking, goal setting, and self-motivation). Other inappropriate behaviors, however, may spring from socioemotional challenges the student is facing in and out of school. Punishing a student, or even prescribing supports to ameliorate the frequency of a student's misbehavior, without also considering these socioemotional antecedents is unfair, unwise, and inefficient. Don't misunderstand—students must behave in a manner commensurate with the school's high expectations; however, when misbehavior stems from socioemotional challenges, the school will best serve the student's needs by leveraging all school-based and community-based resources to assist in these critical areas. Counselors, social workers, and psychologists are members of the schoolwide intervention team and will be invaluable in helping students in the socioemotional domains.

Finally, we must always remember that behavior and academic success are inextricably intertwined. This is particularly true for students who exhibit challenging behaviors. Remember, an often-overlooked antecedent to poor behavior is academic failure. It's rare to find a student exhibiting behavioral changes who has not also experienced academic failure at some point in the past. While supporting the student's behavioral issue, take the time to investigate if academic difficulties exist as well. Helping students experience success, whether behavioral or academic, gives hope and can be the antidote to frustration and poor choices.

Academic Misbehaviors

For academic misbehaviors resulting from lack of self-regulatory skills, reinforcement of instruction on those skills is often necessary. The schoolwide team should assume primary responsibility for ensuring that students who lack knowledge of the rules of school receive the supports they need, whether these supports are provided by classroom teachers or through supplemental supports. For example, students for whom motivation is an area of need would benefit from learning techniques for self-discipline, such as breaking larger assignments into smaller chunks or setting short-term goals for larger tasks, and rewarding themselves with a small prize upon completing a small chunk or meeting a short-term goal. The schoolwide team would coordinate and support students' teachers in providing these supports and would help monitor students' progress.

When determining specific interventions for students with chronic absence problems, it is vital to remember that absence from school is only a symptom of a larger problem. Students miss school for a wide variety of reasons, and the reason for each student must be identified; just as in academic RTI, the intervention must be targeted to a specific cause. The solutions for a student missing school due to medical issues will look different from those for a student who is afraid to go to school due to peer bullying. Curing the root problem will eliminate the symptom of absenteeism.

When attendance issues arise, experience tells us that there are three steps that will help. The schoolwide intervention team can determine who is the appropriate school representative to meet with the family and do the following:

1. Communicate how valued the child is at school and how important daily attendance is to success.

2. Ask, "How can we help?" (The answers are often informational, not practical, in nature).

3. Agree upon an attendance incentive plan. Too often the solution many schools take toward absenteeism is to create "attendance contracts" that outline the punitive steps that will be taken by the school if the problem persists. For a student who already does not want to come to school, and parents who do not feel welcome or connected to the school, it is unlikely that a list of negative consequences will improve these conditions. Instead, it is best if a designated member of the office staff (most commonly, the

principal, assistant principal, and/or counselor), the parent(s), and the student sit together and clearly state the positive consequences that come from regular attendance, planning for short-term and long-terms "wins" for the child as his or her attendance improves. Incentives are limited in their effectiveness, however, if the correct cause of absenteeism has not been identified.

Be prepared to offer supports. Sometimes students do not attend school because there is a challenge contributing to their poor attendance, and in many cases their parents are sympathetic regarding the challenge. Whether academic frustration or socioemotional crises, there may be antecedents to poor attendance to which the school can and should respond. Be prepared to take action.

Social Misbehaviors

Perhaps no challenge within schools frustrates adults more than social misbehavior such as acting out. The reactive, hesitant ways in which adults often respond are deflating and disempowering. Administrators and teachers typically select interventions that produce the most immediate relief, even if the relief is short term.

We have often convinced ourselves that some students are inherently bad and that punishments and negative consequences will lead to more appropriate behaviors. This has resulted in environments of control in which adversarial relationships between adults and students have perversely increased antisocial behaviors while relegating accountability for improved climates beyond the classroom: to the main office or to the home. Our "get-tough" policies—such as suspension, expulsion, and increased security—seem to perpetuate the cycle of acting out, punishment, acting out, while further compromising the relationships between students and adults at schools. As a result, adult–student relationships deteriorate, the connections between academic and behavioral success disintegrate, and the motivation and joy of both adults and students at schools decline.

There is another, better way. A first step is recognizing that student misbehavior stems from two primary impulses: to avoid a task or situation, or to gain attention from adults or peers (Kohn, 1996). The science of behavior has taught us that students are not born "bad." They require regular and frequent feedback on their actions from adults, because without it, they will receive feedback from others that can shape undesired behaviors. Students do not learn best when corrected with negative consequences and reinforcement, but when corrected through positive feedback. They learn behavior best, as they do many other skills, when taught explicitly and directly (Van Veer, 2005).

In chapter 5 we introduced the *Behavioral Analysis Protocol* (page 121), which can help teachers and teams make more informed decisions in their efforts to improve student behavior. One of the positive outcomes of these analyses is that teachers and other staff can learn to recognize when students are about to have an episode of misbehavior. Instead of missing these signs, or unintentionally aggravating the situation, staff can make precorrections. One effective and respectful way of accomplishing this is to design behavior precorrection cards that are discreetly placed on a student's desk, with messages such as "Ensure that you are on task" or "Take a second to breathe—try not to become frustrated." At times, schools may determine that they need to reteach important skills that students have not yet internalized. Counselors, administrators, or teaching staff can provide structured intervention to students during recesses, lunch, or during an elective period using curricula designed for this purpose. Schools can also start by reteaching the lessons that were developed for the demonstration day at the beginning of the year as mentioned earlier in this section.

An essential element of a system of behavioral interventions is the explicit acknowledgment of positive behaviors. This reinforcement and support, particularly for students who struggle with behavior, is more effective than punishment in "intervening" to change behavior.

All staff must commit to acknowledging students when they meet the expectations that have been set. The most powerful form of acknowledgment is sincere verbal praise. However, schools will be most successful when tangible rewards are also identified. Our recommendation is to distribute simple paper slips or "incentive cards" to students when they demonstrate positive behavior. Aside from the cost of the paper and copying, we recommend that schools spend very little or no money on rewards. Our experience is that creativity is more motivating than high-priced prizes. Here are a few examples, most of which will work across all grade levels:

- Many organizations will donate used books to schools. Allow students to select a book when they accumulate twenty-five incentive cards.
- Ask students to turn in their incentive cards to the office, and conduct weekly drawings with winners receiving "front-of-the-lunch-line" passes.
- Allow students to "purchase" preferential parking spots every month at the cost of twenty-five incentive cards.
- Ask staff members to "sell" prizes, such as dance lessons, lunch with the teacher, guitar lessons, or other fun and easy prizes, for a certain number of incentive cards.

At the secondary level, staff sometimes have a more difficult time imagining rewards that will motivate older students. One strategy may be to view as a privilege what in the past may have been viewed as a right. For example, eating lunch anywhere around campus may have been viewed as a right in the past. Now, it's a privilege. Students may eat anywhere they like *if* they accumulate ten incentive cards a week, but must otherwise sit at the lunch tables in the cafeteria.

The distribution of rewards must be easy and routine. All staff members must participate, and it must be easy for them to do so. Some educators worry that rewards are dangerous. To be clear, we are not advocating either paying students or rewarding them for achieving good grades. We are advocating that free or extremely low-cost rewards be identified to tangibly acknowledge positive behaviors. A study of literature on rewards and positive reinforcement reveals that rewards are not inherently negative and that objections to rewards are unfounded. In fact, research has consistently determined that rewards are a core feature of building a positive school culture (Cameron, Banko, & Pierce, 2001; Cameron & Pierce, 1994, 2002). While rewards can be used badly—typically when the student and not the behavior is rewarded—research has not proven that rewards in and of themselves inhibit intrinsic motivation.

The burning question for most schools concerned about school climate and their students' behaviors is what to do when students misbehave. When completed systemically, collaboratively, and consistently, the systems of behavioral supports overseen by the school leadership team will significantly reduce social misbehaviors. Nonetheless, some students will need additional support beyond all that has been described.

Schools must develop a continuum of supports in order to successfully manage the behavior of all students. When students have a difficult time behaving, despite a well-defined and consistently applied behavioral support system, our next response should be helping the student monitor his or her own behavior by providing clear and frequent feedback. This can best be done through a Check-In/Check-Out (CICO) system. These systems serve many purposes. They are effective data-gathering tools that reveal patterns of behavior. They are effective communication tools: from teacher to teacher, from teacher to administrator, and from school to home. Perhaps most importantly, they make transparent to students the success—or lack of success—they are experiencing and help them self-regulate.

Suppose, for example, the identified goal is for a student to be on task without being reminded more than twice in a class period. At the beginning of the class, the teacher and student "check in," and the teacher reminds the student of the goal. Both teacher and student track, during the class, how many times the student has to be reminded. At the end of the class, they "check out" and compare notes on how the student did. AIMSweb has a whole section devoted to this topic, and SWIS has a tab for it as well, but simpler, less expensive systems will work, too.

The goal should never be to invent new ways of punishing students. Yet if you determine that you have run out of ideas at your site, talk to colleagues at other schools and at the central office, and take advantage of school psychologists. They often have specialized training in the area of behavior and can be invaluable in support of students at risk.

Behavior interventions start with a well-designed, well-executed Tier 1, just as academic interventions do. When schools make improving behaviors a priority and follow steps such as those provided here, students will respond. *Concentrating, Screening, and Planning for Behavioral Supports* (page 155 and **go.solution-tree.com**/rti) will help a school leadership team and/or school behavior team plan an effective system for Tier 1, 2, and 3 behavior supports.

Start with building the climate through making commitments to collective responsibility. The behavior of adults is a critical factor in improving the behavior of students. Students can tell when adults at school care for their welfare. Ensure that the adults on your campuses are communicating with a caring attitude. Strive to establish connections with all students, particularly students who are experiencing difficulty with their behavior. Be proactive. We usually know from past years which students may have a difficult time with behavior. Take steps to ensure that the school year begins successfully for these students. Student behavior improves when the adults act consistently and systematically toward all students. Then concentrate instruction by helping students self-monitor and self-regulate their behaviors. Ensure that information is available through convergent assessments to continuously inform and improve the process. Then make certain that all students have access to the levels of support they need to be highly successful.

District Responsibilities for Interventions

Rather than dictate which interventions a school may or may not purchase or use, the central office should focus on building the capacity of school personnel to make increasingly informed decisions about what will best serve the needs of its students.

District leadership often creates a specialized new role such as "RTI Coordinator" or "Intervention Specialist" to support the implementation of RTI in schools. In all too many cases, the district's effort usually stops there; typically, little attention is paid to the learning demands on individuals assuming these new roles, or their need for support and conferred authority from district administrators. Instead, these individuals are expected to transmit particular kinds of knowledge and skills about intervention to school personnel without truly having the knowledge base to help schools make these kinds of important decisions.

Instead, district leaders should create a series of resources and trainings to empower both school site personnel and those holding these new kinds of positions to make better informed decisions about intervention programs, intervention strategies, universal screening, and progress monitoring tools. This type of systemwide capacity is typically built through partnering with a local intermediary organization or university that has a track record for high-quality training and development. A local "learning system" brings together both school- and research-based knowledge of effective practice and provides teachers and school leaders with access to skilled professionals within and outside the system, enabling them to build their own toolbox of resources.

Earlier in this chapter, we identified creating flexible time in the school day for intervention and enrichment as a critical consideration of RTI. District leadership can do a great deal to either support schools in their quest to find and then provide this time to students, or undermine and even sabotage their efforts. District leadership can inadvertently work against school efforts to find time when they place too great an emphasis on strict adherence to the district-developed pacing guide. This allows skeptics to claim that it is impossible to create flexible time for interventions and enrichment because "I can't possibly cover all the material required by the district."

Another way in which we have seen district leadership undermine school efforts to provide this kind of flexible time is by failing to realize that these minutes *are* instructional minutes. In fact, we would argue that these minutes, if used according to the characteristics identified earlier in this chapter, may be the very best instructional minutes a school might provide. Many states have regulations requiring a certain number of instructional minutes for each student, each year. Why would district leadership take the position that highly targeted, timely, research-based interventions administered by highly trained individuals do not represent instruction? Does instruction only occur when a teacher is standing in the front of the room engaging in whole-group instruction?

Finally, district leadership provides a powerful model when its general and special education administrators provide a common, united voice to schools, reinforcing the blended model of "just ed" that we promote in our work.

Armed with effective interventions and time designated during the school day to provide this additional support to students in need, a school has the building blocks of an effective system of interventions. What is still lacking is the ability to guarantee that every student who needs help will receive it. Without this level of certainty, a school cannot achieve its mission of high levels of learning for every child. This is the goal of certain access, which is the focus of our final chapter.

Activities and Tools Summary

Does your school have effective interventions?

See the *Intervention Evaluation and Alignment Chart* (page 153).

Does your school have a plan for a schoolwide system of behavior support?

See *Concentrating, Screening, and Planning for Behavior Supports* (page 155).

Visit **go.solution-tree.com/rti** *to download these activities.*

Intervention Evaluation and Alignment Chart

	Targeted										
	Unmotivated or Failed Learner?	Tier 2 or Tier 3?	Desired Student Learning Outcome?								
	U or F	2 or 3									

Current Site Interventions	Research-Based	Directive	Timely	Highly Trained	Systematic	Alignment Steps					

+ = Intervention is highly aligned.
✓ = Intervention is somewhat aligned.
X = Intervention is not aligned.

Simplifying Response to Intervention © 2012 Solution Tree Press • solution-tree.com
Visit **go.solution-tree.com/rti** to download this page.

Effective Intervention Evaluation and Alignment Chart Protocol

This activity can be used by a leadership team and/or intervention team to evaluate schoolwide interventions, or by a teacher team to evaluate teacher-led interventions. It is recommended that this activity is completed twice a year—prior to the start of the school year, and at the midpoint of each school year.

Guiding Questions

1. **Research-Based:** Do we have evidence that the intervention can work? Do we have evidence that the intervention is working for students currently in the intervention? Score with a + , ✓, or X.

2. **Directive:** Do we require targeted students to attend? Do we hold students accountable when they don't? Score with a + , ✓, or X.

3. **Timely:** How long does it take us to identify and place a student in or out of this intervention? (Goal: At least every three weeks during the school year.) Score with a + , ✓, or X.

4. **Highly Trained:** How well trained and qualified are the individuals implementing this intervention? Score with a + , ✓, or X.

5. **Systematic:** Can we guarantee that every student who needs this intervention, gets this intervention? Score with a + , ✓, or X.

6. **Targeted—Unmotivated Learner/Failed Learner:** Is the intervention for intentional nonlearners (won't do) or failed learners (can't do)? Have we mistakenly placed nonlearners and failed learners in the same intervention? Score with a U for unmotivated learner (won't do) or an F for failed learner (can't do).

7. **Targeted—Tier 2 or Tier 3:** Is the intervention supplemental support (Tier 2) or intensive support (Tier 3)? Score with a "2" for Tier 2 or a "3" for Tier 3.

8. **Targeted—Desired Student Learning Outcome:**
   + Are our interventions targeted to specific standards/outcomes?
   + Are students grouped by the cause of their struggles, or the symptoms?

9. **Alignment Steps:** What actions can be taken to address any column with an "X" on the chart?

10. **The Big Picture:** Look at the list of interventions as a whole. Are there a variety and balance of offerings? For example, are there interventions targeted to both unmotivated and failed learners? Is support offered to both of these groups at Tier 2 and Tier 3?

Concentrating, Screening, and Planning for Behavioral Supports

Steps to Planning	Notes	Actions
1. Explicitly define desired student behaviors and commit to consistently teaching and reinforcing: • Academic behaviors (self-regulatory) • Social behaviors (self-monitoring)		
2. Screen for behavior problems: • Academic behaviors (Self-Regulatory Assessment Tool) • Social behaviors (Student Risk Screening Scale [SRSS])		
3. Develop a Behavior Documentation Form (BDF). • Align BDFs with the School-Wide Information System (SWIS) or the school's student information system.		
4. Screen and monitor attendance. • Review attendance records to identify students with high absentee rates.		
5. Clearly define behavior as a responsibility of the schoolwide team, with input from: • Staff members concerned about student behavior • Experts and novices among staff • Students and parents		
6. Identify expectations and desired behaviors. • Identify key student behaviors, phrased positively. • Identify key settings around campus in which key student behaviors will be explicitly described.		

Simplifying Response to Intervention © 2012 Solution Tree Press • solution-tree.com
Visit **go.solution-tree.com/rti** to download this page.

Steps to Planning	Notes	Actions
7. Teach desired behaviors. • Explicitly, consistently, and repeatedly teach, reinforce, and reteach the behaviors identified in step 6. • Be prepared to reteach after breaks and at the beginning of each school year.		
8. Create a system for monitoring behavior. • Create a BDF. • Build consensus, and communicate how behavioral infractions will be processed.		
9. Identify rewards. • Build consensus and consistently reinforce positive behaviors using agreed-upon tokens. • Strive for a 5-to-1 ratio of positive-to-negative interactions with students.		
10. Identify supports for at-risk students. • Initiate Check-In/Check-Out (CICO) procedures consistently across the school for at-risk students. • Build time into the instructional day for students to receive supplemental support and reteaching in diagnosed areas of behavioral need. • Leverage counseling supports (psychologists, counselors, social workers) from within the school and from the broader community. • Consider providing an adult or student mentor, assigning community service, providing social skills intervention, or creating and utilizing a behavior contract.		

Steps to Planning	Notes	Actions
11. Analyze data, monitor, and adjust. • At least monthly, gather and analyze data on the behavioral infractions of students around campus. • Identify when, where, and what behavioral infractions appear to be most common. • Identify if there are students (groups or individuals) or staff who may need additional support. • Be prepared to reallocate resources if data indicate the need.		

CHAPTER 7

Certain Access: How Do We Get Every Child There?

Certain access: *A systematic process that guarantees every student will receive the time and support needed to learn at high levels. Thinking is guided by the question, How do we get every child there?*

A school can have noble intentions, a collaborative culture, a clear and viable curriculum, effective instructional practices, targeted interventions, and timely assessment processes, but if it does not implement them *systematically*, then these best practices will be meaningless for students who struggle after core instruction. The purpose of RTI is to ensure that *every* child receives time and support to learn at high levels.

Certain access is how a school demonstrates its belief that all kids can learn—it is where the rubber hits the road! Collective responsibility creates the culture and structures of collaboration necessary to ensure that all students succeed. Concentrated instruction defines with laser-like focus what all students must learn, and convergent assessment guides instruction, evaluates teaching effectiveness, and identifies specifically which students are struggling and where they need help. Certain access is how we provide every child the time and support needed to achieve.

Certain is defined as *sure to happen; inevitable.* A school that has a truly systematic process for meeting the needs of every child can confidently tell any parent whose child attends the school, "It does not matter what teacher your child has; we guarantee that your child will receive the time and support needed to learn at high levels." The superintendent of a certain-access district can promise parents, "It does not matter which school your children attend in our district, or which teachers they have. We guarantee your children will receive the time and support needed to achieve." If schools and districts cannot provide this assurance, then what they most likely offer is an educational lottery system.

Random Access

Tragically, very few schools currently have the processes in place to ensure that every student receives the time and support to meet his or her individual needs. In reality, student success at most schools is more commonly determined by luck, economics, and/or parental influence. Consider for a moment how most children's educational programs are determined each year:

- **Pink and blue cards.** At many elementary schools, a yearly ritual determines each child's best chance to learn for the next school year; we call it "The Dance of the Pink and Blue Cards." Each spring, every teacher completes a data card on each student, usually a pink card for each girl and a blue card for each boy. Then, each grade-level team meets and groups the cards into classes. The goal is to create class rosters for the next year, with the hope of making the classes balanced and fair for the next year's teachers. Consideration is most often given to balancing the number of boys and girls (hence the "pink" and "blue" colors), problem behaviors, student ability, and special needs in each class. Far less attention is given to which teachers will best match the unique needs of each student. When the stacks are complete, the principal collects them and then determines which teacher will be assigned each group of cards.

  We are not suggesting that pink and blue cards have no value, as their information can be very helpful when placing students in classes. The problem is that at many schools this is *the* most influential step in determining each student's success. Although this process can be described as *systematic*, it is not designed to meet the needs of individual students.

- **Computerized class assignments.** At the secondary level, the process to determine student class assignments is even more random; instead of teacher sorting, computer logic statements and random distribution make the determination. Each summer, school administrators create a master schedule of classes, deciding when each class will be offered and who will teach each class. These course parameters are entered into the school's student data management software, along with the course selection requests for each student. After all the information is entered, the administrators cross their fingers and press *Run*. The computer then begins to randomly place students into classes. Obviously, the computer is not programmed to consider which sequence of teachers would best meet the individual learning needs of each student, but instead is programmed to sort within the criteria of course title, available sections, and class balance. Often it takes more than one run before the schedule is locked and individual student schedule cards can be printed for the first day of school. An individual student's schedule can change radically each time the schedule is run.

  The use of computer software to assist with student scheduling is not inherently detrimental to student success, and it is unrealistic to think that a comprehensive high school will hand-schedule every student. The problem is that at many schools this is the *only* factor determining each student's placement. Like the elementary "dance," this certainly cannot be viewed as a process that is likely to meet the unique needs of each child, especially those most at risk.

- **Ability grouping.** Many schools determine student class placement based on each child's perceived ability to achieve. The criteria and assessments used to determine each child's proper level vary greatly, from gifted testing, placement exams, universal screening, teacher recommendations, grade point averages, and/or state test scores. While the measurement tools may vary, the purpose is the same: to determine each child's prior knowledge and ability to learn, then to place each child into the "proper" program to meet his or her ability. At most schools, the highest-scoring students are placed in the highest track, often referred to as *gifted, accelerated, honors,* or *advanced placement.* Students scoring in the average range are placed in large, nondescript courses, often referred to as *regular, general,* or *grade level.* Finally, the students deemed significantly below grade level and lacking the skills and aptitude to learn are placed in below-grade-level coursework, commonly referred to as *basic* or *remedial.*

  Some schools justify this practice as "differentiation" to meet the needs of each child, but in reality it is nothing more than tracking students. As Rick DuFour states, "Research has made it abundantly clear that putting the least capable and least motivated students together in a class with a curriculum that is less challenging and moves at a slower pace increases the achievement gap and is detrimental to students" (DuFour, 2010, p. 23). The only thing tracking is guaranteed to do is keep the high-achieving students high, the average students average, and the low students perpetually behind. Why? The students in the highest track typically have access to more highly trained teachers, more rigorous curriculum, and more enrichment opportunities. Conversely, the students in the lowest track are more likely to have inexperienced teachers, lower learning expectations, below-grade-level curriculum, and fewer chances for enrichment (Oakes, 2005). When the high-track students succeed, it confirms the school's belief that the children are gifted, and when the low-track students fail, it validates the school's determination that the children are incapable and potentially learning disabled. The unavoidable result is that the highest track receives what every child needs to be able to learn at the highest levels—and the lowest track does not. Students who are native English speakers and come from well-educated parents who are economically stable are most likely to be identified for the highest learning tracks. Minority students, English learners, and students from economically disadvantaged families most often fill the rosters of lower tracks. It would be hard to justify this system as an effective way to ensure high levels of learning for all children, and it is in direct contradiction to the four essential guiding principles of RTI.

- **State test results.** Because many schools across North America are singularly focused on improving test scores, they resort to assigning students core instruction based on each child's previous year's test results. Students who scored below proficient are often placed in remedial coursework or double periods of math and language arts, and are often stripped of elective classes and placed in test-focused support classes. This approach is fraught with problems. First, students score below proficient on the state test for different reasons. Some lack the prerequisite skills, some struggle with the new grade-level content, while still others face attendance or behavior issues. If all these students are placed in the same course, a single teacher would have difficulty meeting this wide variety of individual needs. Also, test-focused coursework tends to fall into the trap of trying to cover all the material that might be on the test. Student assessments in these classes often follow the state-testing format, which means the curriculum is predominantly taught at the knowledge and computation level. This approach is in direct conflict with the goals of concentrated instruction.

Considering that the fundamental purpose of RTI is to systematically meet the individual learning needs of each child, it would be hard to imagine processes more misaligned to achieve this goal than the ones described.

Because many parents understand the risks of leaving their child's teacher assignment in a traditional school to chance, they work tirelessly to influence the process. They carefully research the best teachers at each course and/or grade level, and armed with this information, they start lobbying to get their child into the preferred classes months, even years in advance. They volunteer to be room parents to get closer access; they meet with the principal; they may beg, cry, plead, demand, and threaten—whatever it takes. More often than not, it works. In contrast, students who are most at risk are the least likely to have parents who manipulate the system on their behalf.

Ironically, for the majority of educators who have children of their own, this scenario is hardly a surprise. We know the importance of effective teaching for our own child's success, so we do not leave our child's teacher placement to chance. Because we work in the profession, we are far more successful than the average parent at navigating the system for our own child's benefit. If the randomness of the traditional student placement process is not good enough for our own children, then it should not be acceptable for any child.

Certain Access

Only when schools create a tiered, systematic intervention program can the promise of certain access be realized. A systematic response begins with the school's ability to *identify* students who need help. After students are identified, the school must *determine* the right intervention to meet the child's learning needs, and then *monitor* each student's progress to know if the intervention is working. If the evidence demonstrates that the intervention is not meeting the intended outcome for a specific student, the school must *revise* the student's support by providing more intensive and targeted assistance; alternatively, if students reach grade-level expectations, the same flexible time and resources are used to *extend* students to even higher levels of achievement. In the rare instances that core, supplemental, and intensive support do not work for a child, the school must carefully consider if special education identification is justified, appropriate, and necessary to meet the student's needs.

While achieving these outcomes—identify, determine, monitor, revise/extend—for every student may seem daunting, it is possible through the coordinated efforts of the school's collaborative teacher and schoolwide teams. It is said that many hands make light work, and with each team taking lead responsibility for specific areas of student learning and support, meeting the needs of every child can become a reality.

Identify Students Who Need Help

Of the five steps that comprise certain access, there is one step that a school must get right every time: *identify*. The school may not initially determine the best intervention for a student, but the school will realize the mistake as it monitors the student's progress and will subsequently revise the program as needed. This process of determine, monitor, and revise is how RTI gets its name: *response to intervention*. But a school cannot perform any of these steps unless the student is identified in the first place. A system of intervention is useless for any student who slips through the cracks.

How does a school develop a flawless identification process? Three identification processes must be utilized. The first two are assessment-driven processes discussed in detail in chapter 5: universal screening and formative assessments. Universal screening is used to identify students who enter the school year significantly at risk in foundational skills, *before* they begin to fail. Formative assessments that measure student progress on current essential standards are the best way to identify students who enter a subject at grade level but later struggle with new content. Chapter 4 provided specific suggestions on how teams of teachers can plan for common formative assessments during Tier 1 instruction. The key consideration to remember is that formative assessments must be able to identify exactly which students have not mastered specific essential standards. In other words, assessment data must reveal student progress *by the student, by the standard, by the learning target*. This ongoing evidence of student learning in Tier 1 instruction will be critical information for use by teacher teams to systematically identify students in need of additional support. But how do we ensure, without a shadow of a doubt, that we are using this information to ensure certain access?

While universal screening data help identify students significantly weak in foundational skills, and ongoing assessment data measure student proficiency on current grade-level learning goals, we know that children are much more than the sum of their test scores. Beyond objective assessment data, there is subjective information that best comes from the school professionals who work with the students every day. These observational data are vital to identifying students for additional help and determining why each student is struggling. For this reason, the third way a school should identify students for additional support is to create a systematic and timely process for staff to recommend and discuss students who need help.

Practically every school in North America has a process to record teacher input on student progress: student report cards. Unfortunately, our traditional grading practices have numerous drawbacks. One of the worst is the amount of time students are allowed to fail before teacher grades are submitted. Most schools have teachers submit student grades on a quarterly basis. That means one-fourth of the year passes before that information can be used to identify students in need of additional help. How far behind can a student get in nine weeks? In many cases, nine weeks is long enough for a student to dig such a deep hole that it becomes the student's educational grave. In addition, grades rarely give information regarding the reasons the student is struggling. What information can a school gain about a student from a letter grade of F, besides the obvious conclusion that the child is failing? Finally, at most schools, the process by which student grades are determined varies greatly from teacher to teacher. Some teachers place a greater weight on effort, others much less. Some teachers let student behavior influence a student's academic marks, others not. Because of this tremendous variance, it is problematic to use traditional report card practices as the primary way teachers share information to identify students for additional support.

An effective staff recommendation process must be timely. We recommend that teacher input be solicited at least every three to four weeks. Participation from all site educators must be required. If even one teacher is permitted to be excused from the process, then the students who are assigned to this teacher are much less likely to receive additional time and support. Consequently, a school would not be able to tell parents that it does not matter which teacher their child has—because it *would* matter.

The process must be deliberate and systematic. All staff members should start the year knowing when the identification process will take place, how the information will be gathered, and what criteria to use for identifying students in need. Finally, the process must be simple and efficient so as not to require teachers an unreasonable amount of time to participate in the process.

Tier 2 Identification Processes for Smaller Schools

The individuals best qualified to identify a particular student in need of interventions are the teachers and staff members who work most directly with the student. At the elementary level, this is usually the child's classroom teacher, but could also include a grade-level team of teachers if they share students. A school could designate at least one grade-level team meeting each month as their "identification" meeting. All staff members who work with students from the designated grade level would attend the meeting, including administrators, special education teachers, specialists, and other school support staff. Each attending staff member should come prepared to the meeting with:

- A list of students who they believe need additional time and support
- The specific needs and concerns for each student
- Recommendations for potential interventions

Students are recommended and discussed collectively, and appropriate interventions are determined. Simple protocols can be developed to keep the meeting focused and efficient.

There are two vital benefits to having in attendance all the staff members who work with a particular grade level or group of students. First, the school can more effectively problem solve the needs of each student. As every staff member who works with the student is in attendance, the school gets a "360-degree" view of the student's entire school day (see fig. 7.1).

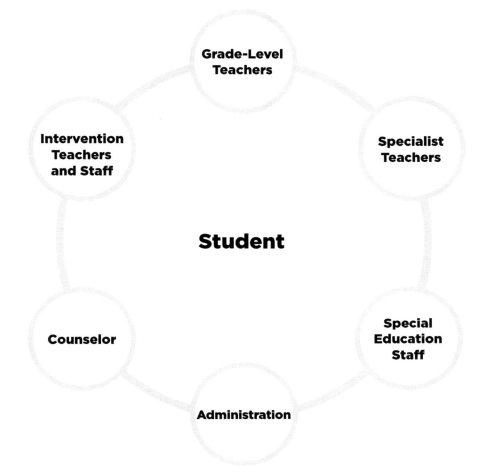

Figure 7.1: A 360-degree view of student learning at Tier 2 at a small school.

So, for example, if there are behavior concerns, the team can determine if the behaviors in question are demonstrated all day (class time, recess, specialist time, and so on), or just in particular settings. Second, because members of the teacher team and the schoolwide team participate, interventions can be coordinated based on whether a student needs support that falls under the lead responsibility of the teacher team and/or interventions led by the schoolwide teams.

This model of Tier 2 identification can also work well for secondary schools in which students are assigned to interdisciplinary teams, where a "village" of teachers shares a particular group of students. Frequent scheduled meetings can be arranged in which the interdisciplinary team, along with other staff professionals who work with this targeted group of students, can meet to identify and discuss students in need of support.

Tier 2 Identification Processes for Larger Schools

While the previous identification process works well for smaller schools, in which a grade-level or interdisciplinary team of teachers shares a specific group of students, this process may not work as well for larger secondary schools. At a large comprehensive high school, there can be hundreds of students at each grade level. It would not be practical to have every staff member who works with the freshman class meet together and discuss the individual needs of every ninth-grader in need of help.

Nevertheless, systematic input from all teachers is critical to the identification process for three reasons. First, if even one teacher is not included in the identification process, then any student assigned to that teacher is much less likely to be identified for interventions, thus violating the goal of certain access. Second, like the small-school identification process, it is best to get a 360-degree view of the child to determine the student's needs and interventions. Collaborative teacher teams at the secondary level are usually formed around shared subjects or courses, so when algebra teachers meet to discuss their students, they will not know if a student who is struggling in algebra is also struggling in any other courses. There is a significant difference between a student failing solely in his or her math class and a student failing in his or her math, language arts, science, and physical education classes. Without a 360-degree view, it is difficult to determine the most appropriate levels of support (see fig. 7.2).

Third, there must be a way for classroom teachers to refer students for interventions led by schoolwide teams. If schoolwide teams are responsible for leading Tier 2 interventions that support students with motivation, attendance, and behavior concerns, there must be a way for classroom teachers to refer students to these types of interventions, as they will know best which students have need for these types of services.

For these reasons, approximately every three weeks, larger schools should have all teachers refer students in need of additional support. The traditional progress-report process, usually done electronically through the school's student data management software, can be used to collect this information, as long as a teacher provides more than a letter grade for each at-risk student and also provides targeted comment codes as to why the student is struggling. For example, a math teacher may refer three students from the first period who are currently failing the class. Along with the letter grade of F, the teacher may add a comment for each student to indicate poor attendance, late or missing work, or low test scores. Administrative and/or counseling staff can serve as intervention coordinators, using this combined student information to get the 360-degree view of each student's needs, meet with the student, determine if schoolwide interventions are needed, and take primary responsibility to ensure that these interventions happen.

Due to the inherent benefits and weaknesses of universal screening, assessment data, and staff recommendations, the key to identifying students for extra help is to not rely solely on just one of these methods, but to use all three. While teacher teams and schoolwide teams take collective responsibility for identifying students for interventions, the teacher teams have the common assessment data and the most accurate observational data, having seen their students in core instruction every day. For these reasons, the process to identify students in need of additional help after Tier 1 instruction is highly dependent on classroom teachers and teacher teams.

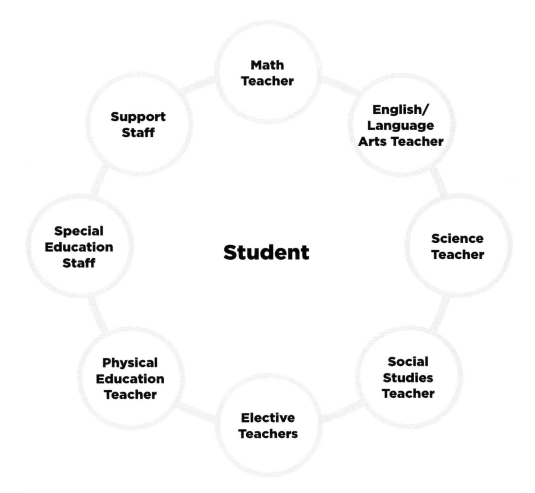

Figure 7.2: A 360-degree view of student learning at Tier 2 at a large school.

Determine Specific Learning Needs and Interventions

After a student is identified for additional time and support, the school must *determine* the specific learning needs of the child, the reason core instruction was not effective, and the most appropriate intervention(s) to address these concerns.

Through our work, we have observed two commonly used approaches for determining interventions for students needing Tier 2 support. In the first approach, when a student begins to struggle, classroom teachers refer the student to the intervention team, which in turn reviews the student's assessment data and determines the appropriate interventions. There are certainly benefits to this approach, as a team can often brainstorm better solutions than an individual teacher. However, this referral process has also negatively reinforced a belief in many general education teachers that they are responsible for only the initial teaching in Tier 1. If students require help after initial teaching, the classroom teacher's response is, Who do I send them to? Especially at schools with a large number of at-risk students, this practice overwhelms the intervention team, site intervention resources, and the RTI process.

In response to this problem, many districts have developed a second approach to determining Tier 2 interventions, in which classroom teachers or teacher teams cannot refer students for schoolwide interventions until they can document the interventions that have been tried in their classroom. This approach places responsibility for the initial response of Tier 2 interventions with classroom teachers. The drawback to this approach is that every student does not struggle for the same reason. The reasons can vary from just needing a little extra practice on a new concept, to lacking necessary prerequisite skills, to requiring assistance with English language, to having severe attendance and behavioral issues. It is unlikely that classroom teachers or teacher teams have all the skills, time, and resources needed to effectively meet every need—making this initial Tier 2 response an impossible responsibility for classroom teachers, failing students and educators alike.

The answer to this dilemma lies not in deciding who is responsible for determining student interventions from Tier 1 to Tier 2, the school's intervention team *or* the classroom teachers. *Both* must be involved. The key is to clearly determine what each group's specific responsibilities are to ensure that all students succeed. This is the purpose of the RTI split pyramid in figure 7.3—to clearly define the intervention responsibilities of teacher teams and schoolwide teams that lead school support resources.

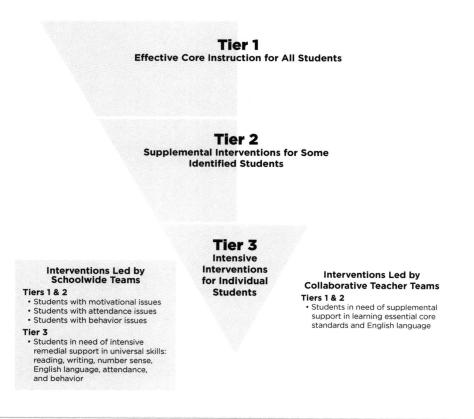

Figure 7.3: The inverted RTI pyramid.

This clarity of responsibility is critical. When only one of these two groups is responsible for determining Tier 2 interventions, the demands are too overwhelming. When "everyone" is responsible for Tier 2 interventions, then "no one" is, unless the buck stops somewhere.

Tier 2 Interventions Led by Collaborative Teacher Teams

Collaborative teacher teams should take the lead in determining interventions for students who have not learned essential core standards and English language. We are not suggesting that it is *solely* the job of teacher teams to ensure that every student learns the essential content, or that other schoolwide resources should not be used to support this team with core instruction, intervention determination, and/or supplemental interventions to support their students in need of help. The point is this: who is going to take the lead? When it comes to students learning essential standards for a particular subject and/or grade level, the teachers who teach that content should be both empowered to design Tier 1 core instruction and lead the school's response when students require additional support.

If a collaborative teacher team should take primary responsibility for delivering effective core instruction of essential standards in Tier 1, as well as for determining the support needed for failed learners in Tier 2, how can a team accomplish this daunting task? This question has already been answered through the previous chapters. Consider for a moment how the previous essential Cs of RTI have created the culture, structure, and focus for a collaborative team of teachers to address this work:

- **Collective responsibility.** The teacher team has consensus that their fundamental mission is to ensure that all students learn at high levels. It is not their job to *teach* their essential standards; it is their responsibility to ensure that all students *learn* them. The team does not view the students as "my kids" and "your kids," but "our kids." To achieve this goal, the school has embedded frequent time in the teachers' professional day for each teacher team to work collaboratively. This process creates the culture and collaborative structure needed for teacher teams to meet their Tier 1 and Tier 2 responsibilities.

- **Concentrated instruction.** It would be virtually impossible for a collaborative team of teachers to accept responsibility for effectively teaching core instruction *and* provide interventions for students who fail to learn if the team is expected to cover the entire state curriculum for their course and/or grade level. To address this concern, each teacher team identifies a limited number of essential standards that will guide their work. With laser-like focus, the team clearly determines the rigor level, prior skills, and common assessments for each standard, as well as a scope and sequence for teaching the curriculum. The team thoroughly unwraps each standard into teacher- and student-friendly learning targets, plans for at least one formative assessment during the unit of study to identify which students are struggling and which instructional practices are proving to be more effective, and purposely designs time in the unit plan for reteaching based on assessment data.

- **Convergent assessment.** To start the year, students are universally screened for the foundational skills needed to succeed in core instruction. Students significantly at risk in these areas receive intensive help supported with schoolwide resources. The team plans formative assessments to guide its preventive support to students weak in specific prior skills needed to learn new grade-level curriculum. Additionally, at least one formative common assessment is administered to monitor student progress during core instruction, evaluate the effectiveness of the core instruction, provide corrective feedback to students, and guide additional support during Tier 1 instruction. At the end of each unit, a common summative assessment is administered to identify students still in need of additional time and support to learn the essential standards.

This continuous, circular, collaborative process is designed to meet the needs of at least 90 percent of students after Tier 1 and Tier 2 instruction, thus enabling teacher teams to take responsibility for this section of the pyramid.

Tier 2 Interventions Led by Schoolwide Teams

As previously discussed, students struggle at school for many reasons, some of which relate to motivation, attendance, and behavior issues. Because the leadership team can best coordinate schoolwide resources to address these areas of need, they are responsible for creating procedures to support students with these issues. Resources may include the school counselor(s), psychologist, speech and language specialist, curricular specialist, instructional aides, and classified support staff. To address these nonacademic areas of need, we make the following suggestions:

- **Motivation.** Collective responsibility must mean that schools take responsibility for academic learning *and* for more "behavioral" aspects of a student's development. Students with motivational issues, also commonly referred to as *intentional nonlearners*, are students who have struggled primarily due to a lack of effort. Motivation is one important aspect of self-regulation, and we have provided information and resources and to address self-regulation in chapter 4.

  Core instruction could and should have been sufficient to meet the child's learning needs—if the student would have applied himself. Intentional non-learners are not usually motivated by grades, nor do they usually understand the long-term consequences of their actions. In response to these challenges, schools must act; a common mistake we see in schools is misdiagnosing failed learners as intentional nonlearners, or intentional nonlearners as failed learners.

  In *Pyramid Response to Intervention*, we detailed numerous interventions to address the needs of students lacking the motivation needed to succeed, including mandatory study hall, homework help sessions, frequent progress reports, study skills support, goal-setting and career exploration programs, and targeted rewards for proper effort. All these solutions rarely require a highly qualified teacher to administer the intervention—what they require are caring, demanding individuals who can hold these students accountable to try. Administrators, instructional aides, campus supervisors, and other school support staff can facilitate these interventions, which in turn allows teachers to focus on what they do best: teach!

The problem many schools face is that they are grouping failed learners and students with motivational issues in the same intervention. This happens when schools target students for interventions based on grades or test scores. If a school requires ten students to attend a language arts intervention because these students are failing their language arts class, it is likely that some of the students are failing the class because they need help understanding the classwork, while others know how to do it, but won't. As the teacher in charge of the intervention begins to tutor a couple of failed learners, what are the unmotivated students likely to do? Probably stop working at the least, and misbehave at the worst. This will require the teacher to stop tutoring and instead stand over the nonlearners to get them to work. This is a lose–lose scenario—the teacher loses the ability to teach, and the failed learners lose the opportunity for extra instruction. Placing students with motivational issues and failed learners in the same intervention is like having gasoline and a match in the same room: together they can blow up the intervention.

A final caution regarding motivational issues: lack of effort is a symptom, not a cause. Intentional nonlearners and failed learners often look the same in a teacher's gradebook—a row of zeros that represent missing assignments. In reality, many failing students develop a façade: they act like they don't care because they have failed for so long that they have learned that it is better to fail by not trying than to fail while trying. If the student gives his best effort and fails, it validates that he is "stupid"; if he fails due to lack of effort, he can at least maintain some level of self-esteem by projecting an attitude of "I could do it, but I don't care."

When a school is unsure whether a student's struggles are caused by lack of effort or lack of skills, we suggest starting by making the student do some work, since all the school knows for sure about a student with a row of zeros in a gradebook is that he or she is not doing any work. Once held accountable to try, the student's efforts will validate whether the student is a "won't do" or "can't do."

One final word, at the risk of repetition. Please do not view academic and motivational (or behavioral or self-regulatory) needs as entirely separate challenges. While correctly and precisely diagnosing the needs of at-risk students is critical, and the supports schools provide will be distinct, schools should not be surprised if students have both types of needs. No matter what explains a student's lack of learning, schools can and must commit to a collective responsibility to providing supports.

- **Attendance.** Chronic absenteeism is one of the most reliable predictors of at-risk youth behavior, such as drug abuse, dropping out of school, and future incarceration. When students show signs that school absences are having a negative impact on their success at school, schoolwide resources should be used to address the problem. While classroom teachers can be part of the solution, it is more difficult for a teacher to take the lead of contacting the parent, discussing the cause of the problem, creating an intervention plan, and monitoring progress. Site personnel, including the school administration, deans, counselors, and office support staff, should lead the process.

Like zeros for unmotivated students, absences by a student are a symptom, not a cause. There are many reasons why a student suffers from habitual absenteeism. The parent might not be diligent at getting the child to school each day on time; a student who is being bullied at school may wake up with a stomach ache (real or purported), too afraid to go to school; some students have made no meaningful connection to an adult or peer on campus; and some students have serious medical concerns. The intervention for the student being bullied will be markedly different than the one for a student with medical concerns. Every absence problem is not as straightforward as following district policy, putting the parent on an attendance contract, and threatening a referral to the student attendance review board at the police station. The key question is, Why is the student absent so much? The answer to this question is the cause of the problem and the area that must be targeted for an effective solution.

- **Behavior.** Anyone who has ever taught knows that students cannot learn until they can demonstrate the positive behaviors necessary to succeed in class. For students weak in self-control and social skills, learning becomes collateral damage. In the previous chapters, we described how a school can create a tiered approach to teaching positive student behaviors and how to respond when students need additional support in this area. At the heart of these recommendations is a schoolwide approach in which student expectations are clear and consistent for every child, in every class. To achieve this goal, there must be a schoolwide coordination of efforts and a schoolwide plan for students in need of behavior interventions. We must be honest with one another, and we must honestly read the research (Kohn, 1996; Marzano, Marzano, & Pickering, 2003), regarding how teachers contribute to appropriate student behaviors. Effective teachers:

  + Model positive behaviors
  + Treat students respectfully
  + Create positive, productive learning environments with clear procedures
  + Establish positive relationships with all students

It is not that classroom teachers are not expected to be part of behavior interventions; the question is, Who will take the lead? It is unlikely that a classroom teacher has a credential in child development, counseling, and/or behavior plans. Fortunately, there are professionals in almost every district who are trained in these areas, including the school administration, deans, counselors, and the school psychologist. For this reason, it makes most sense that the "buck stops" for behavior interventions with these school-wide resources.

It is vital to view these suggested responsibilities as just that: recommendations. As with many aspects of RTI, the best recommendations can be rendered useless if they are implemented in a rigid, protocol-driven process. The thinking behind these recommendations is guided by these simple principles:

- Tier 1 and Tier 2 are not the responsibility of either teacher teams *or* school-wide teams—it takes classroom teachers *and* schoolwide resources.

- When everyone is responsible for interventions, nobody is. For this reason, final responsibility to *lead* certain interventions must be clearly defined.

- When determining who should be responsible for a particular intervention, the school should ask, Who is best trained in this area of need? Look beyond job titles. What does the child need, and who has the skills to address those needs? Do the individuals asked to lead a particular intervention have the time and resources necessary to succeed? Is the intervention fair and reasonable to all involved?

As an example of applying this thinking, we are often asked who should take primary responsibility for Tier 1 and Tier 2 support of English learners (ELs): classroom teachers or schoolwide resources. Honestly, there is no one-size-fits-all answer—what is important is to answer this question with the right thinking. At a school in which a majority of the students are English learners, it is impossible for support staff to address all their needs. When most of a school's student body has a specific need, it must be addressed in Tier 1 core instruction; English language development (ELD) standards must be taught as part of the Tier 1 core curriculum, in general education classrooms, by classroom teachers. This means that teacher collaborative teams would be identifying ELD standards, teaching these standards, and assessing these standards. In this scenario, who would be in the best position to lead the Tier 1 and Tier 2 teaching for EL students? Classroom teachers.

On the other hand, what if a school has a very small number of English learners? It is unlikely that grade-level and/or subject teacher teams would be asked to collaboratively identify ELD standards, teach these standards, or assess these standards as part of their core instruction. Instead, this school may have hired specialized staff to address this need, which means that schoolwide resource would be responsible. For a school that has built a culture of collective responsibility, learning to apply the guiding principles of RTI will not be difficult.

Core and More

One common mistake that schools make when implementing a tiered intervention program is that they pull students from essential core instruction to provide remediation of prior skills—that is, Tier 2 interventions replace student access to Tier 1 core instruction. When students miss essential core instruction for interventions, they never catch up. This is because while the targeted student is receiving interventions to learn a prior skill, they are missing instruction on a new essential standard. Ask classroom teachers why they don't like students "pulled out" of their class for interventions, and they will tell you: "Because the student misses what I am teaching now." For these students, it is one step forward, two steps back.

If the purpose of an intervention is for children to catch up and to ensure high levels of learning, this practice can hardly qualify as an intervention. Students who need additional time and support to learn prior skills do not need core instruction or remediation; they need core instruction *and* remediation (see fig. 7.4).

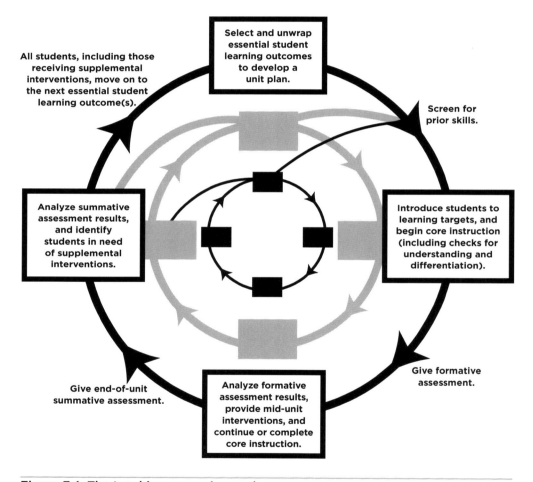

Figure 7.4: The teaching–assessing cycle.

A school can deliver both core instruction and Tier 2 support in a number of ways. First, we recommended earlier that collaborative teacher teams identify the essential learning standards for their course or grade level. This is the content that all students must have access to and from which they should never be pulled for interventions. But this is not the only content that will be taught during core instruction. Besides the standards that every student has to know, there will also be content that is "nice" to know—in other words, content that, if missed, would not hurt a student's ability to succeed in grade-level content next year. Students can be pulled for interventions when "nice to know" content is being taught, but they should not be pulled from core instruction on "has to know" essential standards.

Second, we recommended that collaborative teacher teams include time in their unit plans for reteaching and enrichment. Designating flexible time after the mid-unit common formative assessment, and then again after the summative assessment, allows intervention time for students who need additional time to learn without dropping behind in new instruction.

Monitor Tier 2 Interventions

After a school has *identified* students in need of extra help and *determined* the correct intervention to meet the child's need(s), the school must *monitor* each student's progress. Consider for a moment the name of this process: response to intervention. At the foundation of RTI is a belief that, as educators, we will make instructional decisions based on how children respond to our efforts. If an intervention is working, it confirms that the child's diagnosis is correct, the "medicine" is appropriate, and the child is on track for a full recovery. But if the child is not responding to our interventions, then it means either the diagnosis is incorrect, or we have selected the wrong medicine. Accurate and timely assessment data are essential to make this type of determination.

This is the purpose of convergent assessment: a process of collecting targeted information regarding a specific student that will continually add depth and breadth to an understanding of the student's individual needs, obstacles, and points of learning leverage. Chapters 5 and 6 described in detail how collaborative teacher teams and schoolwide teams can work together to measure student learning and evaluate a school's instructional effectiveness.

For interventions, we refer again to the teaching–assessing cycle. The formative and summative assessments identified in the teaching–assessing cycle (see fig. 4.7, outer ring) are progress-monitoring tools. The data provided from these assessments are vital in determining whether the intervention has worked or if more intensive help is needed.

Additionally, this information is more powerful when students are engaged in the process. When students understand why they are in an intervention, what learning outcome(s) they must master, and how they are doing toward meeting the goal, they are much more likely to hit the target. Progress monitoring should not only guide a teacher's instruction, it should be used to help the learner take ownership of his or her learning.

Revise or Extend Interventions

After a school has *identified* students in need of extra help, *determined* the correct intervention to meet the child's need(s), and *monitored* each student's progress, the school will need to decide whether to *revise or extend* interventions.

When "Some" Help Is Not Enough

At Tier 3, the schoolwide teams take lead responsibility for intensive support of students with severe motivational issues, chronic absenteeism, and extreme behavior concerns. Additionally, schoolwide teams assume lead responsibility for students who are significantly behind in the universal skills of learning: reading, writing, number sense, and English language.

There are three logical reasons for this recommendation. First, these students are not only struggling with mastery of current grade-level standards, they are also significantly weak in critical foundational skills for those standards. In reading, for example, a student might not only have difficulty identifying point of view, but also not be able to decode the text; she not only struggles to write a thesis statement, but has difficulty writing a complete sentence; in math, a student not only struggles with solving equations with exponents, he still cannot multiply; an English learner who is weak in academic vocabulary also does not understand anything the teacher is saying. With needs this great, these students will require intensive, targeted interventions, most often administered by staff highly trained in each area. The school's counselor(s), psychologist, speech and language specialist, curricular specialist(s), and special education teacher(s) are often the individuals best trained to meet these needs. Determining how a school can best utilize these limited resources is the responsibility of the school's leadership team.

Second, students requiring intensive support usually have more than one area of concern. The intensity of their struggles often affects multiple subjects, as well as motivation, attendance, and behavior. As teacher teams are formed around specific learning outcomes, they are not well positioned to take lead responsibility for interventions outside their areas of expertise. Because the school's leadership and intervention teams have representation from all areas of student learning, they are best qualified to lead intensive interventions.

By having this diverse expertise around the table, looking at a student's area(s) of concern from the perspective of their specialized training, the schoolwide intervention team has the best chance to properly diagnose the student's needs and develop a comprehensive and coordinated plan of support.

Finally, these students will need more than *some* help to catch up; they are going to need a lot of help. This usually means the support must be embedded in these students' daily instructional program. This level of support requires designing the school's master schedule to meet these needs. A teacher team cannot create or revise the school's master schedule. This is the responsibility of the school's leadership team.

The goal at this stage of the intervention process is to get a different kind of 360-degree view. From Tier 1 to Tier 2, the goal was to get a 360-degree view from all the staff members who work with a specific child. From Tier 2 to Tier 3, the goal is to get a 360-degree view of the student from the perspectives of all the reasons why a student may struggle in school (see fig. 7.5).

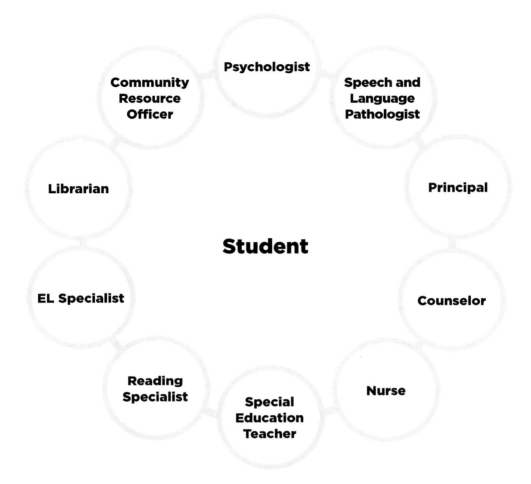

Figure 7.5: A 360-degree view of student learning at Tier 3.

We are not suggesting that classroom teachers are absolved from responsibility for helping students in need of intensive help. On the contrary, these students should still have access to core curriculum, which makes classroom teachers a critical part of the solution. At the same time, it is unlikely that an eighth-grade language arts teacher can teach grade-level standards, assist students in need of some help, enrich the students who have already mastered grade-level skills, and also be responsible for teaching remedial content to students who are multiple years below grade level. This is a nearly impossible task. Additional resources and expertise are needed to address these severe remedial needs, and schoolwide coordination is required to systematically apply these powerful but limited resources.

Remember, Core and More and More

Like supplemental interventions, intensive intervention should not replace a student's access to core instruction. The purpose of RTI is to close achievement gaps, not widen them. Kids need core instruction *and* remediation.

There are rare occasions when a student can be so far behind in remedial skills that he cannot derive any benefit from core, grade-level instruction. In these cases, the child may need to receive intensive remedial instruction to build the skills needed to re-enter the core program. But there must be a plan that demonstrates how the child will get caught up and back to grade level. The removal from core instruction must be temporary—just long enough and intensive enough to get the child back into grade-level instruction. If the child never gets back to grade-level curriculum, then the modifications are not an intervention at all, but instead just glorified tracking—expectations are lowered, and the child is tracked into substandard curriculum. This will ensure that the child will never catch up and ultimately deny the student any chance to succeed in school.

Extending Student Learning

We have heard some schools express concern that creating a system of interventions can potentially come at the cost of students already at or above grade level, as the school is now focusing their collective efforts primarily on helping at-risk students. When a school embraces *high* levels of learning for every child, then their goal becomes not merely to get every student to a minimum level of proficiency, but to maximize every student's academic potential. If a school creates processes to target instruction and provide flexible time to meet the individual needs of each student, these structures do not have to be used solely for the benefit of students struggling below grade level—they can also be used to support students in above grade-level curriculum. The *thinking* is no different.

Certain access demonstrates best how the four Cs are not individual acts or disjointed protocols, but four interdependent guiding principles that create a continuous process focused on student learning. Certain access is guided by the fundamental assumptions of collective responsibility—that all students can learn at high levels, and that we accept responsibility to ensure this outcome for every child. The collaborative teams created to achieve this mission are the engines that drive the work. Concentrated instruction focuses a school's core instruction and interventions, bringing clarity to the essential learning outcomes. Convergent assessment provides the ongoing information necessary to identify the specific learning needs of each student, as well as the effectiveness of our efforts. Without the first three Cs, a school would not have the school culture, collaborative structure, curricular clarity, or learning information necessary to effectively respond when students don't learn. Certain access forges these outcomes in a tiered, systematic process that provides every student the time and support necessary to learn at high levels. Each C represents an essential element needed for students to learn; only when all four are united in a continuous process can they secure the promise of learning for all. See pages 182–190 or visit **go.solution-tree.com/rti** for activities and tools to assist teams. *Getting Started With RTI* (page 182) can help a school leadership team assess its current reality and plan short- and long-term action steps to improve in each of the 4Cs. The leadership team can then use *Designing a System of Interventions* (page 184) to plan a schoolwide system of interventions aligned with the inverted RTI pyramid and team structures described in this book. A handout listing *Additional Resources* (page 187) is also provided.

Where Do Special Education Resources Fit Into the Pyramid?

When we are asked how special education resources fit into RTI, our answer is, "Yes!" The goal of RTI is to get past asking, What help does this student qualify for?, and instead ask, What does this child need, and who on our staff is best trained to provide this support? This is why we purposefully did not follow the typical RTI practice of a four-tier pyramid, with special education represented as the fourth tier. This common approach promotes thinking that special education is separate from the previous tiers—that somehow it stands alone and apart. Equally disconcerting is that it seems to support the misguided approach that the tiers are the "steps" that a school must follow to get a child into special education. Both interpretations are misguided and counterproductive.

To apply the correct thinking to a practical example, consider a school that identifies twelve students who are significantly below grade level in reading fluency. Suppose the school asks, What do these children need, and who on our staff is best trained to provide this support? The best reading teacher on campus is a general education teacher who has a master's degree in reading, holds a reading specialist credential, and is a prior district Teacher of the Year. Because this teacher is clearly the best-qualified person and offers these students the best chance to get caught up in reading fluency, the students will be assigned to her for daily intensive support in their area of need. If seven of the students are current special education students, should that criterion change the intervention? Should the special education students be taken out and assigned to a special education teacher for the same service? While the special education teacher may be well trained in teaching reading, the qualifications of the general education teacher are superior in this area.

Consider an alternate situation: what if the best-trained reading teacher at the school is a special education teacher—should the five general education students be removed from the intervention because they do not "qualify" for the help? This also makes no sense. These students would have to drop further and further behind before they would qualify for assistance from the best teacher—and by then it may be too late to catch up.

In the end, it is not the label that should determine interventions, but the child's need and which staff member is best trained in the targeted area. Considering our more liberal definitions of each tier as being "some" or "a lot" of help, and the blurring of the responsibilities between special education and general education, one might wonder why we need a pyramid at all. Our answer is simple: it is to guide our thinking. A school's efforts to ensure that all students learn at high levels start with all students having access to grade-level curriculum and quality initial instruction—this is Tier 1. No matter how well a school differentiates core instruction, some students will need some help after initial teaching—this is Tier 2. Other students will enter grade-level instruction with significant gaps in foundational skills and/or severe obstacles related to effort, attendance, and/or behavior. These students will need a lot of help to succeed—this is Tier 3.

If a school pulls students from Tier 1 essential standards instruction to get extra help, the students will drop behind and never catch up. If a school only offers "some" help (Tier 2), it will not be enough for students who enter school far behind. On the other hand, if a school only offers "a lot" of help (Tier 3), it will be unable to help kids until they need intensive care. It takes all three levels—all three ways of thinking—to meet the needs of all children. How this thinking is transformed into practice can and should look different from school to school, as the needs of each school are unique, the resources are different, and the strengths of each faculty vary. But the guiding principles are always the same.

District Responsibilities for Certain Access

As schools begin to successfully implement RTI, district office leadership will need to carefully consider how special education resources are allocated, as well as how the central office can provide sites with access to greater expertise for quality problem solving and special education services. Because RTI proactively provides supports for students, few students will require special education identification. But because most districts allocate special education resources to each school based on the number of students currently qualified, this means that schools implementing RTI properly could lose resources because they are not qualifying enough students to justify their current special education resources. This is like the proverbial killing of the "goose who laid the golden egg": the school has used its current special education resources to serve all students, thus decreasing the costly processes associated with special education, yet is ultimately punished for this outcome by losing the very resources that made this outcome possible. Additionally, sites will likely need access to greater levels of expertise in specific learning disabilities to better diagnose student needs, recommend solutions, and potentially provide services. For smaller districts, this can be best accomplished through the local Special Education Local Plan Area (SELPA). These district considerations are vital to the RTI process.

If RTI blurs the lines between general education and special education, then why should schools identify students for special education? What unique role and services should be provided once a student has qualified through the RTI process? What should special education look like within an RTI framework? In the epilogue, we will consider a new vision of what special education can become when supported by effective RTI practices.

Activities and Tools Summary

Does your school have a plan for getting started or getting better at the four Cs of RTI?

See *Getting Started With RTI* (page 182).

Has your school created a tiered system of support to ensure that all students learn at high levels?

See *Designing a System of Interventions* (page 184).

Does your school have a process for determining if it is appropriate to refer a student for special education identification?

Are you looking for more resources?

See *Additional Resources* (page 187).

Visit **go.solution-tree.com/rti** *to download these activities.*

Getting Started With RTI

This activity is designed to help a school leadership team and/or teacher team assess the school's current reality on the essential elements of an effective RTI program, set a long-term vision, and identify specific steps to achieve the school's goals.

	Guiding Questions	Our Current Reality	Desired Reality	Next Steps
Collective Responsibility	Do we believe all students can learn at high levels? Will we take responsibility to make this a reality?			
Creating Teacher Teams	Do we have frequent (weekly) collaborative time embedded during our professional day? Is every teacher part of a collaborative team? Are our teacher teams formed around shared student learning outcomes? Have we identified team norms? Do we hold each other accountable for following norms?			
Creating Schoolwide Teams	Have we created a school leadership team? Is there representation of every teacher team on the leadership team? Have we created a school intervention team? Do our schoolwide teams meet frequently? Have our schoolwide teams identified norms? Do members hold each other accountable for following norms?			

page 1 of 2

	Guiding Questions	Our Current Reality	Desired Reality	Next Steps
Concentrated Instruction	Have we clearly defined the essential learning outcomes that our students must master for success in the next course/grade level? Do all students have access to grade-level essential standards?			
Convergent Assessment	Have we created common assessments that measure student mastery of each essential standard? Do we compare results to identify the most effective teaching strategies? Do we use this information to guide our interventions?			
Certain Access	Do we have frequent time, during the school day, to reteach and enrich students? Do we have a process to frequently identify students for additional time and support?			

Simplifying Response to Intervention © 2012 Solution Tree Press • solution-tree.com
Visit **go.solution-tree.com/rti** to download this page.

Designing a System of Interventions

This activity will assist a leadership team in designing a schoolwide system of interventions. Using the inverted pyramid graphic, consider the following questions, and fill in the boxed sections as appropriate.

1. Universal Screening

    + How will we identify students in need of intensive interventions *before* they start to fail? (See *Universal Screening Planning Guide*, page 113, to assist with this step.)

2. Tier 1 Core Program

    + Have our teacher teams identified essential standards by grade, subject, and/or course?

    + Does every student have access to grade-level essential standards?

    + Is flexible time embedded in Tier 1 to provide differentiated instruction and additional time embedded to meet the individual needs of students?

    + Have we clearly defined the positive behaviors (effort, attendance, social behaviors) that we want all students to demonstrate? Is there a plan to teach, reward, and support these behaviors?

    + How will we measure student progress toward meeting these academic and behavior expectations?

3. Certain Access: Tier 1 to Tier 2

    + How will we systematically identify students who need additional help after core instruction? (See chapter 7 for ideas.)

    + Is every teacher involved in this process?

    + Is this process frequent?

    + What criteria will we used to identify students in need of supplemental support?

4. Tier 2 Supplemental Program

    + What supplemental interventions are currently available at our school? What is needed?

    + Which interventions will be led by teacher teams? (Failed learners)

    + Which interventions will be led by schoolwide intervention resources? (Motivation, attendance, behavior)

+ How can we best utilize schoolwide resources to support Tier 2 interventions?

+ How will we monitor student progress?

5. Certain Access: Tier 2 to Tier 3

+ How will we systematically identify students who need intensive support? (See chapter 7 for ideas.)

+ Do we have a school intervention team to lead Tier 3 Interventions? (See chapter 3.)

+ Is this process frequent?

+ What criteria will we use to identify students in need of supplemental support?

6. Tier 3 Intensive Program

+ What intensive interventions are currently available at our school? What is needed?

+ How can we best utilize schoolwide resources to support Tier 3 interventions?

+ How will we monitor student progress?

7. Special Education Identification

+ How will the intervention team determine if special education is necessary, appropriate, and defendable for a student? (See *Essential Questions for Special Education Identification*, page 198.)

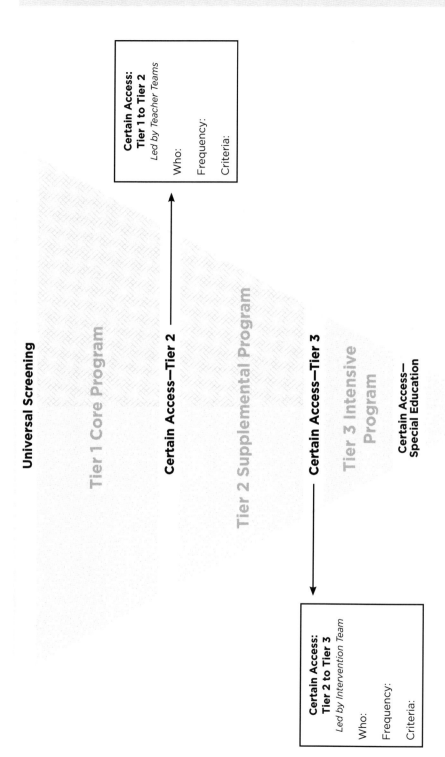

Universal Screening

Tier 1 Core Program

Certain Access—Tier 2

```
┌─────────────────────────┐
│ Certain Access:         │
│ Tier 1 to Tier 2        │
│ Led by Teacher Teams    │
│                         │
│ Who:                    │
│                         │
│ Frequency:              │
│                         │
│ Criteria:               │
└─────────────────────────┘
```

Tier 2 Supplemental Program

Certain Access—Tier 3

Tier 3 Intensive Program

**Certain Access—
Special Education**

```
┌─────────────────────────┐
│ Certain Access:         │
│ Tier 2 to Tier 3        │
│ Led by Intervention Team│
│                         │
│ Who:                    │
│                         │
│ Frequency:              │
│                         │
│ Criteria:               │
└─────────────────────────┘
```

Additional Resources

Name of Resource	URL or Author(s) and Publisher	Description
AIMSWeb	www.aimsweb.com	This site offers full-service CBMs, for a price.
Better Learning Through Structured Teaching: A Framework for the Gradual Release of Responsibility	Douglas Fisher and Nancy Frey Association for Supervision and Curriculum Development, 2008	This book offers an outstanding structured model of teaching and lesson design. Structured lessons are fundamental to Tier 1 instruction and for allowing small-group supports to be delivered during Tier 1.
Center on Instruction	www.centeroninstruction.org	The site provides the best research and meta-analyses in the areas of reading, math, science, special education, and English language learning.
Checking for Understanding: Formative Assessment Techniques for Your Classroom	Douglas Fisher and Nancy Frey Association for Supervision and Curriculum Development, 2007	Instruction and assessment must become fluid companions. Instruction, whether at Tier 1, 2, or 3, must be frequently informed by informal assessments.
Classroom Instruction That Works: Research-Based Strategies for Increasing Student Achievement	Robert J. Marzano, Debra J. Pickering, and Jane E. Pollock Association for Supervision and Curriculum Development, 2001	Marzano et al. consistently deliver the very best research-based practices to inform our practice.
Council for Exceptional Children	www.cec.sped.org	This site provides invaluable information from a preeminent advocacy group for students with special needs.
Developing Self-Regulated Learners: Beyond Achievement to Self-Efficacy	Barry J. Zimmerman, Sebastian Bonner, and Robert Kovach American Psychological Association, 1996	Ultimately, we want our students to self-monitor and be self-motivated. This book will explain how to help students truly become lifelong learners.

page 1 of 4

Name of Resource	URL or Author(s) and Publisher	Description
DIBELS	https://dibels.uoregon.edu	This site provides access to excellent research in the area of literacy and access to exceptional, free reading CBMs for grades preK–6.
The Differentiated Classroom: Responding to the Needs of All Learners	Carol Ann Tomlinson Association for Supervision and Curriculum Development, 1999	The very first line of defense, and the most critical factor in RTI, is strengthening Tier 1 instruction, or "shoring up the core." Differentiating instruction is non-negotiable, and Tomlinson is the source.
easyCBM	http://easyCBM.com	This site offers free CBMs for reading and mathematics for K–8; allows teachers to enter student names, print CBMs, enter data, and print reports; includes norms for each CBM; and allows students to take some tests online.
Florida Center for Reading Research	www.fcrr.org	This is an exceptional site for all things reading. In particular, it provides free, research-based activities for students in all five domains of reading and provides reviews of dozens of research-based, commercial reading interventions.
Intervention Central	www.interventioncentral.org	This site is an exceptional resource for all things RTI, from generating and printing CBMs to finding resources to help monitor site RTI efforts.
LD Online	www.ldonline.org	This site provides great information on learning disabilities and resources for support.

page 2 of 4

Name of Resource	URL or Author(s) and Publisher	Description
Making Standards Work: How to Implement Standards-Based Assessments in the Classroom, School, and District (3rd Edition)	Douglas B. Reeves Advanced Learning Press, 2001	Reeves' work will help schools "concentrate" their instruction by analyzing the priority to be placed on standards.
Models of Teaching (8th Edition)	Bruce Joyce and Marsha Weil with Emily Calhoun Allyn & Bacon, 2008	This book provides background on effective instructional design (the precursor to Fisher and Frey's current work).
National Center on Response to Intervention	www.rti4success.org	This USDOE-sponsored site offers background and resources on RTI.
National Center on Student Progress Monitoring	www.studentprogress.org	This USDOE-sponsored site offers background and resources on progress monitoring.
Office of Special Education Programs (OSEP) Technical Assistance Center on Positive Behavioral Interventions and Supports (PBIS)	www.pbis.org	This USDOE-sponsored site is an absolute treasure trove of all things in the domain of behavioral RTI.
Oregon Reading First Center	http://oregonreadingfirst.uoregon.edu	This is an exceptional site with scholarly, cutting-edge research on reading.
Power Standards: Identifying the Standards That Matter the Most	Larry Ainsworth Advanced Learning Press, 2003	As the title implies, and like Reeves' book, will help schools "concentrate" their instruction by analyzing the priority to be placed on standards.
Project Forum	http://projectforum.org	This USDOE-sponsored site provides background on special education policy.
Reading Rockets	www.readingrockets.org	This site provides helpful information on reading for educators and parents.

Name of Resource	URL or Author(s) and Publisher	Description
Research Institute on Progress Monitoring	www.progressmonitoring.org	This site provides background and research resources in the area of progress monitoring.
RTI Action Network	www.rtinetwork.org	This site is a helpful resource for educators and families and includes an extensive list of FAQs.
The Differentiated Classroom: Responding to the Needs of All Learners	Carol Ann Tomlinson Association for Supervision and Curriculum Development, 1999	The very first line of defense, and the most critical factor in RTI, is strengthening Tier 1 instruction, or "shoring up the core." Differentiating instruction is a non-negotiable, and Tomlinson is the source.
Vaughn Gross Center for Reading and Language Arts	www.meadowscenter.org/vgc	This is one of finest centers for reading resources, particularly for English learners and students with special needs.

A New Vision of Special Education

The previous chapters provided a detailed vision of how the four essential guiding principles of pyramid RTI, the four Cs, can create the culture and structures necessary to ensure high levels of learning for every child. In this vision, collaborative teacher teams design unit teaching cycles that embed differentiation and flexible time into initial instruction. The school has a systematic process to identify students who require supplemental instruction, determine their specific learning needs, and provide effective, targeted interventions to achieve the desired learning outcomes. For the very small number of students for whom this supplemental support is not enough, the schoolwide intervention team, representing different areas of educational expertise, determines the intensive support necessary to meet the child's learning needs. By this point, almost all of the school's students are succeeding. But what does the school do when these three tiers of support do not meet a child's unique needs?

While it is not the primary purpose of RTI to identify students for special education, if a school implements RTI properly, a small number of students will be qualified for special education. Due to the previous efforts at Tiers 1, 2, and 3, the school will be confident that these students truly have disabilities and that their learning difficulties are not due to demographics or the quality of instruction. Students with these special needs are most in need of the very best of public education. Specialized resources, expertise, and learning environments may be needed. To achieve this goal of leveraging resources to ensure high levels of learning for students with special needs, we must move beyond our traditional thinking about how we serve students with special needs and instead create a new vision of special education.

A Failing Model

Nearly four decades have passed since President Ford signed PL 94–142 into law, creating special education in the United States (Education for All Handicapped Children Act of 1975, 1975). Unequivocally, this legislation has produced some outcomes that are morally and educationally significant. In 1970, only one in five students with disabilities (U.S. Office of Special Education Programs, n.d.) were served in American public schools, as most schools denied enrollment to students with special needs. PL 94–142 has changed public education and, arguably, public perception: we have moved from excluding and ignoring children with disabilities to providing them with a free, appropriate public education (FAPE) in the least restrictive environment.

In many ways, PL 94–142 was a civil rights law, guaranteeing every student with special needs the right to attend public school. To that end, special education has been highly successful, as today virtually no child with special needs can be denied access to a free and appropriate public education.

Yet while the outcome is substantial, it has proven insufficient in providing students with the high levels of learning necessary to successfully prepare them for life beyond special education. Today, barely half of all special education students receive a high school diploma (NCSET, 2006), and far fewer go on to postsecondary education (Samuels, 2010). Our traditional special education practices focused primarily on identification and placement, with very little focus on ensuring that identified students learned at high levels. In reality, the guiding principles of our current special education system not only fail to support student learning at a high level, but actually inhibit a school's ability to meet this goal. This model has overidentified students from at-risk demographics as being disabled, has allowed at-risk students to drop too far behind before receiving help, has disengaged general education teachers from the intervention process, and has overwhelmed site special education resources with far too many students to serve.

At most schools, the only systematic intervention process to provide students additional time and support is special education. Most students must fall far enough behind before they qualify for extra help. Either an accepted medical diagnosis or evidence of a learning disability is required to qualify for special education. The traditional process used to identify a specific learning disability is the "discrepancy model"—also known as the "wait to fail" model. For students to qualify for special education assistance, children must demonstrate a discrepancy of at least two standard deviations between their perceived ability and their current level of achievement. Unfortunately, research confirms that once a child reaches that level of discrepancy, it is nearly impossible for the child to catch up (Fuchs & Young, 2006). By the time the help arrives, the student is "terminal." At that point, the extra assistance is rarely "help," but hospice.

We know that collective responsibility and collaboration are essential to meeting the needs of all students, and yet it is hard to imagine a more isolated group of professionals at most campuses than the staff who serve students with special needs. Physically, most schools house their special needs classrooms in the most isolated spots on campus, such as an old office or storage space converted into a classroom or in portable classrooms at the far end of the playground. The same can often be said for the professional spaces provided itinerant support staff such as school psychologists, speech therapists, and counselors.

Even where physical isolation does not exist, professional and legal walls of isolation are all too real. Most state special education regulations have created a "school-within-a-school," designating that special education resources can only be used for qualified students, thus restricting the ability of general and special education teachers to share students. So much time and attention are given to meeting legal requirements that special education staff are forced to spend inordinate amounts of times completing forms, meeting deadlines, and securing signatures, leaving little time to collaborate with peers.

Such practices hurt both teachers and students. The specialized training the special education teachers receive can benefit many students, not just those officially identified for special education. General education teachers could improve their instructional practices through frequent collaboration with special education teachers. Likewise, special education teachers do not always have the same in-depth, subject-specific content knowledge as general education teachers. Special education students need access to this expertise, and special education teachers could improve their content knowledge through frequent collaboration with these teachers.

As educators, we must move beyond providing students with special needs the right to merely attend school, and instead must ensure that they maximize their learning potential. To achieve this goal, we must rethink the way we use special education resources. One of the most powerful aspects of RTI is that it not only provides the structures for general and special education professionals to work together to meet the need of all students, but it aligns federal and state laws to support these outcomes. These critical changes create the conditions necessary for a new vision of special education.

Identifying the Real Special Needs

Transforming special education must begin with a more accurate way of identifying those students who truly have special needs. As RTI systems better serve students with learning challenges, two outcomes are possible. The interventions and supports may meet the at-risk student's needs and close the performance gap between him and his grade-level peers; with continued monitoring and support, he may succeed in general education. If the student's needs do not respond adequately to increasingly intensive, targeted, and individualized supports, however, a referral for evaluation to determine special education eligibility will be made. This evaluation will be highly informed by the types of interventions that were not adequately successful and by the ongoing, and increasingly detailed, diagnoses of the student's needs.

As we have frequently mentioned throughout this book, one of the greatest obstacles to effectively implementing RTI practices we have seen throughout North America is onerous documentation protocols and processes. Most are designed to legally defend a school's decision to qualify a student for special education, and that is a valid concern; careful consideration of evidence and learning data is critical to determining eligibility. But too often these processes are guided by a district's desire to apply predetermined intervention protocols equally to all children. The school collects reams of documentation to prove the student's failure, rather than to evaluate whether the school taught the child properly. We must be confident that the student truly has special learning needs. When considering a student for special education, a school should ask the following questions:

- **Tier 1**
  - + Did the student have access to rigorous grade-level curriculum?
  - + What evidence do we have that our school's initial instruction was effective for similar students?

> + Was the student given additional time and differentiated instruction during Tier 1 instruction?

- **Tier 2**
  + Did we identify the student for supplemental time and support in a timely manner?
  + What were the child's specific learning needs?
  + What was the cause of the student's struggles?
  + What research-based interventions were used to address the student's specific learning needs?
  + What evidence do we have that these interventions were effective for similar students?

- **Tier 3**
  + When was the child referred for intensive support?
  + What quality problem-solving process was used to better identify the child's specific learning needs and the cause(s) of the student's struggles?
  + What research-based interventions were used to address the student's specific learning needs?
  + What evidence do we have that these interventions were effective for students with similar needs?
  + Are there any other intervention or supports that should be tried before considering special education placement?
  + Do we have consensus from the intervention team that special education identification is necessary and appropriate? Is this decision "defensible"?

Obviously, student assessment data will play a critical role in answering these questions. Yet it is not the volume of paperwork that should guide the decision, nor should the determination rest upon a school's ability to prove that they have satisfactorily completed all the required paperwork and protocols. Instead, special education eligibility should be a measure of the school's confidence that it has served the child well, and that the child truly has unique learning needs that cannot be met and/or maintained by the school's general education and RTI resources. Qualifying a student for special education is not in itself the solution to the student's learning need, but it creates opportunities to provide the child even more highly specialized, targeted, and personalized support. As Douglas and Lynn Fuchs recommend, "Students who prove unresponsive to RTI's preventative intervention deserve a revitalized special education tier to address their serious disability" (Fuchs & Fuchs, 2007, p. 18). See *Essential Questions for Special Education Identification* (page 198 or **go.solution-tree.com/rti**) for a tool the school intervention team can use to consider whether special education identification is appropriate, justified, and defendable for a student.

From General Ed and Special Ed to Education for All

The National Association of State Directors of Special Education published a list of eleven RTI myths in 2006. This publication reinforces an important point: RTI is the responsibility of both general and special education educators. Some have loudly stated that RTI is a general education responsibility (Batsche et al., 2005). The reasons for this insistence are understandable. RTI should not simply be an alternative, albeit superior, way of determining if a student has a specific learning disability. RTI's advantages over the discrepancy model are well documented (Fletcher, Denton, & Francis, 2005). But if RTI evolves to be solely the domain of general education, we will lose a powerful opportunity. Special educators may hesitate to contribute their critical knowledge and experience to assist teams of educators in meeting the needs of students as early as possible, as their efforts may not be deemed needed or appropriate at Tier 1 and 2. General educators may hesitate to welcome their contributions for the same reasons. Meeting the needs of all students, whether prereferral or after a student has an IEP, is the responsibility of all educators at all times.

What might a new collaboration between general and special educators look like? This collaboration would include not only teachers but also the itinerant special education staff members so vital to meeting the needs of students with special needs: the school psychologist, speech and language pathologist, occupational therapist, and registered nurse, to name but a few.

For the sake of illustrating the potential power of nonteaching special education staff in supporting general education, let's consider the speech and language pathologist. Speech and language pathologists are experts in language acquisition, a major factor in the difficulty that leads to more students qualifying for special education with a diagnosis of specific learning disability than any other difficulty: failing to learn to read (Spira, Bracken, & Fischel, 2005). As we have learned more about reading, as we screen for reading difficulties earlier and more successfully, and as we use more targeted and well-designed programs and strategies to provide supplemental supports, we are becoming more successful at meeting the phonemic awareness needs of students. Phonemic awareness, however, is a subset of a much broader set of reading and language skills known as phonological awareness. Students who do not respond to phonemically based core instruction and supplemental supports may have challenges based on their ability to process auditory inputs. Discrete sounds, or phonemes, may present difficulties for these students. They may respond to a broader phonological approach. Luckily, there are staff members on every school campus who are experts in language acquisition, phonological awareness, and auditory processing. They are the speech and language pathologists. They can and should be working with students in early schooling in a preventative manner. They can and should be working with all teachers, providing the knowledge and strategies to identify needs and provide targeted instruction. They can and should be screening and more fully diagnosing phonological and auditory needs earlier. Doing all this will require increased levels of collaboration between general and special education staff and an increased commitment to fully funding and staffing key positions. The same scenarios could be described for other special education support staff.

Through this collaboration between general and special education, many students will receive supports that traditionally required special education identification. If general and special education staff work collaboratively through the RTI process to meet the needs of all students, then what is so "special" about special education? Why should students be qualified for special education, and what services should be provided once they have qualified? First, the special training of special education staff should be used to help any students who might benefit from their expertise, not just those students who have earned the right by failing far enough behind. This ability to provide preventive support for at-risk students is a critical new role for special educators. And because the RTI process will address overqualification of students, this will allow special education to focus on the primary role for which it was founded: to meet the unique, intensive learning needs of students whose disabilities are adversely affecting their ability to learn. These services will include both students who are capable of being independent adults but suffer from learning obstacles that far exceed the resources and training of most faculties, and students who face profound disabilities and require specialized curriculum, facilities, and educational staff.

Our goal in writing this book has been to simplify response to intervention. With the four guiding principles, we hope that we have created a way of thinking in which schools and educators are empowered to create systems of interventions that are designed to meet the specific needs of their students with the limited resources at their schools, and to build upon the unique talents and skills of their staffs. Yet we fear that some may equate the word *simple* with the word *easy*. These are not synonymous. If RTI was easy, everyone would be doing it, and we would have record levels of student achievement at virtually every school. Ensuring that every student succeeds at school is difficult, demanding work. There will undoubtedly be challenges and unexpected obstacles for any school with the courage to embrace this work. The journey may be challenging, but we cannot imagine a cause more important or efforts more worthy of a life's work.

C. S. Lewis once said, "We are like eggs at present. And you cannot go on indefinitely being just an ordinary, decent egg. We must be hatched or go bad" (Lewis, 1952, p. 155). RTI is at such a transitional point. Within RTI lies the ability to transform our schools and provide all children with "wings" to reach their fullest potential. Yet at most schools this potential lies dormant, buried under layers of state regulations, district protocols, and traditional school practices that are misaligned and counterproductive to the essential elements of RTI. Over time, this promise will decay into just another failed educational reform unless we, as educators, grasp a new way of thinking about our work. If we are willing to believe that all students can learn at high levels, and embrace that our collective efforts can achieve this outcome, then we can begin to reach this noble goal for every child.

Activities and Tools Summary

Does your school have a process for determining if it is appropriate to refer a student for special education identification?

See *Essential Questions for Special Education Identification* (page 198).

Visit **go.solution-tree.com/rti** *to download this tool.*

Essential Questions for Special Education Identification

These questions are designed to help a site intervention team consider if special education identification is appropriate, justified, and defendable for a student. Unless the intervention team can answer each question affirmatively, then the decision to recommend special education is not appropriate or defendable.

Tier 1:

- Did the student have access to rigorous, grade-level curriculum?
- What evidence do we have that our school's initial instruction (Tier I) was effective for similar students?
- Was the student given additional time and differentiated instruction during Tier I instruction?

Tier 2:

- Did we identify the student for supplemental time and support in a timely manner?
- What were the child's specific learning needs?
- What was the cause of the student's struggles?
- What research-based interventions were used to address the student's specific learning needs?
- What evidence do we have that these interventions were effective for similar students?

Tier 3:

- When was the child referred for intensive support?
- What quality problem-solving process was used to better identify the child's specific learning needs and the cause(s) of the student's struggles?
- What research-based interventions were used to address the student's specific learning needs?
- What evidence do we have that these interventions were effective for students with similar needs?
- Are there any other intervention or supports that can or should be tried before considering special education placement?
- Do we have agreement among the intervention team that special education is necessary and appropriate to meet the needs of this child? Is this decision defensible?

References and Resources

Ainsworth, L. (2003). *Power standards: Identifying standards that matter the most.* Englewood, CO: Lead & Learn Press.

Andrade, H., & Cizek, G. J. (Eds.) (2010). *Handbook of formative assessment.* New York: Routledge.

Baird, M. (2008, May). *LD eligibility and response to intervention: Why this, why now, and why not?* Paper presented at the LRP National Institute on Legal Issues of Educating Individuals with Disabilities, Charlotte, NC.

Bandura, A. (1993). Perceived self-efficacy in cognitive development and functioning. *Educational Psychologist, 28*(2), 117–148.

Bandura, A. (1997). *Self-efficacy: The exercise of control.* New York: Worth.

Barber, M., & Mourshed, M. (2007). *How the world's best-performing school systems come out on top.* New York: McKinsey.

Bardwick, J. M. (1996). Peacetime management and wartime leadership. In F. Hesselbein, M. Goldsmith, & I. Somerville (Eds.), *The leader of the future: New visions, strategies, and practices for the next era* (pp. 131–134). San Francisco: Jossey-Bass.

Batsche, G., Elliott, J., Graden, J. L., Grimes, J., Kovaleski, J. F., Prasse, D., et al. (2005). *Response to intervention: Policy considerations and implementation.* Alexandria, VA: National Association of State Directors of Special Education.

Black, P., & Wiliam, D. (1998). Inside the black box: Raising standards through classroom assessment. *Phi Delta Kappan, 80*(2), 139–148.

Bloom, B. S. (1968). Learning for mastery. *Evaluation Comment, 1*(2), 1–12. (ERIC Document Reproduction No. ED053419)

Bloom, B. S. (1971). Mastery learning. In J. H. Block (Ed.), *Mastery learning: Theory and practice* (pp. 47–63). New York: Holt, Rinehart & Winston.

Bransford, J. P., Brown, A. L., & Cockings, R. R. (Eds.). (2000). *How people learn: Brain, mind, experience, and school.* Washington, DC: National Academy of Sciences.

Brantlinger, E. A. (Ed.). (2006). *Who benefits from special education? Remediating [fixing] other people's children.* Mahwah, NJ: Lawrence Erlbaum.

Brockman, M. S., & Russell, S. T. (2009, November 20). *Decision-making/reasoning factsheet.* Accessed at http://cals-cf.calsnet.arizona.edu/fcs/bpy/content.cfm?content=decision_making on March 7, 2011.

Brookhart, S. M., & Moss, C. M. (2009). *Advancing formative assessment in every classroom: A guide for instructional leaders.* Alexandria, VA: Association for Supervision and Curriculum Development.

Buffum, A., Mattos, M., & Weber, C. (2009). *Pyramid response to intervention: RTI, professional learning communities, and how to respond when kids don't learn.* Bloomington, IN: Solution Tree Press.

Burke, K. (2010). *Balanced assessment: From formative to summative.* Bloomington, IN: Solution Tree Press.

Burns, M. K. (2004). Empirical analysis of drill ratio research: Refining the instructional level for drill tasks. *Remedial and Special Education, 25*(3), 167–175.

Burns, M. K. (2007). RTI will fail, unless . . . *Communiqué, 35*(5), 38–40.

Burns, M. K., Appleton, J. J., & Stehouwer, J. D. (2005). Meta-analytic review of responsiveness-to-intervention research: Examining field-based and research-implemented models. *Journal of Psychoeducational Assessment, 23*(4), 381–394.

Burns, M. K., Tucker, J. A., Frame, J., Foley, S., & Hauser, A. (2000). Interscorer, alternate-form, internal consistency, and test-retest reliability of Gickling's model of curriculum-based assessment for reading. *Journal of Psychoeducational Assessment, 18*(4), 353–360.

Burns, M. K., & VanDerHeyden, A. M. (2006). Using response to intervention to assess learning disabilities: Introduction to the special series. *Assessment for Effective Intervention, 32*(1), 3–5.

California Department of Education. (2000). *Science content standards for California public schools: Kindergarten through grade twelve.* Accessed at www.cde.ca.gov/be/st/ss /documents/sciencestnd.pdf on December 10, 2010.

Cameron, J., Banko, K. M., & Pierce, W. D. (2001). Pervasive negative effects of rewards on intrinsic motivation: The myth continues. *Behavior Analyst, 24,* 1–44.

Cameron, J., & Pierce, W. D. (1994). Reinforcement, reward, and intrinsic motivation: A meta-analysis. *Review of Educational Research, 64*(3), 363–423.

Cameron, J., & Pierce, W. D. (2002). *Rewards and intrinsic motivation: Resolving the controversy.* Westport, CT: Bergin & Garvey.

Catts, H. W., Hogan, T. P., & Adolf, S. M. (2005). Developmental changes in reading and reading disabilities. In H. W. Catts & A. G. Kamhi (Eds.), *The connections between language and reading disabilities* (pp. 41–54). Mahwah, NJ: Lawrence Erlbaum.

Clemens, N. H., & Shapiro, E. S. (2008, August). *Improving diagnostic accuracy in reading within RTI models.* Poster session presented at the annual convention of the American Psychological Association, Boston, MA.

Collins, J. (2005). *Good to great and the social sectors: A monograph to accompany* Good to Great. New York: HarperCollins.

Common Core State Standards Initiative. (2010). *Common core state standards for English language arts & literacy in history/social studies, science, and technical subjects.* Washington, DC: National Governors Association Center for Best Practices and the Council of Chief State School Officers.

Compton, D. L., Fuchs, D., Fuchs, L. S., & Bryant, J. D. (2006). Selecting at-risk readers in first grade for early intervention: A two-year longitudinal study of decision rules and procedures. *Journal of Educational Psychology, 98*(2), 394–409.

Conley, D. T. (2007). *Redefining college readiness.* Eugene, OR: Educational Policy Improvement Center.

Council of Chief State School Officers. (n.d.). *Formative assessment for students and teachers (FAST).* Accessed at www.ccsso.org/Resources/Programs/Formative_Assessment_for _Students_and_Teachers_(FAST).html on May 25, 2011.

Covey, S. R. (1989). *The seven habits of highly effective people: Powerful lessons in personal change.* New York: Fireside.

Dahlkemper, L. (2003). What does scientifically based research mean for schools? *SEDL Letter.* Accessed at www.sedl.org/pubs/sedl-letter/v15n01/2.html on July 8, 2011.

Deno, S. L. (1985). Curriculum-based measurement: The emerging alternative. *Exceptional Children, 52*(3), 219–232.

Deno, S. L., Marston, D., Shinn, M., & Tindal, G. (1983). Oral reading fluency: A simple datum for scaling reading disability. *Topics in Learning and Learning Disabilities, 2*(4), 53–59.

Deno, S. L., Mirkin, P. K., & Chiang, B. (1982). Identifying valid measures of reading. *Exceptional Children, 49*(1), 36–45.

Denton, C., Anthony, J., Parker, R., & Hasbrouck, J. (2004). Effects of two tutoring programs on the English reading development of Spanish-English bilingual students. *Elementary School Journal, 104*(4), 289–305.

Deshler, D. D., & Schumaker, J. B. (1993). Strategy mastery by at-risk students: Not a simple matter. *Elementary School Journal, 94*(2), 153–167.

Donovan, M. S., & Cross, C. T. (Eds.). (2003). *Minority students in special and gifted education.* Washington, DC: National Academies Press.

Drucker, P. F. (1954). *The practice of management.* New York: HarperCollins.

Drummond, T. (1994). *The Student Risk Screening Scale (SRSS).* Grants Pass, OR: Josephine County Mental Health Program.

DuFour, R. (2010). Creating remedial tracks "for the good of the kids." *Education Week, 30*(12), 23.

DuFour, R., & DuFour, B. (2010). The schedule won't let us [Advertisement]. *Education Week, 30*(13), 6.

DuFour, R., DuFour, R., Eaker, R., & Many, T. (2006). *Learning by doing: A handbook for professional learning communities at work.* Bloomington, IN: Solution Tree Press.

DuFour, R., DuFour, R., Eaker, R., & Many, T. (2010). *Learning by doing: A handbook for professional learning communities at work* (2nd ed.). Bloomington, IN: Solution Tree Press.

DuFour, R., & Marzano, R. J. (2011). *Leaders of learning: How district, school, and classroom leaders improve student achievement.* Bloomington, IN: Solution Tree Press.

Dutro, S., & Moran, C. (2003). Rethinking English language instruction: An architectural approach. In G. Garcia (Ed.), *English learners: Reaching the highest level of English literacy* (pp. 227–258). Newark, DE: International Reading Association.

Dweck, C. S. (2006). *Mindset: The new psychology of success.* New York: Random House, Inc.

Dynamic Indicators of Basic Early Literacy Skills (DIBELS). (n.d.). https://dibels.uoregon.edu/

Edmonds, R. (1979a). Effective schools for the urban poor. *Educational Leadership*, *37*(1), 20–24.

Edmonds, R. (1979b). Some schools work and more can. *Social Policy*, *9*(5), 28–32.

Education for All Handicapped Children Act of 1975, 20 U. S. C Sec. 401 (1975).

Fendler, L., & Muzaffar, I. (2008). The history of the bell curve: Sorting and the idea of normal. *Educational Theory*, *58*(1), 63–82.

Ferri, B. A., & Connor, D. J. (2006). *Reading resistance: Discourses of exclusion in desegregation & inclusion debates.* New York: Peter Lang.

Fisch, K. (n.d.). *Did you know 2.0* [video]. Accessed at www.youtube.com/watch?v=pMcfrLYDm2U on July 11, 2011.

Fischhoff, B. (1992). Risk taking: A developmental perspective. In J. F. Yates (Ed.), *Risk-taking behavior* (pp. 133–162). Chichester, England: Wiley.

Fischhoff, B., Crowell, N. A., & Kipke, M. (1999). *Adolescent decision making: Implications for prevention programs. Summary of a workshop.* Washington, DC: National Academies Press. (ERIC Document Reproduction Service No. ED441185)

Fisher, D., & Frey, N. (2007). *Checking for understanding: Formative assessment techniques for your classroom.* Alexandria, VA: Association for Supervision and Curriculum Development.

Fisher, D., & Frey, N. (2008). *Better learning through structured teaching: A framework for the gradual release of responsibility.* Alexandria, VA: Association for Supervision and Curriculum Development.

Fletcher, J. M., Denton, C., & Francis, D. J. (2005). Validity of alternative approaches for the identification of learning disabilities: Operationalizing unexpected underachievement. *Journal of Learning Disabilities*, *38*(6), 545–552.

Fuchs, D., & Young, C. (2006). On the irrelevance of intelligence in predicting responsiveness to reading instruction. *Exceptional Children*, *75*(1), 8–30.

Fuchs, L. S., & Deno, S. L. (1991). Paradigmatic distinctions between instructionally relevant measurement models. Exceptional Children, 57, 488–501.

Fuchs, L. S., & Fuchs, D. (2007). A model for implementing responsiveness to intervention. *Teaching Exceptional Children*, *39*(5), 14–20.

Fuchs, L. S., Fuchs, D., Hosp, M., & Jenkins, J. R. (2001). Oral reading fluency as an indicator of reading competence: A theoretical, empirical, and historical analysis. *Scientific Studies of Reading, 5*(3), 239–256.

Fullan, M. (2007). *The new meaning of educational change* (4th ed.). New York: Teachers College Press.

Gallimore, R., Ermeling, B., Saunders, W., & Goldenberg, C. (2009, May). Moving the learning of teaching closer to practice: Teacher education implications of school-based inquiry teams. *Elementary School Journal, 109*(5), 537–553. Accessed at http://openarchive.stanford .edu/bitstream/10408/49/1/Moving%20the%20Learning%20of%20Teaching%20Closer%20 to%20Practice.pdf on September 24, 2011.

Ganzel, A. K. (1999). Adolescent decision making: The influence of mood, age, and gender on the consideration of information. *Journal of Adolescent Research, 14*(3), 289–318.

Gersten, R., Baker, S. K., Shanahan, T., Linan-Thompson, S., Collins, P., & Scarcella, R. (2007). *Effective literacy and English language instruction for English learners in the elementary grades: A practice guide* (NCEE 2007-4011). Washington, DC: Institute of Education Sciences, U.S. Department of Education. Accessed at http://ies.ed.gov/ncee/wwc/pdf /practiceguides/20074011.pdf on July 8, 2011.

Good, R. H., & Shinn, M. R. (1990). Forecasting accuracy of slope estimates for reading curriculum-based measurement: Empirical evidence. *Behavioral Assessment, 12*(2), 179–193.

Good, R. H., Simmons, D. C., & Kame'enui, E. J. (2001). The importance and decision-making utility of a continuum of fluency-based indicators of foundational reading skills for third-grade high-stakes outcomes. *Scientific Studies of Reading, 5*(3), 257–288.

Gravois, T. A., & Gickling, E. E. (2002). Best practices in curriculum-based assessment. In A. Thomas & J. Grimes (Eds.), *Best practices in school psychology* (4th ed., pp. 885–898). Bethesda, MD: National Association of School Psychologists.

Gunn, B., Smolkowski, K., Biglan, A., & Black, C. (2002). Supplemental instruction in decoding skills for Hispanic and non-Hispanic students in early elementary school: A follow-up. *Journal of Special Education, 36*, 69–79.

Guskey, T. R. (2003). How classroom assessments can improve learning. *Educational Leadership, 60*(5), 7–11.

Guskey, T. R. (2010). Mastery learning. *Educational Leadership, 68*(2), 53–57.

Guskey, T. R., & Pigott, T. D. (1988). Research on group-based mastery learning programs: A meta-analysis. *Journal of Educational Research, 81,* 197–216.

Hagenbaugh, B. (2002, December 12). U.S. manufacturing jobs fading away fast. *USA TODAY.* Accessed at www.usatoday.com/money/economy/2002-12-12-manufacture_x.htm on July 8, 2011.

Haigler, K. O. (1994). *Literacy behind prison walls*. Washington, DC: U.S. Government Printing Office.

Hammond, C., Linton, D., Smink, J., & Drew, S. (2007). *Dropout risk factors and exemplary programs: A technical report.* Clemson, SC: National Dropout Prevention Center.

Hattie, J. (2009). *Visible learning: A synthesis of over 800 meta-analyses relating to student achievement.* New York: Routledge.

Individuals with Disabilities Education Act (IDEIA), 20 U. S. C. §§ 1400 *et.seq.* (2004).

Jellison, J. (2006). *Managing the dynamics of change: The fastest path to creating an engaged and productive workplace.* New York: McGraw-Hill.

Jenkins, J. R. (2003, December). *Candidate measures for screening at-risk students.* Paper presented at the National Research Center on Learning Disabilities Responsiveness-to-Intervention symposium, Kansas City, MO. Accessed at www.nrcld.org/symposium2003/jenkins/index.html on March 7, 2011.

Joyce, B., & Weil, M. (2008). *Models of teaching* (8th ed.). Boston: Allyn & Bacon.

Kohn, A. (1996). *Beyond discipline: From compliance to community.* Alexandria, VA: Association of Supervision and Curriculum Development.

Kotter, J. (2010). *Eight steps for leading change.* Accessed at www.kotterinternational.com/kotterprinciples/ChangeSteps/Step2.aspx on March 15, 2011.

Kulik, C. C., Kulik, J. A., & Bangert-Drowns, R. L. (1990). Effectiveness of mastery learning programs: A meta-analysis. *Review of Educational Research, 60*(2), 265–299.

Leafstedt, J. M., Itkonen, T., Arner-Costello, F., Hardy, A., Korenstein, B., Medina M., et al. (2007). Was it worth it? You bet: The impact of PL 94–142 on lives and careers. *Issues in Teacher Education, 16*(2), 19–31.

Leahy, S., Lyon, C., Thompson, M., & Wiliam, D. (2005). Classroom assessment: Minute-by-minute and day-by-day. *Educational Leadership, 63*(3), 18–24.

Lewis, C. S. (1952). *Mere Christianity.* London: Geoffrey Bles.

Leyton, F. S. (1983). *The extent to which group instruction supplemented by mastery of initial cognitive prerequisites approximates the effectiveness of one-to-one tutorial methods.* Unpublished doctoral dissertation, University of Chicago.

Lyon, G. R. (1996). Learning disabilities. *The Future of Children: Special Education for Students With Disabilities, 6*(1), 54–76.

Lyon, G. R., Fletcher, J. M., Shaywitz, S. E., Shaywitz, B. A., Torgeson, J. K., Wood, F. B., et al. (2001). Rethinking learning disabilities. In C. E. Finn, R. A. J. Rotherham, & C. R. Hokanson (Eds.), *Rethinking special education for a new century* (pp. 259–287). Washington, DC: Progressive Policy Institute and the Thomas B. Fordham Foundation.

Marzano, R. J. (2003). *What works in schools: Translating research into action.* Alexandria, VA: Association for Supervision and Curriculum Development.

Marzano, R. J. (2007). *The art and science of teaching: A comprehensive framework for effective instruction.* Alexandria, VA: Association for Supervision and Curriculum Development.

Marzano, R. J., Marzano, J. S., & Pickering, D. J. (2003). *Classroom management that works: Research-based strategies for every teacher.* Alexandria, VA: Association for Supervision and Curriculum Development.

Marzano, R. J., & Waters, T. (2009). *District leadership that works: Striking the right balance.* Bloomington, IN: Solution Tree Press.

Mayer, D. P., Mullens, J. E., & Moore, M. T. (2000). *Monitoring school quality: An indicators report* (NCES 2001-030). Washington, DC: National Center for Education Statistics. Accessed at http://nces.ed.gov/pubs2001/2001030.pdf on January 10, 2005.

McCann, E. J., & Turner, J. E. (2004). Increasing student learning through volitional control. *Teachers College Record, 106*(9), 1695–1714.

McMahon, M., & Luca, J. (2001). *Assessing students' self-regulatory skills.* Accessed at www.ascilite.org.au/conferences/melbourne01/pdf/papers/mcmahonm.pdf on August 10, 2011.

McMillan, J. H. (2007). *Formative classroom assessment: Theory into practice.* New York: Teachers College Press.

McTighe, J., & Wiggins, G. (2004). *Understanding by design professional development workbook.* Alexandria, VA: Association for Supervision and Curriculum Development.

Moody, S. W., Vaughn, S., Hughes, M. T., & Fischer, M. (2000). Reading instruction in the resource room: Set up for failure. *Exceptional Children, 66*(3), 305–316.

Muennig, P., & Woolf, S. H. (2007). Health and economic benefits of reducing the number of students per classroom in US primary schools. *American Journal of Public Health, 97*(11), 2020–2027.

Muhammad, A. (2009). *Transforming school culture: How to overcome staff division.* Bloomington, IN: Solution Tree Press.

National Association of State Directors of Special Education. (NASDSE). (2006). *Myths about response to intervention (RtI) implementation.* Accessed at www.spannj.org/keychanges/education_materials09/Myths_About_RTI_NASDSE.pdf on July 8, 2011.

National Association of State Directors of Special Education (NASDSE) and the Council of Administrators of Special Education (CASE) at the Council for Exceptional Children. (2006). *Response to intervention: NASDSE and CASE White Paper on RtI* [White Paper]. Accessed at www.nasdse.org/Portals/0/Documents/Download%20Publications/RtIAnAdministratorsPerspective1-06.pdf on July 8, 2011.

National Center on Secondary Education and Transition. (NCSET). (2006, March). Promoting effective parent involvement in secondary education and transition. *Parent Brief.* Accessed at www.ncset.org/publications/viewdesc.asp?id=2844 on August 26, 2011.

National Partnership for Teaching in At-Risk Schools. (2005). *Qualified teachers for at-risk youth: A national imperative.* Accessed at www.learningpt.org/pdfs/tq/partnership.pdf on August 26, 2011.

Neild, R. C., & Balfanz, R. (2010). *Unfulfilled promise: The dimensions and characteristics of Philadelphia's dropout crisis, 2000–2005.* Accessed at http://inpathways.net/Unfulfilled_Promise_Project_U-turn.pdf on July 8, 2011.

Neild, R. C., Balfanz, R., & Herzog, L. (2007). An early warning system. *Educational Leadership, 65*(2), 28–33.

Northwest Evaluation Association. (n.d.). www.nwea.org/

Oakes, J. (2005). *Keeping track: How schools structure inequality.* New Haven: Yale University Press.

Osterman, K. F. (2000). Students' need for belonging in the school community. *Review of Educational Research, 70*(3), 323–367.

Pierangelo, R., & Giuliani, G. (2006). *The special educator's comprehensive guide to 301 diagnostic tests.* San Francisco: Jossey-Bass.

Pippitt-Cervantes, M. (n.d.). *Building blocks of reading proficiency skills needed to read.* Accessed at http://publicportal.ousd.k12.ca.us/199410119113614750/blank/browse.asp?A=383&BMDRN=2000&BCOB=0&C=57721 on September 9, 2011.

Popham, W. J. (2005, April). Standardized testing fails the exam. *Edutopia.* Accessed at www.edutopia.org/f-for-assessment?page=1 on December 6, 2010.

Popham, W. J. (2008). *Transformative assessment.* Alexandria, VA: Association for Supervision and Curriculum Development.

Prasse, D. P. (2009). *Why adopt an RTI model?* Accessed at www.rtinetwork.org/learn/why/whyrti on July 8, 2011.

President's Commission on Excellence in Special Education. (2002). *A new era: Revitalizing special education for children and their families.* Washington, DC: U.S. Department of Education.

ProLiteracy America. (2003). *U.S. adult literacy programs: Making a difference.* Accessed at www.proliteracy.org/NetCommunity/Document.Doc?id=18 on July 8, 2011.

Prometric Services. (2011, May 24). *Internal psychometric guidelines for classical test theory.* Accessed at http://prometric.com/reference/ELD5.htm on July 8, 2011.

Reder, S. (1998). *The state of literacy in America.* Washington, DC: U.S. Government Printing Office.

Reeves, D. (2002). *The leader's guide to standards: A blueprint for educational equity and excellence.* San Francisco: Wiley.

Reeves, D. (2004). *Accountability for learning: How teachers and school leaders can take charge.* Alexandria, VA: Association for Supervision and Curriculum Development.

Reeves, D. (2009, July 14). In education, standards aren't enough. *The Hill, 16*(82). Accessed at www.leadandlearn.com/sites/default/files/articles/090714-the-hill-in-education-standards-arent-enough.pdf on July 8, 2011.

Rouse, C. (September, 2005). *The labor market consequences of an inadequate education.* Paper prepared for the Equity Symposium on the Social Costs of Inadequate Education at Teachers' College, Columbia University, NY.

Rumberger, R. W. (2001). High school dropouts: A review of issues and evidence. *Review of Educational Research, 57*(2), 101–121.

Sadler, D. R. (1989). Formative assessment and the design of instructional systems. *Instructional Science,* 18, 119–144.

Samuels, C. A. (2010). Learning-disabled enrollment dips after long climb. *Education Week, 30*(3), 1, 14–15.

Sarason, S. (1996). *Revisiting the culture of school and the problem of change.* New York: Teachers College Press.

Scarcela, R. (2003). *Accelerating academic English: A focus on English language learners.* Oakland: Regents of the University of California.

Scherer, M. (2001). How and why standards can improve student achievement: A conversation with Robert J. Marzano. *Making Standards Work,* 59(1), 14–18.

Schlechty, P. C. (2001). *Shaking up the schoolhouse: How to support and sustain educational innovation.* San Francisco: Jossey-Bass.

Schlechty, P. C. (2002). *Working on the work: An action plan for teachers, principals, and superintendents.* San Francisco: Jossey-Bass.

Schmoker, M. (2004, February). Tipping point: From feckless reform to substantive instructional improvement. *Phi Delta Kappan, 85*(6), 424–432.

Schmoker, M. (2005). Results *fieldbook: Practical strategies from dramatically improved schools.* Alexandria, VA: Association for Supervision and Curricular Development.

Sergiovanni, T. J. (1996). *Leadership for the schoolhouse: How is it different? Why is it important?* San Francisco: Jossey Bass.

Shapiro, E. S., & Clemens, N. H. (2009). A conceptual model for evaluating system effects of response to intervention. *Assessment for Effective Intervention, 35*(1), 3–16.

Shapiro, E. S., Solari, E., & Petscher, J. (2008). Use of a measure of reading comprehension to enhance prediction on the state high stakes assessment. *Learning and Individual Differences,* 18, 316–328.

Shaywitz, S. (2003). *Overcoming dyslexia: A new and complete science-based program for reading problems at any level.* New York: Knopf.

Shores, M. L., & Shannon, D. M. (2007). The effects of self-regulation, motivation, anxiety, and attributions on mathematics achievement for fifth and sixth grade students. *School Science and Mathematics, 107*(6), 225–236.

Silberglitt, B., Burns, M. K., Madyun, N. H., & Lali, K. E. (2006). Relationship of reading fluency assessment data with state accountability test scores: A longitudinal comparison of grade levels. *Psychology in the Schools,* 43, 527–535.

Silberglitt, B., & Hintze, J. M. (2007). How much growth can we expect? A conditional analysis of R-CBM growth rates by level of performance. *Exceptional Children, 74*(1), 71–84.

Skiba, R. J., Poloni-Staudinger, L., Gallini, S., Simmons, A. B., & Feggins-Azziz, R. (2006). Disparate access: The disproportionality of African American students with disabilities across educational environments. *Exceptional Children, 72*(4), 411–424.

Skiba, R. J., Simmons, A. D., Ritter, S., Gibb, A., Rausch, M. K., Cuadrado, J., et al. (2008). Achieving equity in special education: History, status, and current challenges. *Exceptional Children, 74*(3), 264–288.

Sperling, R. A., Walls, R. T., & Hill, L. A. (2000). Early relationships among self-regulatory constructs: Theory of mind and preschool children's problem solving. *Child Study Journal, 30*(4), 233–252.

Spira, E. G., Bracken, S. S., & Fischel, J. E. (2005). Predicting improvement after first-grade reading difficulties: The effects of oral language, emergent literacy, and behavior skills. *Developmental Psychology,* 41(1), 225–234.

Sternberg, R. (1996). *Successful intelligence: How practical and creative intelligence determines success in life.* New York: Simon & Schuster.

Stiggins, R. J. (1997). *Student-centered classroom assessment* (2nd ed.). Upper Saddle River, NJ: Prentice Hall.

Stiggins, R. J. (2007a). Assessment for learning: An essential foundation of productive instruction. In D. Reeves (Ed.), *Ahead of the curve: The power of assessment to transform teaching and learning* (pp. 59–76). Bloomington, IN: Solution Tree Press.

Stiggins, R. J. (2007b). *An introduction to student-involved assessment for learning* (5th ed.). Upper Saddle River, NJ: Pearson Education.

Stiggins, R., Arter, J. A., Chappuis, J., & Chappuis, S. (2007). *Classroom assessment for student learning: Doing it right—Using it well.* New York: Prentice Hall.

Sugai, G., & Horner, R. (2002). The evolution of discipline practices: School-wide positive behavior supports. *Child and Family Behavior Therapy, 24,* 23–50.

Swanson, C. B. (2008). Cities in crisis. *Editorial Projects in Education.* Accessed at www .edweek.org/rc/articles/2008/04/01/cities_in_crisis.html on March 7, 2011.

Talbert, J. E. (2010). Professional learning communities at the crossroads: How systems hinder or engender change. In M. Fullan, A. Hargreaves, & A. Lieberman (Eds.), *Second international handbook of educational change* (pp. 555–572). Dordrecht, Netherlands: Springer Press.

Toffler, A., & Toffler, H. (1999). Foreword. In R. Gibson (Ed.), *Rethinking the future: Rethinking business principles, competition, control and complexity, leadership, markets and the world* (pp. viii–x). Sonoma, CA: Nicholas Brealey Publishing.

Tomlinson, C. A. (1999). *The differentiated classroom: Responding to the needs of all learners.* Alexandria, VA: Association for Supervision and Curriculum Development.

Tomlinson, C. A. (2000). *Differentiation of instruction in the elementary grades.* ERIC Digest, EDO-PS-00-7.

Tomlinson, C. A., & McTighe, J. (2006). *Integrating differentiated instruction and understanding by design.* Alexandria, VA: Association for Supervision and Curriculum Development.

University of North Carolina School of Education. (n.d.) *Learn NC.* Accessed at www .learnnc.org/reference/number+sense on May 25, 2011.

U.S. Department of Agriculture, Utah State University Extension, & LetterPress Software. (n.d.) *Growing a nation: The story of American agriculture.* Accessed at www.agclassroom .org/gan/classroom/pdf/embed1_seeds.pdf on July 8, 2011.

U.S. Department of Education (USDOE). (1996a). *Eighteenth annual report to Congress on the implementation of the Individuals with Disabilities Education Act.* Accessed at www2. ed.gov/pubs/OSEP96AnlRpt/index.html on March 7, 2011.

U.S. Department of Education (USDOE). (1996b). *Manual to combat truancy.* Accessed at www.ed.gov/pubs/Truancy/index.html on March 7, 2011.

U.S. Department of Education (USDOE). (2001). *Twenty-third annual report to Congress on the implementation of the Individuals with Disabilities Education Act.* Washington, DC: Author.

U. S. Department of Education (USDOE). (2003). *The health literacy of America's adults: Results from the 2003 National Assessment of Adult Literacy.* Accessed at http://nces .ed.gov/pubs2006/2006483.pdf on July 8, 2011.

U.S. Office of Special Education Programs. (n.d.). *History: Twenty-five years of progress in educating children with disabilities through IDEA.* Accessed at www2.ed.gov/policy/ speced/leg/idea/history.html on March 7, 2011.

VanDerHeyden, A. M., & Burns, M. K. (2005). Using curriculum-based assessment and curriculum-based measurement to guide elementary mathematics instruction: Effect on individual and group accountability scores. *Assessment for Effective Intervention, 30*(3), 15–29.

VanDerHeyden, A. M., Witt, J. C., & Gilbertson, D. A. (2007). Multi-year evaluation of the effects of a Response to Intervention (RTI) model on identification of children for special education. *Journal of School Psychology, 45*(2), 225–256.

VanDerHeyden, A. M., Witt, J. C., & Naquin, G. (2003). Development and validation of a process for screening referrals to special education. *School Psychology Review, 32*(2), 204–227.

Van Veer, H. (2005). Fostering reading comprehension in fifth grade by explicit instruction in reading strategies and peer tutoring. *British Journal of Educational Psychology, 74,* 37–70.

Vaughn, S., Wanzek, J., Linan-Thompson, S., & Murray, C. (2007). Monitoring response to intervention for students at-risk for reading difficulties: High and low responders. In S. R. Jimerson, M. K. Burns, & A. M. VanDerHeyden (Eds.), *The handbook of response to intervention: The science and practice of assessment and intervention* (pp. 234–243). New York: Springer.

Virga, J. (2010, November 12). PLCs and self-efficacy: What is the connection? [Web log entry.]. Accessed at www.allthingsplc.info/wordpress/?p=1207 on July 19, 2011.

Walker, H. M., Horner, R. H., Sugai, G., Bullis, M., Sprague, J. R., Bricker, D., et al. (1996). Integrated approaches to preventing antisocial behavior patterns among school-age children and youth. *Journal of Emotional and Behavioral Disorders, 4*, 194–209.

Wallace, B., & Graves, W. (1995). *Poisoned apple: The bell-curve crisis and how our schools create mediocrity and failure.* New York: St. Martin's Press.

Waller, J. (2001). *Face to face: The changing state of racism across America.* New York: Perseus Books.

Wiliam, D. (2011). *Embedded formative assessment.* Bloomington, IN: Solution Tree Press.

Winters, C. A. (1997). Learning disabilities, crime, delinquency, and special education placement. *Adolescence, 32*(126), 451–462.

Wong Fillmore, L., & Snow, C. E. (2000). *What teachers need to know about language.* Washington, DC: U. S. Department of Education's Office of Educational Research and Improvement Center for Applied Linguistics. (ERIC Document Reproduction Service No. ED 990 008).

Ysseldyke, J. E., Algozzine, B., & Thurlow, M. L. (1992). *Critical issues in special education.* Boston: Houghton Mifflin.

Zins, J. E., & Ponti, C. R. (1990). Best practices in school-based consultation. In A. Thomas & J. Grimes (Eds.), *Best practices in school psychology II* (pp. 673–694). Washington, DC: National Association of School Psychologists.

Index

A

ability grouping, 161
academic misbehaviors
    concentrated instruction and, 64, 66–67
    convergent assessment and, 96–97, 99
    interventions and, 147–148
accountability, 24
Accountability for Learning (Reeves), 47
AIMSweb, 105, 150
Ainsworth, L., 48, 54, 82
Andrade, H., 58
Arter, J. A., 58
assessments
    See also convergent assessment
    building common formative, 56–58,
        92–93
    formative, 92
    self-evaluation tool, 29–30
    self-regulatory assessment tool, 97, 117
    self-regulatory problem-solving tool, 99,
        119–120
attendance issues, 171–172

B

Balanced Assessment (Burke), 58
Balfanz, R., 85
Bandura, A., 135
Bangert-Drowns, R. L., 57–58
Bardwick, J., 6
behavior
    See also misbehaviors, academic;
        misbehaviors, social
    documentation forms, 99–101, 124
    impact of teachers on student, 172–173
behavioral analysis protocol, 99, 121–123,
        148
behavior expectations matrix, 69, 76
Block, P., 1
Bloom, B., 7, 57, 58
Brookover, W., 17
Bryant, J. D., 87
bubble-kid approach, 3
Burke, K., 58

C

certain access
    defined, 10, 159
    description of, 162–179
    district responsibilities for, 180
    problem with random access, 159–162
Chappuis, J., 58
Chappuis, S., 58
Check-In/Check-Out (CICO) system, 150
Cizek, G. J., 58
Classroom Assessment for Student Learning
        (Stiggins, Arter, Chappuis and,
        Chappuis), 58
Clemens, N., 102, 103–104
collaboration, making time for, 39–40,
        195–196
collaborative teams, 12
    effectiveness, ensuring, 39–42
    forms, 41–42, 43–44
    foundations, 43–44
    goals, 32
    grade-level, 34
    interdisciplinary, 34–35
    norms, 40–41
    responsibilities in inverted RTI pyramid,
        13, 32, 46
    role of, 31–32
    schoolwide, 36–39
    subject/course-specific, 34
    teacher, 33–36
    Tier 2 interventions led by, 169–170
    types of, 32
    universal screening, 81–82
    vertical, 34
collective responsibility
    accountability, 24
    believing all students can learn at high
        levels, 18–19
    confronting resisters, 22
    consensus, 20–21, 22–23, 27–28
    defined, 9, 15
    district, 23–25
    doable plan, providing a, 21
    ownership/school, 19–23

Pyramid Response to Intervention
Austin Buffum, Mike Mattos, and Chris Weber
Accessible language and compelling stories illustrate how RTI is most effective when built on the Professional Learning Communities at Work™ process. Written by award-winning educators, this book details three tiers of interventions—from basic to intensive—and includes implementation ideas. **BKF251**

Pyramid Response to Intervention
Austin Buffum, Mike Mattos, and Chris Weber
Shift to a culture of collective responsibility, and ensure a path of opportunity and success for every student. Focusing on the four Cs vital to student achievement, this powerful four-part program will help you collect targeted information on students' individual needs and guide you to build efficient team structures. **DVF057**

Pyramid of Behavior Interventions
Tom Hierck, Charlie Coleman, and Chris Weber
Students thrive when educators hold high expectations for behavior as well as academics. This book shows how to use a three-tiered pyramid of behavior supports to create a school culture and classroom climates in which learning is primed to occur. **DVF036**

The Collaborative Administrator
Austin Buffum, Cassandra Erkens, Charles Hinman, Susan Huff, Lillie G. Jessie, Terri L. Martin, Mike Mattos, Anthony Muhammad, Peter Noonan, Geri Parscale, Eric Twadell, Jay Westover, and Kenneth C. Williams
How do you maintain the right balance of loose and tight leadership? How do you establish profound, lasting trust with your staff? What principles strengthen principal leadership? This book answers these questions and much more in compelling chapters packed with strategies and inspiration. **BKF256**